Force Field

*For Lorraine, Glad and Verdi...*
*and the circle of Yin that irons the sharp edges!*

# FORCE FIELD

## HOW TO CREATE AN UNBREAKABLE MINDSET AND UNLOCK YOUR FULL POTENTIAL

## GAVIN SAMIN

Force Field
Author – Gavin Samin
© Gavin Samin 2023

Web: www.forcefieldbook.com
Email: info@forcefieldbook.com

Editing, design and publishing support by www.AuthorSupportServices.com

Cover Art by Francis Fenlon at francis@yellowfoxdesign.com

ISBN: 9781 9223 7524 7

NATIONAL LIBRARY OF AUSTRALIA · A catalogue record for this book is available from the National Library of Australia

# CONTENTS

# PREFACE

## *FORCE FIELD*

Definition: an impenetrable bubble
or invisible protective shield.

# Early years – the 'insecurity' guard

I AM THE ELDEST of three children; I have two younger sisters. My parents separated when I was quite young and contact with my father for many years after that was rare. My mother was a total soldier, running herself ragged chasing after three hyperactive children and doing her best to play the role of two parents. No doubt she was also dealing with her own adult problems including the emotional fallout from her marriage breakdown. I could write a whole book on her heroics and on the plight of single motherhood as seen through the eyes of a son.

As much as my mother tried to provide a positive and stable environment, I was nonetheless burdened with an underlying anxiety about my personal safety and that of my family. This prevailing sense of vulnerability was heightened at night when I was convinced we'd be burgled while we slept or snatched from our bedrooms by an abductor. I also distinctly remember, at the age of ten, being panicked by the story of a young Melbourne girl named Eloise Worledge who'd been kidnapped from her home while her parents slept in the next room. To this day, she has never been found.

I subsequently spent most nights in a hypervigilant state, repeatedly checking my bedroom window was locked and waking up constantly to the sound of what I was certain were footsteps in the hallway. Not surprisingly, I developed chronic sleeping problems. This was not helped by the physical discomfort of having a small transistor radio under my pillow that played all night to block out the silence. I figured if I couldn't hear the noises, then they weren't there. With one ear pressed firmly into the thinnest pillow I could find (it made the radio underneath sound louder), I slept on my side and wedged my index finger in the opposite ear. This was as close to total sound block-out that I could manage and it became the contorted profile of my nightly pre-sleep ritual. None of these imaginary and somewhat macabre intruder scenarios ever materialised, but my nervous system lived them thousands of times over.

Despite my childish safety fears, I nonetheless felt a responsibility as both the eldest child and the only male in the family to conceal these worries. I instinctively embraced the self-appointed role of bodyguard within the household, which included protecting my mother. I recall adopting this mentality as early as nine years old. In a sense, I had positioned myself as the family 'force field' despite being too immature and anxious to successfully execute such a role.

I came to realise as I was compiling this book that I did not escape the single-parent living arrangement unscathed. My personal insecurities were heavily driven by the absence of a male adult or big brother in the house. For instance, when I stayed over at my grandparents' house or a friend's place where their father was home, I slept like a baby. It was like I was 'off-duty' and truly resting in a safe place. The contrast between these scenarios and sleeping in my own bedroom could not have been greater.

The pattern of insecurity continued well into my late teens as I started to confront the range of daylight threats that accompany adolescence. I went to an all-boys public high school, which was hardly a place to expose your vulnerabilities. Simply put, if you outwardly showed any weakness, you were a potential target for being bullied. As such, I masked my self-doubt with an overcompensating sense of external bravado and tried not to be one of the hunted. While my early teenage years were a typical mixture of ups and downs, I experienced a number of distressing encounters between the ages of 14 and 17 that compromised whatever self-confidence I'd managed to assemble up to that point. This included a stressful and quite public episode with a school tough guy; being followed and threatened by a considerably older and unhinged lunatic; and my nine-year-old little sister being stalked by a stranger. In addition to this, someone very close to my mother was tragically killed in a motor accident during this period. Hence, at a stage when I was feeling more vulnerable than ever, my real force field – my mother – had been emotionally demolished. I wanted so badly to be the family rock during this time, but my inherent immaturity made this seem out of reach.

# Role models and superheroes

As a young boy, I was obsessed with superheroes. Of all the attributes portrayed by my favourite characters, the most alluring were those who possessed some form of armour: Superman's bulletproof body, Iron Man's impenetrable suit, Captain America's protective shield and the 'Force' used by the Jedi.

By my mid-teens, I'd moved onto Hollywood action stars like Charles Bronson and Clint Eastwood, both of whom portrayed a fearless and grizzled image on screen. The fact that they were just movie characters was not lost on me, but I clung to them regardless as objects of inspiration and genuine manhood.

At around the age of 16, I watched a documentary that not only triggered my lifelong love of boxing but almost had me believing that force fields might exist. The video was called *A.K.A. Cassius Clay*. For those who may not be aware, Cassius Clay changed his name at age 22 to Muhammad Ali. The documentary featured some of his greatest fights and revealed his supreme confidence and strength of character. Here was a man who was funny, articulate, charismatic and good-looking (his own words!), yet when he was called to fight, he was also probably one of the hardest men in heavyweight boxing history. Aside from his actual fighting skills, Ali's mental toughness and self-belief were astonishing, and he was virtually impossible to intimidate. To me, he was a real-life superhero, equipped with a battle-tested force field. A captivation with martial arts superstar Bruce Lee soon followed, fuelling a fascination with the martial arts that remains fully active to this day.

Immersing myself wholeheartedly in the strong character philosophies of these real-life warriors provided me with the first glimpses of a model for dealing with my underlying vulnerabilities. I came to realise that I couldn't habitually retreat from everything that scared me, nor could I go through life avoiding difficult people or uncomfortable scenarios. To feel and exhibit the fortitude I admired so much in others, I'd have to take a page out of my heroes' books and learn how to toughen up both physically and mentally. I couldn't make things around me less intimidating, but I could make myself stronger.

# Martial arts and beyond

I ventured into my first kung fu class at Narwee Scout Hall in 1981. My friend Brad had been training with the club for some time and was already very good. On and off over the following couple of years, I attended classes with Brad and this represented the humble beginnings of my enduring martial arts journey.

After leaving high school, I studied hotel management while working my way up to leadership roles in the restaurant and conference business. At some point during this period, the kung fu club closed and my training sat idle. I was later introduced to the martial art of karate and trained on and off for a while in a nearby church hall. Unfortunately, I was heavily entrenched in shiftwork during this time, which made commitment difficult.

In 1992 at the age of 25, I left the hospitality industry and started working for a newly opened karate school in Sydney. Go-Kan-Ryu Karate (GKR Karate) had been operating in Adelaide, South Australia, for around eight years and was about to launch in New South Wales. It offered an opportunity to train in the martial art as part of my work and provided a pathway for a potential long-term career that could eventually lead to achieving my black belt. To me, this was a dream come true. To others around me, it seemed like I'd run away to join the circus because I'd left a stable management role in a conventional industry to pursue something untested and whimsical.

My work with GKR began at the very bottom. This included me knocking on doors in the evenings to promote memberships for their new locations, and then karate training during the day in an accelerated learning program. Since this unassuming start point, I have spent thousands of hours in the dojo sweating, stretching, punching, blocking, kicking, sweeping, falling, wrestling, sparring, winning, losing and learning. As each year passed, I could sense my technique developing significantly, and the exposure to a number of in-house instructor training programs saw my management and communication skills coalesce aptly with my improving karate standard.

Leadership opportunities emerged over time within the organisation as it expanded throughout Australia, New Zealand and the United Kingdom. In 2003, I was appointed the title of international vice president and senior instructor, overseeing karate and student development across the three countries. In 2017, I achieved the rank of 6th Dan Black Belt and was soon after awarded the title of *Shihan* (Shihan is the Japanese word for 'master' or 'expert instructor'). At around the same time, I became the chief operating officer and assistant chief instructor of GKR, which is currently a 35,000-plus member karate organisation.

Throughout my time in these roles, I have conducted countless special seminars and black belt training camps, assessed and graded over 2,000 black belts of various levels, taught tens of thousands of students from five years of age to 85, and made several trips to both Japan and Okinawa to train in karate's original birthplace. I have also been heavily involved in the selection, recruitment and development of hundreds of successful karate management personnel and senior directors. My central responsibility is to provide high-performance business coaching and 'trainer training' tuition for our leadership group, which over the years has included more than 3,000 karate instructors. I apologise for this rampant display of self-promotion, but my editor insisted I learn to play the trumpet for at least a few paragraphs!

Having worked and trained with so many individuals over the course of my career, there's been very little on the wide-ranging scale of human behaviours that I have not encountered or been responsible for addressing. In this book, I have combined these experiences with years of study and ardent self-examination to produce what I believe is a solid and well-rounded formula for peak performance. This personal management strategy includes the accumulated expertise derived from both my wins and losses, my triumphs and my mistakes.

# INTRODUCTION

AS A BASIC PHILOSOPHICAL starting point, it's essential to acknowledge that we cannot expect governments, institutions or other third parties to accommodate our desires. While the basic framework of 21st century society provides a certain degree of structure and opportunity, our life's journey can still nonetheless resemble an obstacle course. Some of these obstacles will be external, while others will be self-created. How we handle these roadblocks when they present themselves will determine whether they maintain a permanent hold over our life or a temporary one. If you're old enough to read this book, then you've already faced your fair share of these challenges and possibly started to reflect on how well your personal management strategy is dealing with them. Over time, we come to understand that it's not always feasible to blast our way through life's obstacles, nor should we instinctively retreat from them out of fragility. What matters most is that we remain mentally and physically adaptable enough to make adjustments in our approach when our working plan isn't serving us. If the actual terrain is different to how our own cognitive map is presenting it, then our map and its intended routes need updating.

The aim of this book is to share a formula for creating your own force field, which essentially represents an optimal management strategy for confronting and overcoming challenges experienced throughout your life. A 'force field' metaphorically represents the

> The force field engages in threat demolition, while also being your solution architect.

building of strength from the inside out – it symbolises the development of a protective aura that is equal parts offensive and defensive. In other words, the force field is not a static barrier, but more so a dynamic energy that radiates out into your immediate life experiences. This outgoing force makes it more difficult for incoming dangers to penetrate as they are met head-on by an opposing wave of problem-solving skills, guts and intensity. Hence, the force field engages in threat demolition, while also being your solution architect. It can help you address the external hazards as and when they enter and weaken the internal fragilities before they can seep outwards.

Our force field's potency is dependent on the attention we allocate to four key areas:

→ The WISDOM we accumulate
→ The WEAPONS we assemble
→ The WARNINGS we heed
→ The WAYS we practise

It's about how we acquire knowledge, develop skills, navigate around (or through) the hazards and take the necessary actions. The successful synergy of these components is intended to make us better life pilots by equipping us with the capabilities to power through certain trials and to successfully circumvent others. Inarguably, some of our wins in life come from fighting, some from letting go, some from negotiating, some from copping a loss and moving on, and some from accepting that there is no good solution. Achieving prosperity in any field is not about winning all the time; it's about having a winning attitude towards the inevitable setbacks.

Within these four core areas are a series of subcategories, each of which plays a role in strengthening the framework of their parent topics. The multiple chapters emphasise that a force field is not a single thing but a package of mental, physical, emotional and spiritual elements. These ingredients combine to strengthen our resolve and allow us to perform at a high level despite the negative influences, both internal and external, that seek to penetrate our emotional membrane from time to time. Creating our own psychological and physical suit of armour (shield) makes us more robust in the face of dangers and greatly enhances our chances of success in any field we pursue, whether it be personal, professional, sporting or otherwise. Synonymous with the shield is the *sword*. It reminds us that, sometimes, the best defence is offence and that we cannot simply defend our way through difficulties. Hence, the force field represents both the shield and the sword.

It is hoped that the stand-alone chapters in this book allow you to peruse the contents either randomly or in page order without disrupting comprehension. This acknowledges that while the topics may be linked as part of their greater theme, they can also be addressed separately. Furthermore, it's *not* necessary to perfectly relate to every topic; it's more important to let it hit you where it hurts and build strength where you need it. I believe we should

> The force field represents both the shield and the sword.

conduct our lives so as to be an example rather than a warning. This will not always be easy. At times there will be struggles, and the force field is about developing the capabilities to win these everyday skirmishes.

While entire books have been written on some of the single topics contained herein, my intention is to provide a practical level of understanding rather than dive textbook-deep into heavy theory. Right or wrong, I'd rather provide a usable exposure to many important topics than write a thesis on just a few. That said, I encourage anyone who deeply connects with some of the subjects covered to seek out more in-depth material via sources outside of these pages.

The intended takeaway from these notes is that even if you start out weak, you can end up strong, and what scares you doesn't necessarily have to stop you. Developing the most constructive mental response to challenging situations is part of our force field's composition, and it enables us to stay mobile and functioning while distress or pain works its way out of our system. This transformation takes place by design and not by default. While the normal passage of time provides us with many different experiences, it is up to us whether we convert these encounters into wisdom. Failure to thoughtfully reflect on our negative outcomes can reduce these experiences down to random and unexamined memories at best, or irreversible scar tissue at worst.

> Even if you start out weak, you can end up strong.

In sharing the best of my personal growth discoveries, I have little interest in sounding impressive and care much more about being relatable. In essence, while I see myself as a fundamentally average person, my aim is to be an above-average teacher who, through self-education, perseverance and sound personal management, is able to consistently embody the key principles being preached and communicate them to others in an impactful way.

# PART I

## THE

# WISDOM

## WE ACCUMULATE

# It starts with wisdom

THERE'S BEEN SOME DEBATE in personal coaching circles over the years as to whether new beginnings start with motivation or with education. The best argument I have heard against the pro-motivation origin theory is that an energetic burst of activity will only take us to our desired destination if we are pointing the right way to start with. If you inject motivation into someone who is aiming in the wrong direction, then they will simply arrive at the wrong place faster. Practising the wrong way just makes us better at the wrong way.

We cannot plant good seeds into nutrient deficient soil and expect a positive outcome, nor can a great structure be erected on unsteady ground. There's a good reason why a soil test is the mandatory first step taken by building contractors prior to digging the foundations as it provides unequivocal feedback on the 'lay of the land'. Without this education, the builder can tackle his new project with all the zeal he can muster, but still create something which is structurally unsound.

> Acquiring knowledge can be expensive, but it's nothing compared to the cost of ignorance.

Education is where it all begins – irrespective of the setting – because it encourages right thinking and dictates our initial trajectory. Right thinking develops from a combination of study and experience. Experience can come as a result of personal exposure or from observing the outcomes of other people's thought processes. These components culminate into wisdom which is the effective application of right thinking! Knowledge represents what you know, and wisdom is what you do with what you know. Most importantly, wisdom is the scaffolding around which our force field is constructed, and it ensures we never end up being *that* person with all the gear and no idea.

Acquiring knowledge as a lifelong avocation can be expensive, but it's nothing compared to the cost of ignorance. It's time to get smart!

# THE STUDENT

FULL DISCLOSURE. I'VE NEVER been a criminal and rehabilitated after prison. I've never experienced a potentially fatal weight gain, then lost it all via the latest spartan diet and exercise regime. I've never abused drugs or alcohol and gotten clean. I've never been addicted to gambling or been associated with shady underworld figures. I've never been rich and lost it all, or penniless and become an overnight billionaire. I didn't have an abusive upbringing and I wasn't raised in poverty.

In other words, I've not experienced the ill-treatment or brutal hardships that some people have endured to augment my backstory or make any of my existing achievements sound more heroic. There is no way most of us could compete hardship-wise with what the truly impoverished or unfortunate have suffered. While I unequivocally respect anybody who has triumphed over major adversity, my personal story is not a comeback tale. Thankfully, the offering of life guidance or performance coaching is not restricted to those who have survived extreme personal catastrophes.

That said, over the course of this life I've experienced my fair share of grief and suffering including the heartbreaking loss of loved ones, witnessing the physical and mental suffering of close family members, the feeling of being alone and without support or protection, the lament over stupid things I've said, the exasperation over poor decisions made, and the deep regret regarding things I've done and things I didn't do. While this laundry list of challenges could be broadly viewed as part of life, their effects are by no means trivial, and we are not naturally equipped to handle them deftly when they occur.

Whether your existence up to this point has been shaped by major calamity or not, there have undoubtedly been multiple triumphs and hardships along the way that have provided opportunities to learn lessons and increase your life IQ. Inherent curiosity is born of our desire to accumulate wisdom and involves regularly examining our approach to challenging situations and assessing whether adjustments need to be made going forward.

> It is imperative that you remain teachable.

Competitive sport provides an ideal classroom for learning how to problem-solve. The score at half-time dictates if your gameplan needs revising. If you are fighting someone in a martial arts match or sparring session, you need to make corrections quickly if what you are doing is not working. Whether your coach or instructor is providing external feedback, or if it's simply the score that's prompting your internal search for a better way, for your own personal growth and wellbeing, it is imperative that you remain teachable.

# The black belt

Different martial arts practices have varied ways of acknowledging excellence, with the black belt being the most universally recognised qualification. There is indeed a degree of mysticism surrounding this rank, with some of it justified and some of the expectations and beliefs exaggerated. While testing criteria can differ from one martial arts style to another, a common denominator is that achieving black belt means you have trained physically hard for many years, greatly improved your ability to protect yourself, and hopefully developed a mature and restrained character.

The black belt concept signifies worth in the dual practices of self-defence *and* self-development where combat skills and good character are in lockstep. The self-defence component could be viewed as resilience in the face of external threats including physical dangers or intimidation, while self-development implies the ability to manage and learn from our internally derived psychological burdens.

This book is not specifically about martial arts, nor is it necessary to be practising a martial art to understand its core themes. However, the force field concept shares many parallels to the ideal outcomes typically derived from self-defence training such as enhanced vigilance, strength and resilience.

Achieving a black belt in any martial art does not initiate a cosmic realignment of your immediate surroundings by reducing the number of potential threats you are exposed to. Nor does it make you invincible or impervious to pain. What it can do is make you less vulnerable to dangers and improve your ability to respond in a measured and courageous fashion. These valuable life skills can develop over time provided you adopt a studious approach towards all aspects of your training.

True character growth is not an automatic by-product of strenuous physical exercise alone. Moreover, it comes from a deliberate intention to approach the most important aspects of your training and life as a *student*. Becoming a black belt doesn't make you a perfect fighter, but it should make you a perfect student – in and out of the dojo.

Developing wisdom is a lifetime pursuit of the true martial arts practitioner and this should be no less important to any individual seeking high achievement in their field. With wisdom comes the understanding that the person we become is of greater value than the material objects or physical skills we acquire. Our solidity is more impactful than our prowess or our bank balance. Our ability to overcome the disappointment of losses is as important as developing the skills needed for victory.

The martial arts have taught me plenty about managing fear, handling physical limitations, accepting my own vulnerabilities, performing under the weight of expectation and genuinely admiring the abilities of others. It has helped me to understand that hard work beats talent when talent doesn't work hard; that repetition is the mother of skill; and that I can use my body to train my mind. It has shown me how things look worse from the sideline than when in front of you, and that on any given day even the best can be beaten.

Martial arts also instilled in me the universal method for becoming competent at any task by helping me appreciate the magic of technique. Virtually every high-level athlete or performer has a specific process that can be studied and emulated to produce a consistent outcome. Notwithstanding the fundamental advantages of genetics in top athletes, it is still possible for someone who is not blessed with natural mental or physical gifts to develop above-average skills. The martial art way or '*do*' (Japanese translation) also reminds us that we never stop learning – that we can never know it all.

If we were to spend our entire lives adopting a student's mindset, then aspiration, practice and progressive outcomes would take priority over us reaching an arbitrary summit.

A highly successful businessman once said to me, "Don't want what I have – want what I know." This meant the things he'd learned were more important than his material success. As we aim to create our own force field, our innate student is compelled to assemble a solid foundation of grounded and steadfast character traits that keep us moored to our core values irrespective of distractions, setbacks or temptations.

Many centuries ago, creeds such as the *Bushido Code* promoted a range of character-driven virtues as part of the samurai warrior mindset. As the feudal environment within their culture subsided, these principles morphed into guidelines about how chivalrous men should act in their personal and professional lives. In modern times, these qualities can be sought and practised in daily life by men and women equally.

Pursuing the highest standards of personal character should be the cornerstone of any self-improvement exercise. The martial arts Black Belt Code provides as good an example as any to follow.

黒
帯

# BLACK BELT CODE

| | |
|---|---|
| **Integrity** | where speaking and doing are the same action |
| **Honour** | possessing a sense of duty and commitment |
| **Loyalty** | maintaining a fidelity towards those to whom you are indebted |
| **Modesty** | exercising discretion and humility in all circumstances |
| **Respect** | applying due consideration for the desires and feelings of others |
| **Patience** | a calm tolerance of delays or difficulties |
| **Discipline** | doing what needs to be done irrespective of feelings |
| **Courage** | action in the presence of fear |
| **Resilience** | to endure or recover from difficulties (aka… having a 'good chin') |
| **Perseverance** | to stay the course without being discouraged by setbacks |
| **Presence** | remaining focused on the present; difficult to distract |
| **Calm** | mentally still and clear |
| **Balanced** | objective, considered, impartial |
| **Even-tempered** | pleasantly predictable; difficult to annoy or make angry |
| **Generous** | giving of time and knowledge |
| **Mindful** | awareness of self and surroundings |
| **Moral** | adopting mature ethics in all interactions |

The true black belt strives to conduct themselves outside the dojo as they do inside. In other words, there should be no such thing as wearing two hats – and this same sense of ethical consistency should apply to the non-martial artist. For example, being punctual, well-mannered and respectful is not just applicable to job interviews and first dates; it should be a default behavioural setting.

> The more we prepare beforehand, the less we'll need to repair afterwards.

Given that these black belt characteristics are not necessarily instinctive or dictated by genetics, the overriding purpose of adopting the student's mentality towards them is to help us evolve into better life-managers. Whether we like it or not, we'll either need to become adept at managing ourselves and our immediate environment, or expert at either (a) failing and/or (b) apologising. The more we prepare beforehand, the less we'll need to repair afterwards. The harder we work on ourselves, the less time we'll spend in recovery or cleaning up the remnants of our missteps.

# A well-managed journey

There are some unavoidable misfortunes in life such as rare illnesses, freak accidents and untimely deaths. However, considerably more of the hardships we regularly experience are self-created; they are the unintended consequences of poor decision-making, ineffectual self-management or ignorance. History is full of accounts of early explorers who set out on reckless pioneering expeditions only to hit rocks, run out of food, lose crew members, be forced to eat their dogs (or each other) and ultimately die brutal and lonely deaths. This type of disaster makes for a much better movie plot than the responsible explorer who planned properly, listened to well-educated advisers, charted a course, stuck to it with discipline and arrived at their destination with full crew intact.

Given the option, most of us would choose to live our lives without unnecessary difficulties or self-imposed dramas. We'd like to think we could achieve a broad spectrum of success that includes living well into old age with family, friendships, finances and health intact.

Unfortunately, the tale of the 'well-managed journey' is not very sexy – but it should be! Fame and glory seekers would no doubt find such a solid and dependable life path to be a little beige, and it would certainly fly in the face of the 'gung-ho, kick butt, take no prisoners' message regularly peddled online by a number of success coaches.

> The 'well-managed journey' is not very sexy – but it should be!

The harsh reality is that we are living in an era where performing consistently well, in the broader success metrics of wealth, health, family and friendships, is increasingly rare. None of us have to search too far into our family or friendship network to find instances of serious sibling conflict, marital breakdowns, financial distress, mental illness, career frustration, friendship fractures, substance abuse or poor general health. Right or wrong, many of these sociological difficulties were typically seen as characteristic of low-income communities in years gone by, but they are now ubiquitous across the full stratum of society. Therefore, navigating our lives through or around these circumstances should be viewed as a measurement of success in itself.

In reference to the early pioneers, my endeavour is to illuminate and glamorise the story of the common explorer who achieves their degree of 'everyday success' by carefully charting their course and executing a well-managed journey.

'Everyday success' could be described as spending most of your time engaged in fulfilling activities while maintaining the right balance between work, home, finances, health and relationships. It represents a form of personal and professional equilibrium that allows us to keep all of life's most crucial characteristics in a healthy place. Sometimes, we refer to this as 'living our best life'.

This balanced approach provides a secure underpinning for all and any subsequent personal growth enrichment and makes competence an integral part of our personal brand and identity. I believe we should all strive to personally identify as over-achievers rather than high achievers. This may seem like semantics, but the term 'high achiever' tends to measure success in comparison with others whereas 'over-achiever' suggests you've punched above your weight and achieved more than your born characteristics and childhood environment suggested you could. While it's nice to see other people achieving great things around us, exceeding their accomplishments should rarely be part of our internal fuel formula.

# The 'secret'

The term 'secret' means something that is kept unknown or unseen by others. For many years, a number of business coaches, motivational speakers and authors have portrayed the successful characteristics of accomplished individuals as highly coveted secrets that they, and perhaps a handful of others, have managed to obtain: 'The secrets of success', 'The secret ingredient', 'The hidden laws of… ', or just plain *The Secret* are all well-worn staples of self-help parlance. I therefore offer my contribution to this theme: The real secret is that almost nothing is secret.

> The real secret is that almost nothing is secret.

The knowledge we seek to strengthen our constitution and thrive in our most valued pursuits is available everywhere and all the time. This includes public libraries, bookstores, Google, YouTube and so on. But we won't find any of it if we are not searching. While it's true that great opportunities will occasionally fall into our laps, we will fail to recognise their arrival if we haven't done our homework.

Wisdom is more than knowledge, yet it starts with knowledge. Whether you adopt a martial arts code or follow some other enriching philosophy, maintaining a student's mindset ensures you become wiser as you age and avoid becoming the person with 30 years' experience but only one year of expertise.

# WISDOM #2

# PERSPECTIVE

WISDOM IS THE HIGHEST rung on the intellectual ladder and, presumably, it forms because of worldly experience and considered thought. Broadly speaking, wisdom is the consistent application of an enlightened outlook, which could be defined as a series of constructive and fluid conclusions as to how the world works. One of the chief contributors to the formation of these conclusions is our perspective.

Perspective is placing a proportional amount of attention on an issue relative to its degree of importance. It represents our view, our angle, and our interpretation or perception of events and things that happen around us. How we interpret something we see or hear has a significant bearing on how we respond to it. Recognising the role perspective plays in our daily interactions is made easier when we consider that in any situation, there is:

- what happened (the facts)
- what we think happened (our perspective of what happened)

- what we think about what we think happened (the conclusions we draw from our perspective of what happened).

Given the above, it's easy to see how two people can interpret the same issue or outcome in two very different ways.

To suggest someone has a sound perspective is to indicate they have a mature and sensible mentality towards a particular subject or towards life in general. Exercising perspective is characteristic of adopting a balanced view and suggests we keep our thoughts, behaviours and emotions regarding pertinent matters in their rightful ratio. The path to true wisdom is reliant on the development of an even-handed and considered perspective, where objectivity exceeds bias and where logic and emotion are given equal votes.

Drawing measured conclusions towards key topics such as relationships, progress or disappointments results in more thoughtful and productive behaviours. This can often be dependent upon an individual's default disposition. For example, negatively charged people tend to adopt downbeat perspectives and are more likely to be pessimistic or cynical in their outlooks. We'd all like to think that we're nobody's fool and that learning how to separate the wheat from the chaff is an important life skill. But habitually adopting suspicions towards other people, the economy or global politics only discolours our world view and encourages contempt at every turn.

By contrast, an optimist will likely give an issue the benefit of a fair trial, look for an opportunity to learn something new, develop a more mature outlook and take extra time to arrive at a more constructive conclusion. This more sophisticated perspective encourages us to be discerning without being cynical, cautious without being pessimistic and trusting without being naïve.

In acknowledging the influence that someone's disposition has on how they interpret specific subjects, we must remember that dispositions are generally developed – not inherited. The majority of our ineffective core beliefs have likely been fashioned from years of exposure to the wrong sources and the subsequent accumulation of corrupted data. In these circumstances, the decisions we make are not 'wrong' because they are based on the data we have collected; rather, it is the corrupt data we have accumulated that produces bad decisions. This observation reminds us again to stand guard at the door of our minds.

While we can be forgiven for initially onboarding other people's attitudinal inclinations during our formative and adolescent years, our desire to become independent thinkers should urge us to gut and renovate certain perspectives where needed. Ultimately, possessing a narrow or overly judgemental perspective is likely to mean we look out the window at beautiful scenery and only notice the small spots of dirt on the glass. If our perspective filter is dirty, it becomes difficult to recruit our clearest thinking.

## Perspective shapes our philosophy

Progressively, our perspectives amalgamate into an organised set of values known as our personal philosophy. This shapes our subjective reality and reinforces that things are indeed what they seem. In effect, we usually find what we are looking for – good or bad.

Immovable certainty is a trait reserved for zealots and the uneducated, whereas the mature and open-minded individual remains

> Immovable certainty is a trait reserved for zealots and the uneducated.

flexible enough to allow for shifts, whether it be minor fine-tuning or full-blown re-examination. This helps us to navigate our way through life's challenges, maintain credibility, remain relevant and stay connected with the generations who follow. It also fosters better decision-making and preserves our significance as thought leaders within our family or community.

Each of us has personal opinions and our views on important topics dictate how we vote, who we listen to, talk to, love and hate, and how accepting we are of who is running the country. These views and their resulting behaviours can lead us towards a successful outcome or an inescapable disaster – and everything in-between. Perspectives will therefore dictate our trajectory and our destiny.

# Make time for learning

Many people today find themselves trapped in a hedonistic virtual world that instantly delivers every indulgence to their personal handheld device. The addiction to light entertainment and explicit content is rivalled only by the irrational worshipping of food and the glamorisation of insobriety, baseless fame and overt attention seekers. These distractions serve to hijack people's mental focus as they are jettisoned into a 24/7 world of sports (and now sports betting), news headlines, melodramas and social media sideshows.

With such a long list of distractions, it is difficult for these 'busy' people to find time for self-examination. Worse still, when they look left and right, they see that they are pretty much within the pack, watching and talking about the same things as most others within their social group. This shared environment often provides false comfort by making people think it is acceptable (or at least harmless) to be infatuated by facile issues such as who the bachelor is going to choose, which bathroom renovation looks better or what bombshell comment the judge will make about the deflated souffle.

There are some exceptions where individuals immerse themselves in vacuous amusements yet still attain success. In much the same way, the occasional person can smoke a packet of cigarettes each day and still live until they're 95. In playing life's odds, however, we should do our best to create the most favourable conditions for progress and personal achievement. Feasting on a diet of low GI attractions (low *genius index*) will most likely produce a significant cumulative downside in respect to financial success, good health, career advancement or personal happiness. It is crucial for us to acknowledge that our minds have a large but limited capacity and if we fill them with garbage, there is little space for anything else.

How a person thinks is a major factor in determining their life path. We should be constantly examining our views for relevance and accuracy in the light of new experiences. Having the willingness to challenge our current working perspectives is the first step. Then, as we blend the old with the new, the outcome either strengthens our existing ideas or we adopt new and improved ones.

The winds that blow are unpredictable. Sometimes they are at our back and other times in our face. Navigating our way through the inclement periods of life is akin to that of a skilled yachtsman who adeptly adjusts the angle and tension of his sails to traverse a path across an opposing gale. Reaching his desired destination is more about his response to the conditions rather than how favourable or unfavourable the conditions are. The yachtsman's navigational adjustments mirror the mental and emotional fine-tuning that our fluid perspectives and personal philosophies enable us to make throughout the course of our lives.

Failure to capitalise on the potential power of adaptive thinking is likely to blow us off course during adverse circumstances. In these

> In many cases, upgrading our perspectives is more about removal than addition.

instances, our opinion rigidity will see our movement resemble the windsock, which simply tracks the same direction as the prevailing wind and deposits us wherever the externalities dictate.

Accumulating a set of constructive perspectives that move us towards a desired experience or destination can provide us with the critical thinking utility that makes us more resilient in the face of challenges, and thereby strengthens our force field. In many cases, upgrading our perspectives is more about removal than addition. Letting go of an illusion or stripping away destructive beliefs can often make us wiser than discovering a new truth.

In the process of sorting through your personal list of beliefs to eliminate, the distinction to make is not whether your current perspectives are right or wrong, but more so whether they are helpful or unhelpful. Focus less on whether your gripe about something is justified or not and focus instead on whether that viewpoint is serving you well.

For instance, if a woman believes that men cannot be trusted, this has a significant bearing on all her future relationships with men. Based on her past experiences, there may very well be factual evidence to support her view, but failure to relax that belief could mean she either continues to attract untrustworthy men or she creates an unhealthy suspicion that repels the honest ones. Likewise, if a man adopts the global belief that women are too emotional, he is likely to be perpetually accused of insensitivity due to his dismissive attitude towards what may be justifiable grievances from women he works or socialises with. Ultimately, we will only see and hear what our bias allows us to.

In terms of effectiveness, your personal philosophy can be measured on whether it is moving you forwards or backwards. Over time, life will serve us a relatively even dose of sweet and sour, and simply wishing for less of the sour is futile. In our pursuit of higher goals, we would do well to remember that the best place to start is the five to six inches between our ears.

# WISDOM #3

# MIND FIELDS

THERE ARE MANY PARTS to your life for which you should accept full responsibility. Unfortunately, your thoughts are not always one of these parts. In a sense, your mind has a mind of its own. Day in, day out, thoughts appear and disappear – and then sometimes reappear. They arrive without warning and leave without ceremony. These thoughts continue to gatecrash your conscious headspace until you draw your last breath. Some of them are positive, but it's possible that more are negative and present themselves in the form of worry, fear, regret, anger or sadness.

In the self-help world, there are many schools of thought that advocate positive thinking; the presumption here is that you need to have more control over your internal narrative. It is disappointing when we discover that we have no more control over what thoughts enter our minds than we do over what our dog might be thinking at the same time. Acknowledging this helps bring attention to our relationship with these thoughts and liberates us from liability in relation to their content. We can be no more responsible for our thoughts than we can be for red lights, full moons, thunderstorms or solar flares. We cannot control all of our thoughts – only our responses to them.

Thoughts are not the problem – believing them or mistaking them for reality is where we come unstuck. Metaphorically speaking, thoughts can be compared to ocean waves. As they barrel towards the shore, we usually have the choice to ride the wave (or thought) or float above it as it rolls under us. In most cases, riding the wave is a voluntary exercise, as is the activity of latching on and being affected adversely by thoughts.

> We cannot control all of our thoughts – only our responses to them.

This choice is not widely realised, resulting in most people being unable to differentiate between who they are and what they are thinking. To these people, there is no distinction between thought and reality. What they imagine becomes real and affects them like it happened, in much the same way that young children can believe the movie they are watching is real.

It is like believing your nightly dreams represent truth, when these uncontrolled nocturnal showreels reflect little more than the haphazard firing of your unconscious imagination. In most cases, they represent an extension of the experiences you knowingly or unknowingly absorbed throughout that day or past days, or things that may worry you about the future. As mystical as it may be to entertain the possibility that dreams are 'real' and act as the prophet of future events, a simpler rationale is that they symbolise the same random mental machinations that we encounter constantly and involuntarily when awake.

# Are you out of your mind?

This is a question you may be asked if you've proposed something crazy or nonsensical. From a practical perspective, however, being 'out of your mind' is not a bad idea sometimes.

Thanks to a number of pioneers, the concept of mindfulness has become a staple in Western psychology and has found its way into the national healthcare services of many countries. It has even been widely recognised as a valuable tool in institutions like the military as an effective method for reducing stress, enhancing emotional intelligence and handling unpleasant thoughts or feelings.

Mindfulness is deliberately paying close attention to what is happening both internally and externally in a specific and non-judgemental way. At its core, mindfulness helps us distinguish between who we are and what we think. For us, on a personal level, it stimulates a more direct contact with the world rather than just living through our thoughts. It involves consciously bringing awareness to what is immediately happening with an open mind. It encourages us to just notice what's around us and let things be.

Practising mindfulness means we become good at noticing stuff and are less inclined to build opinions or be overly reactive to that stuff. It allows our nervous system to know itself better and interfere with itself less. This provides a unique clarity that heightens our moment-by-moment sensory experiences.

It is important to accept we are not in control of the conception, duration or composition of our thoughts and that trying to subdue, regulate or vanquish them is a fruitless exercise. The 'quiet mind' is a mirage. The best we can do is improve our ability to discriminate between the thoughts we embrace and those we decide to witness as they arrive and leave.

It is much easier to understand this concept than to practise it, given that our unconscious mind is not adept at discerning between what's real and what seems real. This illustrates that the most significant impediment to living more mindfully is the mind. Being mindful means that when the thought appears, we notice its arrival and simply acknowledge our awareness of it. If the thought is irrationally negative, then simply allow it to float by.

Aside from being attached to a thought, we can also become lost in thought. This is where we are thinking without knowing we're thinking and doing so at the expense of experiencing. This automaticity of mindlessly following our thoughts around can distort our interpretation of reality. The often rudderless and chaotic behaviour of our monkey mind – our chattering uncontrollable thoughts – creates a mental discord that has the potential to engineer unhappiness. Our goal is to observe destructive and unhelpful thoughts without judgement or analysis and cultivate the art of living consciously by remembering that our reality is not necessarily governed by what we think.

Once we understand the genesis of our thoughts, we can appreciate that the currents and swells of our mind have nothing to do with us. Instead, we can simply observe without attachment and not overreact each time the waves appear. We can make peace with our mind and accept it for what it is and what it does. The ultimate reward for developing this wisdom is a respite from much of life's tumult.

# Separating behaviour from thought

Our memories, thoughts, feelings and beliefs create inclinations within us to act in particular ways. For example, if we're feeling cheerful and self-assured, we behave differently than if we are sad, angry or fearful. However, if we mindlessly follow our emotional impulses, we relinquish responsibility for our actions and then become hopeful that the right thoughts or emotions materialise at the right time somewhere down the track.

The most important goal when trying to separate your behaviour from your thoughts is to reclaim your personal authority to behave in a manner consistent with your goals, irrespective of your thoughts or feelings. With a careful and measured approach, it is possible for our thoughts and emotions – positive and negative – to surge through us without any discernible opposition or attachment, and no longer automatically dictate our actions.

# IMPERMANENCE

PIVOTAL TO THE DEVELOPMENT of wisdom is making peace with the temporary nature of things. This is one of the most important philosophical principles for any human being to embrace. Temporary is a relative term, and by most people's interpretation, it indicates something short-lived. The literal meaning of temporary refers to anything that is not permanent. In other words, everything in this life is temporary on a fundamental level.

> The wise can be compared to water and the unenlightened to rock.

Life, it has been said, is like a river of passing events. No sooner is one thing brought into sight than it is washed away for something else to take its place. This other thing will, of course, be swept away as well at some point. Change is a natural constant that the wise and the unenlightened respond to in contrasting ways. The wise can be compared to water and the unenlightened can be compared to rock. Rocks do not transform; they break down or wear away with time. Water is the ultimate example of true flexibility because it maintains its internal composition while perfectly adapting to the shape of its surroundings.

Nothing is fixed or lasts forever – including the mind. Each moment is a new moment of mind, and our thoughts, emotions and sense of reality change from moment to moment. The cells within our bodies are constantly being broken down and restored. Externally, both the natural and man-made world changes around us moment by moment, day by day and year by year. Family and friends come and go; they are born and they pass. We hope that love is everlasting, and we cling vainly to our material possessions.

But our efforts to acquire and hold on to what we have will ultimately end at zero. This is the conclusive and definitive irony – only by embracing our mortality (our impermanence) can we really appreciate what we have now.

# Every day is a dying day

We tend to cycle through our days as if they were endless, rarely acknowledging the inherent frailties of life and taking little heed of how much time has already passed. We mindlessly consume time as if extracting it from an abundant supply – even though each day could be our last. Our lives really do resemble sand passing through an hourglass. It's this liberating realisation that needs to jolt our attention into living each day as if it were precious.

> We mindlessly consume time as if extracting it from an abundant supply.

As we age, we are forced to accept that there is less time left than has already been and that the hours ahead are not as guaranteed as the ones we have already lived. This realisation makes our ongoing attention, work ethic, self-awareness, generosity and personal growth more critical. Every moment is literally unique and irretrievable. This viewpoint should urge us to be bold and to act as if there were no limits to our potential.

Many people create intricate belief systems to diminish the finality of death, but the concept of impermanence reminds us to live our life like it is temporary. As morbid as it may sound, it is dying that makes life so significant. This is why we should be encouraged to practise living each day with the end in mind.

If we were to live more with an 'every day is precious' ideology, we would certainly be enlightened enough to appreciate the mobility and relative freedom of our youth, young adulthood and middle age. If we make it to old age, we could be regarded (or disregarded) as 'seniors' – a common euphemism that implies being slow of thought and speech, in constant physical pain, and allied to a pantry of soft foods. By this stage of our lives, we will have inevitably experienced many losses, all silent preparations for the eventual loss of our own life. My mother reminds me regularly that growing old is not for wimps.

In the end, impermanence laughs at us because all that is mortal will expire; all matter turns to dust, and we will inevitably lose everything we love. This can be a confronting and perhaps frightening outlook. But, if we can interpret this fear as a perfectly reasonable uneasiness that helps extract maximum joy and meaning from the present moment, then it can be both instructive and inspiring.

# External changes demand internal changes

Acknowledging the concept of impermanence prompts us to make peace with change in our lives. This could represent changes in our health, relationships, appearance, physical or mental capabilities, business, the economy and so on. Most people tend to be the same behaviourally and philosophically at 50 as they were at 20 – inertia or habit becoming the predominant driver of their actions rather than conscious choice or open-minded inspection.

If we allow ourselves to become too immersed in habit, become overly risk-averse or afraid of change, we face the possibility of becoming little more than a compilation of unexamined patterns driven by the mindless reiteration of past events or mistakes. Truly accepting change as the greatest constant in our life assists us to navigate the passage of time with dexterity and a sense of contentment. From a practical perspective, however, we must ensure that thoughts, wishes and intentions are not mistaken for actual change, especially where recurring patterns of maladaptive behaviour are concerned.

## Solidity vs fluidity

Virtually everything around us, and biologically within us, is in a constant state of change, and we must be prepared to roll with it when necessary. Our obsession with viewing things as 'solid', when they are actually not so fixed, invariably creates an internal friction that frustrates us to no end. Stress is created when we apply resistance to 'what is'.

Perhaps the greatest metaphor exemplifying this is how the surf lifesaving community coaches its young nippers to respond if they find themselves being pulled out to sea by a rip. Rather than attempting to take the seemingly shorter route of swimming directly back to where they entered the water, they are taught instead to 'go with the flow'. The rip will drag them out beyond the breakers and begin transporting them sideways along the beach for a certain distance. Eventually the rip dissipates, and the swimmer is left in relatively current-free waters and can swim back to the nearest shoreline. It also teaches them that they need to save their strength early on so they can make it back. Fighting against Mother Nature's flow by stubbornly trying to swim back through the rip would almost certainly lead to exhaustion and drowning.

Acceptance is often the most constructive initial response we can make to a moment or experience. Sooner or later, we all must accept the inevitability of change and apply the wisdom of flexibility and non-resistance. As we get older, attitudinal or behavioural rigidity only produces dissatisfaction, given that nothing ever stays the same. Until we come to this realisation, we will continue to swim against the tide and be wedded to suffering.

> Change is inescapable but growth is optional.

Change is inescapable but growth is optional. Anyone who stops changing and learning becomes old. Uncertainty is the only certainty and knowing how to live with insecurity is the only thing that can offer us genuine and ongoing emotional security.

# SUCCESS

SUCCESS IS AS MUCH about perspective as it is about a result. Money is traditionally the most common unit of measurement for success in Western society. But if your goalposts are constricted to an amount of money, then you won't feel successful until you're financially wealthy. The real danger in focusing only on money is that it may blind you from your other non-financial accomplishments and successes. How you define success determines how you calculate it and dictates how you organise your priorities in life.

The topics in this section represent some of the most valuable pieces of advice I've received and practised in relation to success.

## Establish what matters most

Socrates famously stated, "The unexamined life is not worth living." This means that a life lived absent of tenet or forethought is a life vulnerable to external forces and the decisions and behaviours of others. Furthermore, Socrates contested that an individual who does not plan or give deep consideration to their life is like a stranger in

> Consistency is more important than intensity.

a foreign land without a compass. For such people, any turn in the road is as good or bad as any other, and if they end up somewhere worthwhile then it will have been by accident. Basically, if you don't know where you're going, any road will take you there.

Success should be seen as a marathon rather than a sprint. In terms of the effort exerted and the rewards experienced during the race, consistency is more important than intensity.

I view success with a wide lens as being the deliberate and balanced management of the following personal elements:

1. Time
2. Health
3. Energy
4. Relationships
5. Money

Each person allocates greater importance to some of these categories than others. However, the more even the balance of time and energy apportioned to each one, the more 'whole' their success will be. Many of us have heard the time vs money argument, and it's a good debate to have. There are countless top executives who are financially rich yet time poor. There are also those who have plenty of time but very little in the way of material freedom. Adding to this, it is almost cliché to reference the man who was laser-focused on building his business over many years, only to find himself divorced (sometimes more than once), disconnected from his children and physically burnt out at the end of it. Ironically, single or multiple divorces will likely separate this man from his highly sought-after affluence anyway. This is not winning when measured by the aggregate of the above key elements.

# Define your success in relation to the five key elements

We all need to define what constitutes a successful position in terms of our money, time, energy levels, relationships and personal health. How would you characterise success in relation to the following basic questions?

- ➢ What would your ideal workday/week look like?
- ➢ How would you like your body to look and feel most of the time?
- ➢ If you have a partner, what would you, as a successful couple, do or share on a regular basis?
- ➢ What actions would you consistently take that made you feel you were being a good parent or son or daughter?
- ➢ What would your bank balance or asset position need to be?
- ➢ What material possessions would you like to hold?
- ➢ How often would you like to travel each year and where to?
- ➢ Would you need to be giving of your time, knowledge or money to others less fortunate, and if so, what would this entail?
- ➢ By what age would you ideally start living this life?

By developing more clarity around our definition of success, we realise that success is an ongoing feeling rather than a single point in time. If we conduct life in such a way that we feel fulfilled in these five critical areas, we are winning the day, the week, the month and winning at succeeding. When we experience this feeling of proportion with greater consistency, we become more balanced in our pursuits and less solely reliant on a lofty financial position to be happy.

These daily, weekly and monthly winnings all have a cumulative value: they create positive chain reactions that generate momentum and progress. This compounding mechanism reminds us that incremental change can bear exponential fruit. Even if you are employed in a basic job with a modest income, you can still feel unashamedly fulfilled and spiritually wealthy in that role and use this to bolster your self-worth and sense of success. Simply put, success is not so much a cause of happiness, but happiness is a major part of success.

# Ignite your inner contrarian

If you think, act and talk about the same things as the average person, then it's unlikely that you will exceed the average in terms of wealth, income, fitness and so on. If you aspire to be an over-achiever, you have to be prepared to go against societal or workplace norms. Statistics tell us that the overwhelming majority of working people are engaged in unsatisfying work that pays them less than they aspire to and takes up too much space in their minds – even when they are not at work.

If you are striving for something that is uncommon, you must be prepared to practise uncommon disciplines to get there. This could involve being engaged in a business enterprise instead of receiving a safe wage, or sacrificing part of your leisure time and devoting it to learning something valuable.

Moreover, any attempt to go the extra mile or remove an unrewarding routine from your life should be stoked with an awareness that you can either have it easy now and hard later, or hard now and easy later. The promise of cumulative progress from continually doing that little bit extra can be a powerful driving force. It's easy to follow the status quo but to be successful in anything, we cannot seek what is popular or easy over what is worthwhile. In making our choices and decisions, we must also consider that the opinion of the majority is not the measure of what is correct. This reminds us of the age-old quality vs quantity debate where, in this instance, the credible individual should be given greater credence than the group-thinking mob.

> To be successful, we cannot seek what is popular or easy over what is worthwhile.

## 'Well done' is better than 'Well said'

The difference between who you are and who you want to be is what you do. No amount of reading or memorising positive material will give you the success you desire. It is only the understanding and application of right thinking that can make a difference. For many people, the knowledge-to-action gap is substantial. They may know what to do but fail to do what they know. Success is unalterably connected with action, and successful people keep moving. They may make mistakes, but they don't quit.

As a business owner, you don't get paid for your time. Rather, you get paid for the value your actions create. When you apply this principle to your health, you realise your body won't change relative to the number of hours you spend flicking through low-fat recipes but more so by what you ultimately choose (or choose not) to put in your mouth. It's important that we approach worthwhile activities knowing there won't always be an immediate or perceptible result each time we engage. When we review how we measure our efforts, we can understand that sometimes success is largely about swinging the bat and not always about winning every inning. Life is a participation sport, not a spectator sport. Perhaps even more poignantly, there are those who analyse and commentate and those who play.

# Don't be distracted by criticism

*"The only taste of success some people get is to take a bite out of you."*

—Zig Ziglar

In the early stages of our martial arts club's expansion, we were more than prepared to think outside the box and weren't afraid to try things that had not previously been attempted in that field. As such, there were plenty of 'peacocks' in the industry trying to derail us with overt criticism and threats of violence as we opened new schools around the country. This bothered me in the early stages as I was relatively young and overly concerned with the approval of others.

I soon came to realise, however, that these people didn't actually know me personally and weren't visualising my face whenever they passed judgement. In the end, the vocal protests and threatening behaviour dwindled to something that more resembled a group of people who liked another football team attacking you for having an allegiance to your favourite club. What I witnessed, for the most part, was a combination of rivalry and jealousy.

I look back at the early criticisms we received from opposition clubs and acknowledge that one or two of them may have been warranted. At the time, though, we were committed to achieving certain outcomes for the greater good, which compensated for some of the initial shortcomings in our approach. Had we let the criticism from our competitors overly influence our forward thrust, it's unlikely we would have endured long enough to keep improving our standards and methods over time.

Your competition in almost any field will display the following behaviours if you're doing well and *only* when you're doing well:

1. When you first arrive, they will ignore you.
2. When you start to get traction, they will denigrate you.
3. When you start to succeed, they will try to copy you.

In the present day, social media has spawned a veritable galaxy of negativity that demands high-profile actors, politicians, educators and the like be able to absorb an unearthly amount of brutal and ruthless criticism. The cost of fame and success has grown exponentially as a result, making the construction of our own person deflector shield (force field) even more crucial.

# Moderate your expectations

While it's established that hopelessness and low expectations have a debilitating effect on progress, the opposite – high expectations – can also generate disappointment. We are bombarded with many images of success each day via TV, billboards, advertising and social media that are superficial and unattainable. If you're always aiming at achieving or acquiring the 'next thing', then consequently there is no time or emotional space to enjoy the 'now thing' you may have just accomplished.

Moderating expectations does not mean you should aim low. Rather, this is cautionary advice to those who are perpetually disappointed with their own outcomes or frustrated by the high achievements (or behaviour)

> Moderating expectations does not mean you should aim low.

of other people. You can decide what you really want without meaninglessly comparing yourself to others or by subscribing to the self-serving urgings of modern advertising.

# Make friends with failure

It is next to impossible to explore the topic of success without allowing space for its opposite – failure. Failure has several other appearances in future pages, so in this section I only provide a brief synopsis of its fundamental relationship to winning.

Success, as they say, is not forever and failure is not fatal. Moving towards or maintaining success is not about avoiding failure because you won't. The real question is whether you let failure toughen you into action or pacify you into inaction. Ultimately, failure is simply a result; it's a learning experience, a chance to find out what doesn't work and perhaps even an opportunity to develop your sense of humour.

Many people allow an unwanted result in their life to negatively impact thoughts about their future. For example, if they find their bank balance is low after years of working (the unwanted result), they may conclude that achieving a wealthy status is beyond them and then use those thoughts to build an overriding theme of struggle going forward. These people will likely maintain their poor financial position.

The present state of our health, career, relationships and bank balance is primarily the physical manifestation of our previous attitudes in action. To improve our results in the physical world, we must first change our internal thoughts and attitudes. How we handle failure is one of the most beneficial matters we can address.

# Prepare for good luck

When contemplating the role that good luck is likely to have in your future, you must first acknowledge the countless instances of good luck with which you have already been blessed. If you've made it to 21 years of age and you're living in a free country, then you've already had more good fortune than you could possibly imagine. The trick is to be able to appreciate what you've been gifted instead of moaning about your bad luck, and to recognise good luck when it presents itself.

Luck is where preparation meets opportunity, and the preparation part is 100 per cent our responsibility. It's not always possible to dictate the arrival or abundance of opportunities, but you can be ready to profit from them.

Sport provides us with many obvious examples of individuals or teams who successfully capitalised on opportunities presented to them by either their opposition or by some unique twist of fate. One of the best examples is when Australian Olympic speed skater Steve Bradbury was at the 2002 Winter Olympics in Salt Lake City. Bradbury captured the world's attention when he won the gold medal in the 1,000-metre event after all of his opponents were involved in a major pile-up at the final turn in the race. Bradbury was coming last at the time but skated through the scattered bodies to breeze over the line in first place. The reflex response from the casual observer was to label his win as a spectacular stroke of luck, but this fails to acknowledge both the thousands of hours involved in his extensive preparation and the fact he had to qualify to be in that final in the first place. It's true that a unique and unexpected opportunity was laid out in front of him that day, but he had to be prepared in order to profit.

It seems, ironically, that the people who enjoy the most luck are the ones who depend on it the least. Successful people appear to earn their good luck. Through courage, know-how, planning, good instincts and hard work, they seize openings and capitalise, and can appear to be lucky. A positive mindset heightens the ability to recognise these opportune moments, whereas a more downcast temperament fosters negativity and blinds an individual from subtle signals of good fortune.

# The front foot

'Getting on the front foot' is a phrase often referenced in the sport of cricket. It refers to the technique that a batsman adopts when attempting to play positively and/or aggressively. As the name suggests, it involves stepping your front foot down the pitch to meet the ball earlier, potentially catching it on the half-volley and negating any movement the ball may have off the pitch. It is also the precursor to the most classical and revered shot in cricket – the cover drive. Operating on the back foot, by contrast, is synonymous with being defensive.

To maximise our chances of recognising good fortune and mobilising our skills at the right time, we must adopt the 'front foot' mentality to those things in life we treasure the most. From a practical viewpoint, this means we build an image of what we want, and then start acting like we already have it. In the dojo, we understand that we have to train like a black belt before we become one. We often need to see or imagine something mentally before we can ever obtain it physically.

# WISDOM #6

# MONEY

MONEY'S DOMINANCE IN OUR lives and its notoriety for causing division more than justifies its own chapter. Discerning how one can best exhibit wisdom when it comes to money is indeed the million-dollar question as we seek to enjoy its spoils and not be engulfed by its negative consequences.

The concept of money is one of the strangest phenomena in our lives. On one hand, it is a universal identification of productivity, means, status and lifestyle, while on the other it is central to many forms of corruption, exploitation and misery. Money's influence is pervasive in all levels of society and is alluring even to those who supposedly spurn it. This is not surprising. It has been an integral part of our thought space since we were old enough to notice our mother hand the ice-cream man a piece of coloured paper in exchange for a soft serve.

The sense of ownership we attach to our money ranks right up there with our children and our spouse, yet very few people admit to this. Furthermore, it's unlikely that those who denounce money's significance would react passively if the money they had was somehow taken away.

Money is also a highly charged topic. We have all heard the warnings about not discussing politics and religion at parties and anyone who has violated this edict could testify to its veracity. Discussing politics is akin to discussing money, since most political arguments are centred around whether money is being distributed fairly by the government of the day.

Differences of opinion about money have destroyed successful business partnerships, split families, filled therapists' waiting rooms, manipulated the stock market, and contributed to suicides and many other things. People even fight over someone else's deceased estate because they believe they have a claim to it, as is evidenced by the extraordinary number of siblings presently contesting their parent's will. Needless to say, most people take their money very seriously.

# The root of all evil

Money often gets a bad rap, but if money could defend itself, its first rebuttal would surely be to point out that it is merely numbers on a piece of paper/plastic (well, it's a digital record now). By itself, money is neither good nor evil and could simply be seen instead as a form of energy. It is also morally neutral in every sense of the word and can serve the highest and the lowest within a society. These perspectives rightfully lay the responsibility for the outcomes money creates firmly at the feet of the individual using it.

As an unashamed *Star Wars* fan, I've often thought that the concept of 'the force' was a perfect euphemism for wealth. The force is a magical power that is ubiquitous throughout the *Star Wars* universe but its exploitation for either good or evil is dependent on the values, character and ambitions of the person harnessing it. The 'dark side' (think Darth Vader) describes where this force is used to further pursuits such as greed, lust, domination and malevolence. The comparatively noble *Star Wars* Jedi warriors have chosen the way of balance, peace, leadership, restraint and benevolence. They have power but endorse the responsible use of it.

# Money doesn't buy happiness

This phrase gets thrown around regularly, mostly by people who have very little money. In many instances, it is their dismissive way of expressing that if they don't have much, then it isn't important anyway. In its simplest form, however, money represents safety, security and basic survival. It cannot be scoffed at or disregarded, especially if one has a family.

People of low financial means may be forced to think about money most of the time in relation to food, shelter and simple subsistence. Wealthy people may also think about money in relation to status, investments, business projects, travel options or making sure they don't lose it. Wealthy people obviously have problems too, but they have less to do with basic survival. No doubt there are lonely and miserable rich folks as well as gratified and happy poor people but, on the whole, the majority of people would choose to have more money than less if they were given the option.

There are literally millions of honest, hardworking people who toil conscientiously for their entire lives, yet never become wealthy. In most cases, this result is more about the average person's expectations and level of financial ambition than it is about their level of occupational skill or qualification. Many people do not foresee themselves becoming wealthy and inadvertently earn, spend and save throughout their lives in such a way as to confirm this belief.

> Our outlook on money determines our effectiveness in attracting it.

By contrast, people who aspire towards wealth and adopt an affirmative approach towards its acquisition are more likely to exhibit entrepreneurial drives, pursue higher-income careers and further study opportunities to multiply their income through investments or business ventures. Our outlook on money, therefore, determines our effectiveness in attracting it.

It's often been a working class view in Australia to portray the rich as unscrupulous and the poor as everyday heroes, as if wealth were a crime and poverty a virtue. This somewhat sanctimonious opinion attempts to equate being voluntarily poor with goodness or humility. It's not my intention to debate the rights or wrongs of this viewpoint, but suffice to say, people who embrace this stance will likely struggle to attain any sort of wealth themselves.

Achieving financial success does not necessarily depend on you becoming 'rich'. Rather, it is about creating a comfortable sufficiency and solidity, and an abundant flow of monetary freedom throughout your life. This more functional attitude towards wealth acquisition and money management liberates you from subsistence concerns, such that monetary shortages no longer dominate your thoughts.

Many people settle for a lot less money in their lives than they could actually attain. They tend to underestimate what they can achieve and the financial status they can reach, yet somehow accept that others can do more. Some feel they are too deeply in debt to start accumulating a sizeable amount of money and bail out of the race in middle age – or earlier. Others choose to identify with extremely negative examples of affluent individuals who have achieved their wealth via corrupt means and make the sweeping assumption that wealth is always a result of exploitation. In any case, if we are to achieve a level of financial abundance in our lives, then we must start to view money as an obedient servant that we employ to create a desirable lifestyle. Scarcity and lack can only exist when we make room for them in our minds.

# Hidden attitudes towards money

It's necessary to flush out any negative beliefs you have towards money or financially successful people if you wish to embark on a wealth-creation path. Considering your response towards some of the following scenarios is a constructive first step towards detecting any negative or conflicting money mindsets:

- ➤ When you see someone driving a prestige car, does it motivate you to achieve a similar result someday or are there underlying feelings of jealousy, resentment or suspicion?
- ➤ If you see someone driving a top-of-the-line Mercedes sports convertible cut in front of another car, what is your immediate reaction?
  - − What a crazy driver! (an observation)… OR
  - − Typical arrogant Mercedes driver thinks he's more important than everyone else on the road! (a biased judgement)
- ➤ If you hear a friend just sold their business for 30 million dollars and is going to retire at 40 years of age, how do you feel about that?
  - − Are you genuinely happy for them?
  - − Are you curious about how they achieved this impressive result?
  - − Does it motivate you to hear this or deflate you?

- – Do you think they are lucky?
- – Is there part of you that thinks this isn't fair or just?
- ➤ If you're a person in your 20s or early 30s, have you allowed the conventional view that young people can no longer afford to buy a house affect your motivation to save for a deposit?
- ➤ Materially speaking, are you secretly competing with others?
- ➤ If you regularly spend more money than you make, what do you conclude is the reason for this?
  - – Everything costs too much… OR
  - – Your income is too low for your current lifestyle choices.
- ➤ What would be your instinctive response to an ongoing affordability predicament?
  - – Look for ways to drive your cost of living down… OR
  - – Look for ways to earn more income.

These scenarios are not meant to cast judgement or imply there is a right or wrong answer, but they will give you an idea as to where your thoughts about money are positioned. They provide a glimpse into attitudes that subtly undermine efforts to attract financial success. People are rightfully allowed to choose if they live a working class, middle class or 'business class' existence, as long as they accept the reality that in most developed societies it is a choice. When we view money as unimportant, however, we fail to live in the real world.

# It's OK to be motivated by money

We are driven to accumulate money throughout our lives, so you might as well make it your servant rather than your jailer. You do not have to be any less caring, selfless or spiritual if you succeed financially.

It is ironic that many individuals who have little money (or who carry a poor attitude towards money) can begrudge a person who has accumulated millions of dollars through business or risk-laden investments yet be guilt-free if their weekly lottery ticket makes them an instant millionaire. For many of these people, winning the lottery is the A to Z of their financial plan.

# It's OK *not* to be motivated by money

It's important for each person to establish what true wealth means to them, and there are plenty of examples of wealth in the world that money can't buy. For instance, you can buy designer fashion but not style; fancy cars but not class; education but not intelligence; cosmetics but not beauty; and sex but not love. The unpleasant truth is that ostentatious material possessions only tend to increase our appetite for more 'things' rather than satisfy us with what we have. When we see well-heeled but classless clowns burning up their financial surpluses on banal gestures, excess, size, noise, bling and pretentious affectations, it's easy to make an argument for its tackiness. At the end of the day, though, these are human issues – not money issues. You can't fix the money; you can only fix the human.

# The happy medium

It is well documented that the financial prosperity of a nation unintentionally brings with it a raft of societal problems, notably pollution, congestion and obesity. This is a direct product of an increasing lean towards excess in affluent Western cultures. Each individual must therefore take responsibility for their own space and do what they can to practise a more balanced view of affluence.

Abundance can endure without making anyone materialistic or overweight and can satisfy healthy yearnings without leaving a person jaded or damaged. Many people are said to 'love money and use people', but this phrase must be reversed to 'love people and use money' if we are to strike the right ethical balance when pursuing financial wealth.

# Financial attraction

Money is not something you need to chase; rather, it's something you attract by the person you become. Not all virtues attract money, but I am referring to the point where an individual's character, attitude, boldness and interpersonal skills intersect with the commercial world.

Some people fail to attract wealth because they don't believe they are cut out for that level of financial success. This is particularly relevant where people have chosen to start a business or be involved in some form of profit-based enterprise. Their first question is often: What should I charge for my product or services? To some extent, there is a tangible starting point to this calculation, especially if the product has come from somewhere and carried a raw manufacturing and distribution cost. The more difficult task for many people is in determining what their time and expertise are worth, as is the case with a service-oriented business.

The mantra to adopt in this instance is: Don't focus on charging less; focus on giving more! When you dedicate yourself to raising the top (the top being the quality of your service) rather than lowering the bottom (providing less service), then everybody wins. If you cut your fees to the bare minimum and then give back in kind, everybody loses. Ramp up the level of service and create a commensurate fee that shows you value what you offer.

As a general rule in business, we need to be wary of setting a price based on the condition that people of limited means will always be able to afford it. A better idea – both commercially and morally – is to charge enough so that you can afford to subsidise (through discounts) those of limited means if you choose to. A healthy fee is only unappealing to the vaguely curious or uncommitted customer.

> Don't focus on charging less; focus on giving more!

# Priorities

Time is more precious than money – you can always acquire more money, but you can't gain more time. As the saying goes, "We're not here for a long time – we're here for a good time!" Money is going to be a part of your life no matter where you live, what you do for a living or who you choose to be with. You might as well make friends with it and earn all you can. Be mindful, however, that its importance in your life is kept in its rightful place: behind your health, relationships, moral standard and mental and emotional wellbeing.

In an advanced country with abundance all around, there is no shame in trying to become financially successful. People in developing nations would die for the opportunities we take for granted – and indeed many die in their attempts to immigrate – and it is OK to take advantage of the incredible environment we are lucky enough to be born into.

Financial success is about good management of both your thinking and your physical wealth itself. Self-control and discipline enter the picture in a big way here. Poor people spend their money first and save what's left. Wealthy people save their money first and spend what's left. Most people struggle to make these sacrifices if the prize they are aiming for isn't clear enough.

If you had enough money to live on for the rest of your life, what would you do with your time?

When you have the answer to this question, try to find work in that area if you can. This is the ultimate wealth! If something you truly love cannot be practically transformed into a career, then pursue the next best thing by finding something you are good at or have a knack for. Your goal from here is to build a sound financial path from within this enterprise.

# WISDOM #7

# STOICISM 101

STOICISM IS AN ANCIENT Greek school of philosophical study that promotes personal ethics and a methodology for seeking practical wisdom in life. Its central virtues represent the pursuit of values such as wisdom, justice, courage and temperance. Stoicism is a vast area of study, and one which I am only intending to provide a brief and hopefully practical introduction on.

> Philosophical examination teaches us how to live well and become better human beings.

Philosophical examination teaches us how to live well and become better human beings and also aids us to overcome many of life's ordeals and hardships. While some schools of thought are better suited to purely academic debate, Stoicism is one of the more practical philosophies. It provides us with a framework that is well-suited for conveyance into modern values and tenets.

Stoicism focuses on two primary questions:

➤ How can we lead a fulfilling and gratifying life?
➤ How can we become better human beings?

Stoicism's functional goal is to achieve inner peace by learning how to handle hardship, apply self-control, be mindful of impulses and fully realise our transitory human existence. This fascinating blend of logic, science and ethics were all meditative practices that helped the Stoics live in accord with nature and not against it. In a sense, they developed their own philosophical force field.

Stoicism promotes principle-centred decision-making and provides mental strategies that augment the human experience both internally and externally. It seeks to achieve this by minimising negative emotions and by amplifying a sense of gratitude and joy.

However, Stoicism remains misunderstood by many people, being viewed as emotional coldness and the ability to endure pain or hardship without the display of feelings. In its purest form, Stoicism is referred to as an 'ascetic' system, meaning that it is characterised by self-discipline and abstention from all forms of indulgence, typically for spiritual reasons. The archetypical Stoic person generally shows little or no external reaction to challenging situations, remaining cool and rational under pressure with an even temperament and measured response.

While these sorts of portrayals can infer a life absent of passion and spontaneity, a more modern version of the practice leaves room for a variety of practical adjustments, all of which can enhance one's experiences and responses to life's challenges.

To provide a practical starting point for Stoicism's value in contemporary life, we need to do two things:

1. Control things that are within our power such as our own attitudes, opinions, dogmas, beliefs, judgements and yearnings.

2.  Reflect an indifference or apathy to the factors which are not in our power, namely things that are external to us such as the weather, the economy, world events or other people's beliefs and opinions.

In taking this view, we adopt the position that nothing external could be either good or evil. It says that *it is what it is* and demands an individual gives greater priority to the quality and nature of their response.

Whenever we casually observe individuals who lead a productive life, we can easily distinguish the basic elements of their expertise, determination and hunger for success. More covert and easier to overlook is the internal system within the individual: the series of principles that govern their cognitive processes and behaviour. For example, whenever failure impinges or the need to adapt is required, how does the individual respond? How do they talk to themselves? What is their outlook?

# The founders of Stoicism

Stoicism, as it's studied today, focuses heavily on the principles of its renowned and foundational leaders: Epictetus, Marcus Aurelius and Seneca.

## *Epictetus*

Epictetus was born a slave on the eastern borders of the Roman Empire around 55 CE. He had a passion for philosophy that began early in his life and, with permission from his owner, he studied Stoic philosophy for many years. Following the death of that era's tyrannical and ruthless emperor, Nero, Epictetus began to teach Stoic philosophy in Rome and then later in Greece, where he founded a school of philosophy. Among his students was the future emperor of Rome, Marcus Aurelius.

## Marcus Aurelius

Marcus Aurelius is considered to be one of the greatest Roman emperors in history. During the war campaign, he kept a personal journal which ultimately became known as *Meditations*. These notes served as a guide for Stoic principles that centred around humility, self-awareness, duty, loss, mortality and nature.

## Seneca

Seneca was a Roman Stoic philosopher, diplomat and adviser to the emperor. His intellectual legacy includes dozens of essays and 124 letters that reflect on areas such as friendship, civil responsibilities, moral obligation, education, modesty, self-awareness and personal discipline.

What does all this mean as we attempt to thrive in a modern world that is awash with health warnings, financial complications, personal pressures and career demands? Following a contemporary adaptation of the Stoic philosophy can provide a very practical code for disarming our daily trials. How we interpret what happens dictates our resultant behaviour and this is where the real benefit lies. When following the Stoic principles, we must acknowledge that all emotions are responses that come from within.

Outside forces are not negative in and of themselves. Our emotional state is more dependent on our acceptance or rejection of these events rather than an event or person. Our philosophy determines how we interpret life's inequities and what conclusions we draw as a result. It is not outside forces that make us feel something; it is what we tell ourselves about what has occurred that creates our feelings.

Our conclusions generate an emotional response and a subsequent behaviour. Improving our behaviour begins with defining our personal philosophy and the Stoic blueprint provides an invaluable guide.

# Control what you can and accept what you can't

Mindfulness practice is a critical component of Stoicism and can be used as a tool to help recognise events in your life that you do and do not control. Becoming aggravated with circumstances outside of your influence only wastes energy and cultivates negative emotions.

Interestingly, the Stoic tradition is also well illustrated by a mythical story about the Buddha. Mara was an antagonist and enemy of the Buddha and sought to destroy him by sending a formidable army. Mara ordered his soldiers to throw flaming rocks at the Buddha, but as they approached, the rocks transformed into flowers and fell to the ground. Undeterred, Mara then instructed his army to fire arrows, but again the arrows turned to flowers once they entered the Buddha's sphere. There was nothing Mara could do to damage the Buddha because the Buddha had mastered the ability to cultivate a happy disposition independent of outside events.

In this example, the flaming rocks and arrows represent our negative external circumstances. We cannot change these events, but we can change our attitude towards them. By coming to this realisation, our mind and moods can become impenetrable.

# Contemplate the loss of your valuables

*"Do not indulge in dreams of having what you have not, but reckon up the chief of the blessings you do possess, and then thankfully remember how you would crave for them if they were not yours."*

—Marcus Aurelius

From time to time, we should take a moment to consider life without the people and possessions we currently have in order to truly appreciate them. If wanting more things leads to dissatisfaction, then where does happiness originate? The Stoic answer to this eternal question is gratitude. We must appreciate all that we have and learn to discover joy in it. We live in an extraordinary period of history with unfettered access to resources and technology that provide us with an unprecedented standard of living.

Instead of appreciating this, we can take it for granted. One of the key Stoic practices is to envisage that some of these valuable possessions have been taken away. This applies to material belongings as well as things of a personal nature. It may sound depressing initially, but by imagining these losses we come to more fully appreciate what we have.

> In the final wash, things come and go but virtue remains.

Hence, if an external item that you place a high value on is taken away, the resulting Stoic response urges you to be grateful that you had that object to begin with rather than being upset about its loss. To the Stoic, everything is 'on loan' from the cosmos. Your house – it isn't yours. Your car – it isn't yours. Your partner – isn't yours. All the clothes and shoes in your wardrobe – aren't yours. All of your possessions belong to providence. Providence gave them to you and fate can take them away, even if you are vigilant and thrifty. This realisation counsels us to practise non-attachment, especially in relation to material objects. In the final wash, things come and go but virtue remains, and therein lies the treasure.

# Refrain from overindulgence

*"Wealth consists not in having great possessions, but in having few wants."*

—Epictetus

Here is another warning against being seduced by modern society's materialistic nature. Our rampant consumer society is driven by an inherent concept of lack and, as such, seems to create more desire than it fulfils. Marketers and advertisers have succeeded in converting society from being needs-based to wants-based. Even if you tangibly have everything you need, it won't be long before you're convinced that more is required. The end result is that our hard-earned money is consumed on the latest fad as we're convinced we'll be more satisfied – that is until the next model comes out in six months' time. If we strive to want less and remove ourselves from the crosshairs of internet and social media marketers, we may learn to become more satisfied with what we have.

# Be genuinely cheerful in all your interactions

Seneca explains that by adopting the Stoic mindset, our happiness can become independent of outside factors. If we strive to be cheerful all of the time, we can be emotionally fulfilled by the full human experience *as it is*. In this case, if we were then to desire more, we may expose ourselves to greater frustration. This is not meant to infer that Stoics cannot relish in life's finer things or its shiny indulgences from time to time; it just advises us not to view these items as mandatory for our happiness. The Stoic philosophy maintains that genuine fulfilment in life only comes by providing service and positivity to the world through helping others. Hence, the phrase, "What you feel you need is what you need to give." If you'd like to improve your mood, then go and cheer someone up.

> What you feel you need is what you need to give.

# Practising values beats preaching them

> *"Don't describe your philosophy – be it!"*
>
> —Epictetus

This simple message is proclaimed more than it is followed. When all is said and done, more is *said* than *done*. Stoic philosophy requires a healthy dose of self-awareness and an above-average ability to take personal responsibility for one's outcomes. It challenges us to consistently act based on our personal values and to live by a basic moral code. It reminds us that no one is listening – but everyone is watching.

The Stoic is more summoned by the call of duty than they are seduced by empty pleasures. Their role then is to ensure that they act in accordance with these duties and commitments and personify the character traits they expect of others. This is particularly vital for any person in a position of leadership, whether it be a coaching scenario, workplace position of authority or even as a parent. Mothers and fathers would do well to accept that their children are not listening to them very much, but they're unconsciously watching them like a hawk, emulating their habits and behaviours, both good and bad.

# Recognise there *is* life after failure

The Stoic ideology of remaining positive in the face of disappointment overlaps with references made in previous chapters about destigmatising failure. The Stoic view is to fail forward and not interpret losses as terminal. It sees failure as a subjective item that requires personal confirmation in order to be realised. As an example, if I choose to define the mere completion and production of this book as a success in itself, then I am less reliant on the approval of others to define it as a success or failure. By creating this virtually imperishable mental construct, we can summon the self-discipline and commitment to see long projects through to their completion without fear of failure or judgement.

Recovering from any failure is a mindset and a practice, and the general Stoic decree asserts that where there is no failure, there is no growth.

# Be guided by your principles

Without a mature and pragmatic philosophy to guide us, we are vulnerable to the myriad of excuses and distractions that continually tap us on the shoulder. To enjoy a life of maximum prosperity and achievement, we must learn to be guided by our principles rather than our moods.

> We must be guided by our principles rather than our moods.

In order to gain optimal benefit from these tenets, it is best not to view Stoicism from an all-or-nothing perspective. It is here that the philosophical overlap between Stoicism and the balanced scales of Buddhism directs us well, urging us to focus on *excellence* over *perfection* and *flexibility* over *dogma*. The ultimate goal of adhering to such a belief system is to transform our experiences for the better through positive and constructive behaviour.

In the hustle and bustle of contemporary life, an effective practice must be portable. Adopting a more Stoic approach starts with simple things such as finding a few moments throughout the day, however fleeting, to just sit and be still. Turn off your phone, take a few deep breaths and reflect on your interactions throughout the day. And when you're working, be ruthlessly present. Focus intently on the task at hand, and do it with concentration, care and patience.

# WISDOM #8

# INTERDEPENDENCE

THE CONCEPT OF INTERDEPENDENCE is a central teaching within the Buddhist philosophy and is sometimes referred to as 'interdependent co-arising'. Its study within the context of Buddhism runs deep but a simplified view of this theme can offer many practical benefits.

The word 'interdependent' means 'mutually dependent' or 'dependent on each other'. Interdependence is a model that proposes everything and everyone is interconnected and interrelated. It suggests that everything in our world is composite and that all things can be dissected into the components that make it up. It implies that nothing has its own irreducible self-nature; that all existence is relational; and that all things result from the co-working of many circumstances and causes. Adopting these principles will generate a vastly different outlook than if we exclusively attribute our success to the shallow notion of rugged individualism.

In the 21$^{st}$ century, virtually every nation is heavily interdependent and interconnected. As a result, destroying your neighbour (or your trading partner) means destroying yourself in the long run. You need your neighbour; the more they prosper, the more content they are and the less they will trouble you for support. More than ever, especially with the growing number of nuclear countries, all of our futures depend on positive global relationships.

The transcendental view is that interdependence is a fundamental law of nature that not only applies to higher forms of life but also to the smallest creatures. Insects, for instance, are social beings who, without any laws, education or religion, survive via mutual cooperation with their environment. This is based on an innate recognition of their interconnectedness.

In acknowledging this, we gain deeper insight into the true nature of existence and begin to view our daily interactions with others a little differently. We begin to understand that nothing is an island unto itself; no single thing is separate all on its own and no one thing is completely self-reliant. This applies to our material actions, mental constructs and emotional activities. These realisations endow us with a greater level of patience and compassion and an insight to act with greater appreciation towards others.

> We begin to understand that nothing is an island unto itself.

A more concentrated inspection of our daily creature comforts can uncover our interdependence. The morning dose of caffeinated life support is a good example. The beloved coffee could not exist without the vendor who ordered the large sachet of beans and the delivery vans distributing these beans to all the stores in your city each with a driver behind the wheel. Then there's the fuel in each van's tank and the complex array of manpower that pumped oil out of the seabed and refined it for the supply of each fuel tank. Going further, there are the process workers who roasted and packaged the raw coffee beans, the ship that transported the beans, and the people who manufactured and maintained both the ship and the containers. Consider also the farmer who cared for the soil and planted the crop, and the pickers who picked the beans. Departing momentarily from the human hands that have contributed to our coffee, we then appreciate the sunshine and rain that made the plants grow...

Every one of the above conditions also had its own intricate web of causes that contributed to its unique arising. This simple example may appear to be digging a little too deep for some, but it reminds us of how many people contribute to the enjoyments that enrich our lives.

# Compassion

The concept of interconnectedness implies that we are a product of our environment. For example, an individual who acts in a rash or aggressive manner has likely been exposed to many contributing factors that have combined to create malcontent. Years of societal and family conditioning can generate an unhealthy array of pent-up and repressed emotions which may have affected their behaviour. Perhaps they had little choice but to act the way they did. If we take time to consider the originating source of a person's negative disposition, then we may respond with more compassion towards them. We can recognise the stress of their day, the frustration of their week, and perhaps even the way they were brought up and treated as a child. We may end up conceding that if our lives and upbringing were switched and we were them, we might react in a very comparable manner.

# Community

A deeper look at the dependent origin of all things moves us further away from the sense of duality that pervades most modern cultures. It diminishes our tendency to adopt self-defeating theories such as 'us vs them', 'good vs evil', 'winner vs loser' and other forms of competitive individualism. Embracing a sense of community enables us to see beyond the flawed concept of separation and embrace the interdependent relationship between all things. Once we reject the paradigm of isolation and accept the intimate connections all around us, we can experience the profound union between ourselves, other people and other things. Everything impacts everything else. We rely upon one another. All of us.

> Everything impacts everything else. We rely upon one another. All of us.

# Humility

Our planet is one big living system that we are interconnected with, along with all its life forms. While it's true we celebrate being at the apex of intelligent life on earth, we are nonetheless equal in many ways with animals, rivers, plant life and so on. At any given minute, Mother Nature could swat us all into oblivion if she so wanted. You and I are only here because she lets us stay... that is, after she decided we could arrive here in the first place. You can be the toughest or the wealthiest individual alive, but you've been granted tenancy on the planet by something greater than yourself, and your achievements have been co-constructed by a team of people and things you've never met. It is an exercise in maturity and practical wisdom to adopt a humble attitude towards your successes and to acknowledge the vital roles that other people, nature and good fortune have played in your achievements.

This view helps us move beyond an egocentric view of our existence towards appreciating our wider universal interdependence. By developing appreciation and goodwill towards all beings we inherently expand our life and provide a wider context in it for humility to manifest.

# Responsibility

Accepting the interconnectedness of all things in nature and society is not intended to present as a political view or be an assault on individual achievement. Nor is it meant to undermine the concept of taking personal responsibility for one's own situation. *Outside* of our own inner world, we desire a civilised, respectful and cooperative environment. We are better placed to experience this if we behave altruistically, with total awareness of our interconnectedness. We can learn to skilfully connect and be a part of our community, while still being a unique individual.

Being aware of our interconnectedness grants us the wisdom to make ethical decisions with greater skill and compassion. The potential consequences of our seemingly innocuous actions are clear to us, and we see the impact we have on others and our environment. We understand that *my peace is your peace* and that we all live downstream from one another.

# PART II

# THE

# WEAPONS

## WE ASSEMBLE

# The sharpened blade

HAVING ESTABLISHED A SOLID foundational mindset from which we plant our feet and aim straight, the focus then turns towards the contents of our personal tool kit. Much of the time and effort spent assembling our philosophical priorities can be nullified if we enact our newfound wisdom with blunt instruments. Experienced chefs know that the sharpened blade cuts more cleanly and effortlessly than the blunt knife. Additionally, and somewhat ironically, kitchen hands are more likely to cut themselves working with a blunt blade than a sharp one due to the extra force required to penetrate and slice neatly. You can't whip butter with a toothpick any more than you can chop down a tree with a hammer.

> The sharpened blade cuts more cleanly and effortlessly than the blunt knife.

In Weapons, we aim to identify and refine a skill set that is supplementary to our evolved mindset. In some instances, these tools provide a protective barrier against the array of incoming ordnances we experience when venturing outside our comfort zone. At other times, our honed weaponry is activated combatively as we thrust and pierce our way forward towards our desired goals. Inevitably, we must tool up to move up!

# MOTIVE

A LACK OF PURPOSE or sense of direction is greatly responsible for many people's underachievement. This is not to say that most people are lazy or without thought for their futures, as there are countless earnest and hardworking individuals. Whether it concerns our career, health or any other worthwhile value, we can rarely depend on the actual task itself to provide us with the internal fuel to keep at it over the long term. While it is a truism for most of us that we have to work, it would be a shame to spend 45 years of our lives in an unfulfilling workplace, toiling from one month to the next with no greater motives than to pay off the mortgage and live for the weekend.

Aside from the work environment, there is also no shortage of people trying to manage their health and fitness. You will regularly hear people say they *have* to get back to the gym, *have* to restart that diet or *have* to start jogging again. All these assertions carry the same tone: they must force themselves to do something they find inherently unappealing, laborious and perhaps even painful. It's little wonder that many people fail to gain traction with these quests.

One of the greatest obstacles to succeeding in any long-term endeavour is the sense of monotony that often arises when progress requires a consistent routine to be followed. While repetition is the mother of all skills, repetition can also be inherently boring and diminish people's staying power. This feeling of tedium sees an endless line of individuals drop out of university, change jobs every few years, fail at their diet, quit the gym, drop the guitar lessons and so on.

It's undeniable that people are trying hard, but the problem for many is aimlessness rather than idleness. What you are doing will almost certainly lose its lustre after a time (if it ever had one), but why you are doing it can remain exciting as long as you learn how to attach something inspiring to its outcome or process. This combustive energy that fuels our forward momentum can only be accessed if our motives are clear, significant and measurable.

> The problem for many is aimlessness rather than idleness.

With these three components in place and our end goal firmly fixed in mind, the means and propelling force to drive us towards it are a constant. You will happily work because you have now attached those tasks to a significant desire. It's not about the work; it's about the motive.

# A lesson in peak states

At the age of 25, I left a safe management job and a relatively decent salary for a role in a completely different field. I knocked on doors six days a week with no base salary and only earned income via sales on a 100 per cent commission basis. Even though I was young and without family or substantial outgoings, I still remember the sense of financial vulnerability that accompanied this new performance-based remuneration structure. I could no longer afford to measure my productivity based simply on time spent or tasks completed. My financial success was based purely on productivity – the end result.

This is not to imply that a salaried role is void of performance expectations. At some point, a succession of poor results catches up with us regardless of our payment structure. A slack worker will eventually be culled, just as a driven worker is usually rewarded. In my earlier jobs, however, if I arrived at work half asleep, hungover or grumpy, I could usually struggle through the day with a 'pass' level of efficacy and still be paid the same income as when I bounded through the door, fully lit and in top form.

When working in an 'unprotected' environment such as running your own business or where the income is purely profit based, the remunerative feedback for positive outcomes is proportionate and often immediate, as is the financial punishment if you are ineffective. Within my new work environment, when I generated a sale I was paid. If I didn't, I went hungry – it was as simple as that! It therefore became critical that I maintained a peak motivational state while engaged in my work.

This meant that my mood had now become directly connected to my day-to-day income. A poor state or low motivation invariably meant no income. This was a harsh consequence for being off my game, but an ultimately valuable lesson in how to get in touch with my peak energy reserves. As such, one of the first phrases I was exposed to in the early days of my business education was that success is at least as much about the 'why' as it is about the 'how'.

Contrary to a well-held view, it is still possible to enjoy your work while performing monotonous tasks (like knocking on doors). It is also possible to achieve income security while being paid performance-based commissions. For these two scenarios to apply, it is necessary to put motive ahead of task. In my case, the role

I had taken was essentially a karate apprenticeship where we trained during the day and promoted our public classes in the evenings. This regular karate training and the goal of one day achieving my black belt was the overwhelming driving force for me as I went about my daily promotional tasks. I knew that every day I worked and every door I knocked on was also another karate training day under my belt, which incrementally moved me another step closer to black belt.

I enjoyed the work because I had attached a greater motive towards doing it – as long as I stayed connected to this motive, I was able to maintain a peak mental and emotional state which guaranteed consistently strong results and a dependable income.

Before too long I discovered that it was not about how good I was or how long and hard I worked; it was how badly I wanted it that counted the most. I learned that the hungry person almost always beats the sharp person. The hungry person can often make it work even if they lack some of the basic skills or knowledge. On the other hand, the sharp person could still fail through lack of drive and determination even though they possessed all the right skills for the role. These examples are not raised to undermine the importance of skills or qualifications, but more to point out that if you want it badly enough, you will find a way. If your 'why' is big enough, then the 'how' can be figured out.

# Motive (noun): a reason for doing something

Motive is the root word and the root cause of motivation. There are times when motivation comes easily, and others when it is nowhere to be found. The more linked we feel with our desired outcome, the easier it is to generate the driving energy required to take action.

Procrastination and lethargy are motivation's two greatest adversaries and their effects on us can be truly paralysing. Most people know for instance that regular exercise and eating well are good for them and will make them feel better. They don't avoid these activities through ignorance of their value, but more so because they are not motivated to make a start. They wait for the wind to meet their back and lurch them forward from their stationary post. Frequently it's a long wait. More often than not, in fact, it will be a headwind – not a tailwind – that they'll contend with at the start.

One of the least acknowledged aspects of motivation is that it often arrives *after* you have started a new activity, not always before. Motivation is often the result of action, not the cause of it. Motivation often says, 'Start without me!' Irrespective of whether it was there to start you off or turned up late to keep you going, motivation is always preceded by a key motive or goal. The more compelling the target, the more propulsive the drive.

> Motivation is often the result of action, not the cause of it.

While the reasons for a person's continued failure to take action can be linked to personal fears, insecurities and other psychological complications, what can be assumed is that these people's obstacles were bigger than their motives.

Eventually, the consequence of *not* doing something grows greater than the pain of doing it and it becomes easier to change than to sit still. This emotional tipping point is triggered by the arrival of a strong motive and signals the defeat of inaction. For some, this tipping point is a health scare, and a good scare is often worth more to a person than good advice. From a weight-loss perspective, many people cite their catalyst for change as being debilitating fatigue or the horror of seeing themselves in an unflattering photo. It is a pity that we often require a calamity to fire up.

When motivation arrives and challenges procrastination and lethargy, we eventually find that it's easier to drag our butts down to the gym than it is to sit on them and feel unhealthy. It becomes easier to make that awkward sales call than to feel the stress of a low income and a diminishing bank balance. The drive to resist a given temptation becomes stronger than the addiction. This is the essence of motivation.

Our eventual call to action represents the crossing of a mental threshold… usually after much stalling and often in the face of a looming deadline – it becomes more agonising to do nothing than to do something. At the end of the day, the prize needs to be greater than the price if we aspire to beat back the internal resistance and take action towards a worthwhile goal.

# The sweet spot

As noble and virtuous as our lofty motives can be, we may still require some additional assistance to drive ourselves forward. In order to freely access the storehouse of motivational dynamism within your body and mind, it is necessary to tap into your chief energy centre - your subconscious mind. To do this effectively, the goals and rewards that we create as our primary motives need to be aligned with the central interests of our subconscious, for example, to *feel safe, have fun* and to *feel powerful*. The juice, as they say, has got to be worth the squeeze. If your reasons for pursuing change or a particular outcome are not grounded in one or more of these three key areas, then your access to the energy source will be denied or impeded.

# Cut to the truth

The gym is always a great example for identifying our hidden drivers. On the surface, many people state that their decision to join was based on practical or commonsense things such as improving fitness, toning up, fitting back into clothes or increasing strength. To the subconscious mind, however, these reasons are relatively bland and are unlikely to allow access to the body's wellspring of motivational energy.

When a guy rocks up to the gym for his first day and the personal trainer asks his reasons for joining, very few young men openly reveal their likely inner motive: to look tougher or more attractive to their partner (or a future partner). While this may seem like a vain or superficial pretext for exercise, it is an extremely powerful motivator because it taps into some of the subconscious mind's primary set of values: fun and feeling powerful.

I'm told that for young women, gym work is typically about the ABT (abs, butt and thighs), and for guys it's the good old GPS (guns, pecs and shoulders). I acknowledge that these are obviously generalisations! Watching parts of the body grow or shrink when we work out is deeply connected to our motivational energy and probably the reason why most gyms have wall-to-wall mirrors (even though they are said to be for checking technique!). While exercise also benefits our internal organs, how many people would continue with regular gym sessions if the benefits of their workouts could only be measured by a cardiograph or blood test? When a young man at the gym was once asked why he rarely used the treadmill, he said, "Chicks can't see cardio!" I rest my case. In the end, we don't have to admit our true gym motives out loud – we just need to install the mirrors.

Similarly, many famous musicians have spent thousands of hours plying their trade while they were growing up. The number of scales and rudimentary practice drills needed to be carried out on their instrument to achieve such brilliance is enormous. While the purist in us assumes that such dedication was nourished by an intense love and respect for their art, many male artists concede that the primary motivating factor for creating music and succeeding in the business was to attract the attention of girls! We can appreciate the honesty expressed here and use it to inform us further about the secret to accessing our own motivational reserves – find something related to fun or excitement to get you motivated.

While the above examples may seem simplistic, they nonetheless support the notion that the zeal and enthusiasm needed for the active pursuit of a goal is best recruited from within the body by convincing it that the effort will equal pleasure, personal power or safety and security.

Knowing this, our minds must now get to work and start creating positive associations with activities or tasks that we value. For example, if you're determined to ride your home exercise bike for 30 minutes each day, then bring the bike in front of the TV and watch your favourite streaming series while you ride. It doesn't matter if the only thing you look forward to on some days is the TV program – what matters is that your backside sits on that bike and pedals for 30 minutes a day. If you have a home gym that you rarely use, consider investing in some mirrors for that room. You can look at yourself the whole time you're working out and there's no one to catch you doing it – and, of course, it's excellent for your technique as well! If there's a particular food you are aiming to avoid, then try making a deal with yourself where a week of successful abstinence will be rewarded by going for a massage. Two litres of water a day for a whole week is not an easy task for many people, but what if the reward for seven straight days was a Gold Class movie or dinner at your favourite restaurant?

On the surface, this can seem like you are playing mind games with yourself – and that's because you are! The more you actively include elements of fun, pleasure or power into your most important aspirations, the more successful you will be at getting started and staying committed. Try it on!

# Feeling safe

When I worked in a 100 per cent commission job, I was continually fascinated at how often my peers would perform at their best during the week just prior to their rent or mortgage being due. Furthermore, those who still lived at home with their parents consistently earned less than those who lived out of home despite often possessing more talent and skill. Irrespective of their individual circumstances, however, all of them somehow seemed to do just enough in the nick of time to pay their rent or keep themselves alive financially.

This is really no different to the school assignment we sat on for two months, only to leave it all until the last week to get started, then work all day and night without sleep and just finish within an hour of the deadline. It's amazing how the fear of something bad happening fires up our motivational engines.

The key here is to try and access the GOYA mentality (get off your ar… armchair) before the harsh consequences of inaction are on our doorstep. This requires us to turn our 'shoulds' into 'musts'. At the 'must' stage, we find the energy and drive to get started and follow through, whereas the 'should' list tends to be a motivation vampire!

# Imagination

*"Imagination is more important than knowledge."*
—Albert Einstein

This phrase encourages us to look beyond what we are currently doing and achieving. Cultivating an inspiring 'why' demands we recruit our powers of imagination and become good at visualising our success before it happens.

Without imagination, we struggle to see beyond our existing knowledge base or skill set and fail to set goals that force us to stretch. In these instances, we are more inclined to put the 'how' first because our existing capabilities represent the extent of our vision. Imagination takes us into the dream phase and can be a looking glass into a better future. The more we visualise this improved version of ourselves and our lives, the more we arouse our motivational forces to drive us forward.

Utilising the power of daydreaming works so well because your subconscious mind doesn't distinguish between what you visualise and what you physically observe with your eyes. If you ever need evidence of this, think about how much anxiety you can physically experience by imagining something bad happening. Worry is literally imagining negative scenarios. It doesn't have to actually happen to cause real fear or stress.

On a more positive note, there are ways you can use this process to your advantage. The relatively boring activity of jogging or running can be stimulated by imagining yourself throughout the run winning a race, scoring the match-winning goal or hitting aces all over the tennis court. Picturing yourself playing a musical instrument in front of a raucous and fully engaged live crowd can give you the juice to privately practise songs many more times than you could tolerate under normal circumstances.

Creation follows vision. Many of us need to wake up and start dreaming if we truly wish to shed our existing skin and become something greater. The first priority of top performers is to visualise what they want. How they are going to get it, who they need to work with and what they need to learn comes second. In the end, if we fail to conceive our own goals and dreams, then someone else will hire us to build theirs.

# Perseverance

Learning you have the fortitude to persevere with a task beyond its initial honeymoon period is, in itself, a motivating force. Perseverance's relationship to motivation is vital as it encourages us to go at it again and again, stoking the sense of optimism that each step forward is one step

> The primary product of perseverance is momentum.

closer. Each time we relaunch, we are given the opportunity to experience the rush of motivation that kicks in when we start anew.

The primary product of perseverance is momentum. As Newton's First Law of Motion expounds, an object tends to stay in motion once it has been deployed along its path. Inertia sees to it that there is less motivation required once we have started a new behaviour or habit. Once the task has begun, it is easier to continue moving forward, often resulting in it being easier to finish than it was to start.

# Specificity

A vague notion of a desired outcome rarely generates the motivation required to change or grow. It is extremely difficult to manage or be inspired by something you cannot measure. Clarity is power, and the more specific your vision for your target is, the greater the potential for its achievement. Nebulous ambitions such as wanting to 'earn more money', 'lose weight', 'get fit' and 'have more time' are explicit enough to identify a direction, but too formless to generate sustained motivational energy. If you really want to get it done, then you need to get vivid.

In the midst of all our personal goal setting and planning, it is worth remembering that we often do more to help others than we do to satisfy our own desires. When we include the hoisting of other people's sails wherever we can, it assists us as we draft our own list of inspirational reasons to strive. In doing this, we also learn how to use our work and other activities as a means of spiritual growth.

# Personal identity

Aside from being driven by where you'd like to go and what you'd like to acquire, of even greater importance is who you want to be. Despite being born with certain physical characteristics and a number of psychological predispositions, you are, in many ways, still extremely malleable – if you want to be! Your unattractive traits and habits are not rusted on, and you are not hostage to the same insecurities and reactions that you've accumulated up to now.

> Your unattractive traits and habits are not rusted on.

With this in mind, we ask ourselves, 'Who do I want to be?' From this, a list of other questions is generated: 'How do I want to be perceived?', 'If I developed a reputation around my friends, family or work colleagues, what would I like this reputation to be?', 'Am I thought of as successful, funny, open-minded, easy to talk to, professional, conscientious, diligent, caring, attentive, thoughtful, powerful, resilient, loyal, ethical and morally sound?' Or, 'Do people think of me as lazy, self-centred, unreliable, obnoxious or volatile?' There are many questions we can ask ourselves about who we are and how we are perceived.

By creating our own motivating personal-identity goal, we can draw out our best behaviour which inspires us to act like the person we would ideally like to be. It's not possible to overstate how important it is to feel proud of who you are. Don't look at other people who impress you and lament all the ways you are not like them. If you see something you like, take it onboard and make it part of your shield, your sword, your heart and your honour!

# My identity

I am personally motivated to behave and think more in accordance with my ideal identity each time I stop to consider my basic hierarchy of values, which are:

- to be a good son
- to be a good father
- to be a good partner
- to be a good brother
- to be a good friend.

I aspire to be good at *being* all of the above. These ambitions help me recruit the necessary motivation to act dutifully towards the important people in my life. Moreover, I like myself more when I am in harmony with these values and feel a greater sense of overall motivation towards other relatively peripheral areas.

# WEAPON #2

# SELF-DISCIPLINE

SELF-DISCIPLINE IS MORE THAN just a weapon. It is perhaps the ultimate superpower! It could be best described as doing what you need to do when you need to do it whether you feel like it or not. It's the ability to carry out a resolution long after the mood in which it was made has passed.

As an example, pretty much everyone is upbeat and positive in the first few days of a diet or new exercise program. We begin making different choices, adjust our behaviour and adopt new habits. Typically, these changes are driven by enthusiasm for our new plan and it's not uncommon for us to experience positive results in a relatively short time.

But at some point along the way – sometimes not that far along the way – we invariably hit a wall. This either causes or coincides with a waning of our enthusiasm. That natural fuel which was driving us at the start of our plan has partly extinguished and, as the novelty factor diminishes, motivation wears thin. All that remains is our daily choice to persevere or stop. It's at this point that we need to recruit a secondary mobilising force to ensure we persist and keep our resolutions on track.

> Discipline is the generator that kicks in when the motivational power cuts out.

Discipline is the generator that kicks in when the motivational power cuts out. When you desire something strongly, it naturally manifests the motivation that turns up the heat in your mind and body. It activates a dynamism that pushes you through the challenges between you and your goal such as laziness, procrastination or negative outside forces. You don't actually require discipline or willpower at this point as your body's natural biochemistry is formulating your own brand of personalised rocket fuel to thrust you forward.

The ability to be driven by a want or desire from time to time is, by itself, unexceptional. Yet despite this, very few people experience a sustained level of success with their personal budgets, diets, relationships or fitness levels. Motivation alone, therefore, is not the 'difference maker' and that's why we all need a back-up generator, which is discipline.

When you exercise discipline or 'will' something to be done, you rely less on feelings and more on your cultivated sense of duty; on keeping true to the commitments you made to yourself or others; and on your allegiance to those who you may lead in your business, sporting team, friendship circle or family. Essentially, you rely only upon your power to act irrespective of your feelings or the conditions at the time. It's just the right thing to do or it needs doing, so you do it.

Unlike motivation, self-discipline is a rare trait that is most often the definitive quality separating leaders from the rest of the pack in any field. Learning how to overcome the resistance that prevents us from taking consistent action is a task well worth pursuing. You may be a great starter, but without self-discipline you are likely to burn out after the initial sprint and fail to cross the finish line.

By exercising self-discipline or willpower, you don't have to rely on motivation. The key here is to use motivation when it's on hand and rely on willpower when it's not. This is the magic of the twin-engine drive mechanism that we all have the potential to utilise. Sometimes it takes motivation to get you moving and discipline to keep you going. Other times, discipline is your starter-motor and motivation serves as your afterburner. Many clever people fall by the wayside because they fail to recognise this dual-ignition concept.

You don't have to be great to start, but you do have to start to *be* great.

This all sounds like common sense, so why isn't it very common? The simple and unvarnished answer is that sometimes it's hard! It's not easy to break old habits, say no to strong temptations and regularly venture outside of your comfort zone. But if we wish to excel in any field, sooner or later we're going to have to turn professional. Pro-athletes perform at a high level on a consistent basis irrespective of conditions, injuries, sickness or scoreboard pressure. Amateurs, however, tend to be fair-weather players who rely on external conditions to yield in their favour. Whether it's in business, in sport or in life in general, we need to play like a professional!

Given how crucial self-discipline is in the process of pursuing our goals, its development as one of our chief superpowers needs to take a high priority. When faced with an internal willpower challenge, we must learn that our minds prompt and help our bodies do what's necessary, and in turn our bodies (through action) prompt and help our minds to feel like continuing. It works both ways.

Willpower challenges are a form of competition between two parts of ourselves. While our internal process is that of one person, we are often in two contrasting minds. We can be completely different people depending on which portion of our brain is more active. It is possible, for instance, that a person may choose chocolate one day, and then make a more responsible decision to eat an apple the next. The simple analysis is that the chocolate illustrates the short-term gratification decision, whereas the apple represents a choice that is more connected to a long-term objective, in this case, to develop or maintain good health.

> People who succeed long term have crafted ways to embrace delayed gratification.

The reality for most people is that their brain is going to meet this willpower challenge one way today and another way tomorrow. Like a child one day and an adult the next. The 'weak' version of themselves one day and the stronger, more disciplined version the next!

People who succeed over the long term have crafted ways to embrace delayed gratification and to be a better version of themselves as their default setting. We must therefore strive to create a synergy between our thoughts and actions that converts our will into an all-weather, all-terrain vehicle capable of driving over obstacles and powering past temptations.

# Discipline leads to freedom

This statement can initially seem incongruous given that most of us view discipline as something harsh and undesirable and see freedom as doing whatever we feel like. However, people who have attained financial wealth, long-term business success, good health and lasting relationships have done so through a process of self-mastery that was born out of personal discipline. In the end, we are only free to the extent that we have released ourselves from the automaticity of unproductive habits.

The well-worn grooves from the past may appear to be fixed in place but self-discipline empowers us to cut a future path of our own choosing – free of impulse or reflex. When engaging in any activity, do so as a conscious choice rather than a mindless habit.

As such, we must examine ways to become a more disciplined version of ourselves on a regular basis by fertilising our mind with upgraded and empowering perspectives. We can also identify practical behavioural choices that build mind-muscle and condition the brain to make decisions in alignment with our long-term goals.

# The magic is in the first few punches!

Serious martial artists don't just train in the dojo. Home training is a major part of the ongoing discipline. Typically, however, the ease of access to your garage or backyard training area is countered by the endless temptations that exist at home. This makes it difficult sometimes to summon the motivation to put on your training clothes and start your at-home workout, irrespective of the activity.

The best advice here is to forget motivation or at least forget relying on it to kickstart your training session. It will most likely show up five minutes after you've started and thrown those first few dozen warm-up punches, kicks, push-ups or sit-ups. This is why we say *the magic is in the first few punches*, because once you've started to move your body and the first beads of sweat appear on your forehead, you start to feel like training and a surge of motivation and enthusiasm roars onto the scene. Before you start, you may not feel capable of doing anything for more than ten minutes, but once you begin you may end up training twice as long as you originally intended. What happened? It's quite simple. You started to physically feel good ten minutes in and, at about the same time, your self-worth puffed its chest out and announced through your internal biochemistry that you're a champion for doing something hard when you didn't feel like it. This is really who you want to be deep down, and when you exhibit these behaviours in the face of resistance, your inner voice cries out, 'Legend!'

This internal glory cycle usually begins with you feeling lethargic and disinterested yet more often than not ends up representing the start of your otherwise empowering daily routine. Remember that no more than ten minutes on the other side of your starting point, the *legend* is waiting.

# What you practise is what you create

Through mostly good choices and disciplined action, in my 50s I am the same weight as I was in high school and have never fluctuated more than two kilos above or below that weight, other than through illness. While I train four to five days every week, eat fairly sensibly and only occasionally drink alcohol, some people have ventured to say that my weight stability and fitness are due to having a naturally slim body type (lucky genes!) However, I'm sure that if I suddenly put on ten kilos of useless mass, those same people wouldn't be saying, "It's such bad luck that he put on that weight." And nor should they. If bad lifestyle choices put the weight on then it's probably good ones that kept it off. It's no different in principle to saying that a top fighter or sportsperson is naturally talented. While they may have been born with an athletic body type, it undermines the thousands of training hours and buckets of sweat that they have dropped over many years if we frame their excellence as something that just came 'naturally'.

Ask yourself, 'What would the strongest, most fearless part of me do right now?' Then do it! There's an old-school saying, "A boy does what he wants to do, but a man does what he has to do." This phrase is a call to become more responsible and serves to remind us that while doing what we *must* may not always result in short-term happiness, it is in fact the path to adulthood and, indeed, to greatness. When a boxer signs up for his next fight, there is nothing in his contract that says he has to enjoy his training camp.

# Improving your willpower

Contemporary neurosciences have made remarkable discoveries over recent years in relation to mapping brain activity. Specifically, using Functional Magnetic Resonance Imaging (fMRI), neuroscientists have been able to accurately identify the portions of the brain that 'fire' when we make certain decisions. They have evidenced that the most pertinent part of the brain from the perspective of maximising self-discipline and willpower is the prefrontal cortex. Essentially, this is the decision-making headquarters of the brain.

Another fascinating concept that has excited the neuroscience field is what's known as 'neuroplasticity'. This is the brain's ability to rearrange itself by forming new neural networks. This process takes place naturally throughout our lifetime as a result of our experiences, both good and bad.

Neuroplasticity is a way for your brain to fine-tune itself for efficiency. This remarkable capacity also allows the brain to rewire itself after a psychological trauma or even a brain injury. The encouraging news here is it reinforces that our ingrained practices *are* changeable, and we are not hostage to our past mental habits or reflexes.

Anyone intending to fortify their willpower and self-discipline must first determine what practices they can adopt to fully engage the prefrontal cortex in their decision-making processes. The more alert and stimulated the prefrontal cortex is, the more we make decisions aligned with our long-term plans. The less it plays a part in our basic choices, the more we are driven by short-term gratification, which often works to counter our greater intentions.

There are practical adjustments you can make to your regular schedule that help your prefrontal cortex operate at its optimal level.

*Get more sleep* – While some people claim to need very little sleep, reliable studies have revealed that less than six hours of sleep per night can deplete the brain's ability to make good choices.

*Meditate regularly* – Meditation focuses on developing an awareness of the mind's activities and considers how these thoughts can manifest into meanings, judgements and behaviours. This leads to more 'conscious' decision-making and exerts a dominance over unhealthy impulses. Small changes can make a big difference! Studies have shown that an extra one hour's sleep and just ten minutes of meditation a day can see brain structures exhibit positive physical changes within as little as three weeks.

*Regular physical exercise* – Aside from the positive effects the production of endorphins can have on your brain function and mental clarity, regular exercise instigates positive chain reactions such as eating more responsibly, drinking more water and getting to bed earlier. It may also result in a sounder sleep, and so the constructive cycle kicks in. This is called having a 'global training effect'. Exercising regularly leads to better decisions all round.

*Maintain a low glycaemic diet* – Dramatic fluctuations caused by high glycaemic foods encourages erratic mental activity that is characterised by rapid surges and drops. Low glycaemic foods help to level out the brain's mood chemistry and create a stronger and more resolute constitution.

This enhances our ability to make better long-term decisions, which in turn helps us make better future dietary choices. Eventually, this process resembles more of a loop than as something having a start and finish line. Ultimately, we are converting our behaviour and decision-making patterns from being driven by habit or cravings to being determined by conscious and considered choices. Every time you say no to a temptation, the power that the temptation had over you is transferred to your future willpower.

*Deliberate exposure* – Sometimes referred to as *surfing the urge*, this is an uncomplicated strategy that tests and strengthens your powers of self-discipline. It involves deliberately exposing yourself to a temptation and paying full attention to the physical discomfort this creates. The intention is to prove to yourself that you have more power over that temptation than it has over you. In a sense, you are seeking out the challenge and letting it know you are not afraid of it.

The most permanent pay-off comes when we approach the urges mindfully:

→ Notice your craving or thought.
→ Accept your feelings without judgement.
→ Slow your breathing; give your mind and body a chance to pause and plan.

→ Look for the behaviour or decision that helps you achieve your goal. In this case it is to abstain!

This exercise teaches you to trust that you can tolerate the accompanying physical sensations and that, if you just wait with patience, they will eventually go away. It demonstrates that they are merely passing experiences you are not compelled to act on.

# Dealing with willpower failures

Think of a recent time you experienced a willpower failure. Maybe you ate something bad for you, stayed up too late, watched something on TV when you had work to do, skipped the gym for a whole week or something similar. First of all, welcome to normal! Secondly, how should you react? Does feeling guilty or getting angry at yourself improve your chances of having more discipline the next time around? What's surprising to many hard taskmasters out there is that the answer to this question is always no. It's actually better to forgive yourself for occasionally letting your discipline slip rather than beating yourself up.

An interesting study was conducted illustrating the negative ongoing effects of being overly self-critical after a willpower blow out. It involved convincing a group of people who were all actively involved in a weight-loss program to break their diet and eat something high in sugar (donuts I believe). Afterwards, the test group was split in half with one group being given basic counselling on how to deal with the breaking of their healthy eating regime. This involved reminding them of their common humanity: that everyone is imperfect, and every now and then we take a step back while climbing because this is invariably how change happens. Overall, the group were reminded that breaking their discipline says nothing about who they are, but more about the process itself.

The counsellors also highlighted that what the participants did next was more important than worrying about what had happened.

The other group was not given any debrief. The participants were put back into a room where they had free and unlimited access to many different types of sweet treats for several hours.

The experiment resulted in those not given a debrief consuming twice as many sweets as those who were debriefed, without exception. This was a clear victory for the encouragement over self-criticism argument as it proved that guilt and shame tend to put us in a state that is more susceptible to temptation, placing us further away from the version of ourselves that is attached to our long-term goals.

> The harder you are on yourself, the greater the likelihood you will relapse.

This case study urges us to think more about the big picture in instances where we experience a personal willpower failure rather than dwelling in a short-term mistake mode. The harder you are on yourself, the greater the likelihood you will relapse… and relapse worse than before. This truth can apply to all aspects of one's life.

# Have a conversation with your future

Many people unconsciously disconnect themselves from their future self, as if the person they will be in 20 to 30 years is a stranger they haven't met yet. In virtually all cases, however, the complete opposite is true. Unless measurable changes are initiated at some point between now and then, you will be basically the same person in 20 to 30 years with the same personality, values and beliefs.

However, the more you can identify with and relate to your future self, the better long-term decisions you are likely to make now. Conversely, if you see little correlation between your current and future self then your 'now' decisions will tend to be short-term based with little consideration for long-term consequences. After all, you are less likely to make decisions to benefit a 'stranger' in the future when you could do something instantly pleasurable or convenient now for someone you currently love – yes, that's you!

If your future self could write a letter to your current self, what encouragements or warnings would such a letter contain? What could you start working on now in relation to your health, relationships or financial wellbeing that your future self would be grateful for?

# Charge your power grid

It is tempting to believe we can achieve our life's ambitions through good old-fashioned optimism and positive visualisation alone. Perhaps it would help if we told everyone around us what our goals in life were. But it is said that the strongest muscle in the human body is the jaw. Talk is cheap! Ultimately, what you practise will determine what you have much more than what you say. Whilst taking action may not always be easy or convenient, it's good to remind ourselves that the pain of discipline is nothing compared to the pain of regret!

It's probably taken you some self-discipline to even pick up this book in the first place and read as far into it as you have. In a sense, you've already exhibited your intention to improve some part of yourself by doing so. All that's left when you finish reading this page, this paragraph, this book or anything else you deem to be of value to your future is to move!

Don't wait to feel good before you start and don't be perturbed if it's not easy at first. Seeking short-term comforts or solutions without consideration for the future is like licking honey from a razor's edge.

Do it now!

> Seeking short-term comforts is like licking honey from a razor's edge.

# WEAPON #3

# GRATITUDE

*"If you look at what you have in life, you'll always have more. If you look at what you don't have in life, you'll never have enough."*

—Oprah Winfrey

GRATITUDE IS A FEELING that expresses appreciation for the things we already have. Being grateful for one's lot can be more challenging than it sounds in this corporate-striving and consumer-driven environment. Enough never seems to be enough!

Commercial advertising goes out of its way to convince us that we don't have enough – or that we *aren't enough*. It specialises in inventing problems or creating shortcomings that aren't there, and then conveniently appears with a basket of ready-made solutions – a type of 'crisis capitalism'.

Many of us in developed countries suffer 'first world' inadequacy disorders due to our lack of appreciation for the gifts and opportunities we have in front of us. If you were born in Australia, the United States, the United Kingdom or any other developed country, then you've already been dealt a good hand. 'Born on third base' is a term used to describe people who become heir to generational wealth, but this could be extended to include the majority of us born into comfort. This is particularly relevant when we consider the level of destitution that millions of people around the world experience daily.

The Buddhist philosophy takes the subject of gratitude even further. Their sense of good fortune extends to having been born human! They sometimes refer to their 'glorious human rebirth' meaning that we could have arrived on this earth as insects or some other animal. It is not overstating our blessings to consider this viewpoint.

Developing a sense of gratitude is about perspective. While some people complain about traffic, weather, their football team's losing streak, or the undercooked steak they were served at the restaurant, there are those at the other end of the scale who have recently encountered near-death experiences. These folks are just happy to be alive, happy to see their children's faces again and overjoyed to see another sunrise!

The time, place and cause of our death remain a cosmic secret until near the end, which is a candid reminder that ultimate control in life is unattainable. Every day above ground is truly a blessing and life is an unearned gift. We have much to be grateful for.

Despite this seemingly positive disposition, there are some who fear that being overly thankful for their current position may diminish their drive to achieve greater things. However, by nature of its form, gratitude can also be associated with increased energy, optimism and humility and need not breed an unhealthy complacency. Gratitude does not stop us from pursuing our targets, but it does remind us not to be deterred if we face obstacles or setbacks. Life's delays are not life's denials.

The general sense of thankfulness that adopting an attitude of gratitude creates allows us to remain proportionally humble on occasions where we do succeed or experience victory. It ensures we do not overlook the wide and varied array of obstacles that stayed out of our way long enough to help us achieve that goal.

This concept is at work with decorated war veterans who are reluctant – on many occasions – to accept accolades of bravery for their survival on the battlefield. While many of these men were highly trained, fulfilled the necessary combat preparations and minimised the risks as much as possible, they often concede that their survival in that bloody battle was as much about good luck as anything else. They know that their fallen comrades were every bit as prepared as they were, but the indiscriminate nature of flying bullets and exploding ordnances meant that there'd be next to no rational explanation for who made it out alive and who didn't.

Those who lack a sense of gratitude or fail to acknowledge the role that good fortune can play in their lives often struggle to give or receive praise. These people define their success as a 100 per cent individual triumph, and often compound this error by adopting a self-righteous and overly judgemental attitude towards the slow progress of others.

Adopting a sense of gratitude is undeniably enhanced by embracing interdependence. As stated earlier, no one lives a truly independent existence. Just because you don't personally know the hundreds of people who contributed to the design and manufacture of your new car, doesn't mean that it wasn't a team effort to get it sitting in your driveway. There is almost no end to the depth of appreciation you can direct towards the vast network of strangers involved in your daily life.

The deepest and most rewarding level of gratitude is one that recognises these realities and regularly gives thanks either directly through speech or inwardly through insight and grateful thoughts. It's very easy to overlook how much more we receive from others in life than we give.

Adopting an attitude of appreciation and gratitude can produce a number of tangible benefits.

# Gratitude generates optimism

Given that gratitude is essentially the practice of focusing on what's good in life, it's easy to understand how it is strongly correlated with optimism. If our current circumstances are fortuitous, then we are more likely to believe that our future will look equally bright.

Author Jonathan Carroll stated, "One of the saddest realities is that we never know when our lives are at their peak. Only after it is over and we have some kind of perspective do we realise how good we had it a day, a month, five years ago." The practice of gratitude enhances our appreciation for the talents we possess and helps us realise these gifts in the moment rather than noticing them retrospectively.

> Gratitude raises an individual's social capital.

A gratitude-driven positive outlook creates a contagious quality within our family and social environments. People are more drawn towards those who make them feel good, whereas they'll avoid the 'negator' who complains about life and its imbalances. You could say that gratitude raises an individual's social capital.

An optimistic attitude can also help us bounce back from a loss or disappointment, and drastically reduce the time we spend sulking by making us more resilient.

# Gratitude can change our story

Contrary to how it may seem, memories are perceptions too. While we may think 'what's done is done', embedded in our recall is the subjective interpretation of 'what was actually done'. Memories are more than one-dimensional recordings or data stored on our cerebral hard drives. There are many ways that our memories can change over time depending on the degree to which we feel grateful in the present day.

We may remember incidents as being worse than they actually were. Parents, for instance, can retrospectively be viewed as lenient or stricter depending on your current relationship with them. Having a grateful temperament makes us more likely to experience our memories with a sense of appreciation and may even renovate our neutral or negative thoughts into more positive versions.

At the end of the day, there will be an end – one day! By making it to the age of 30, it's an indisputable truth that you have already dodged a multitude of bullets and had countless near misses with your health and safety. Let's face it, making it out of the womb is a miracle. Having witnessed childbirth firsthand on three occasions, I'm surprised that single-child families are not the norm. One birth would be enough for most men if they were the carriers.

In any case, if you're still breathing, every day is another chance to turn it all around if things aren't going your way. It all begins by changing your perspective on how fortunate you are to have been born at this time and place in history. It's the best time to be alive. Every day is precious. Make sure you notice!

> Every day is another chance to turn it all around.

# WEAPON #4

# COURAGE

*"Scared is what you're feeling.*
*Brave is what you're doing."*

—Emma Donoghue

IT'S IMPOSSIBLE TO EXAMINE the topic of courage without studying the nature of fear.

Many have attempted to deconstruct fear by reducing the word down to different meanings for the acronym of FEAR, such as 'False Evidence Appearing Real' and 'Face Everything and Respond'. For many people, FEAR more closely resembles 'Forget Everything and Run'.

Entire coaching industries and book shop aisles have been created to deal with the topic of fear… and for good reason. Fear is quite probably the most destructive human emotion that anyone can suffer and, in many ways, represents the death of reason. In most cases, fear makes us weak, has the tendency to paralyse constructive thoughts and actions, causes a withering of one's spirit, undermines confidence, inhibits performance and lames resolve. It can also distort our interpretation of things and create obstructions and demons where none exist. What we fear comes to pass far more swiftly than what we hope – mainly because we make it so. Fear is a powerful motivator that rarely takes us where we want to go.

Whether we like it or not, fear is part of our biology. It is responsible for helping us evade many of life's dangers and helping us make it to old age. The most productive attitude to adopt towards fear is to accept that it is a necessary, integral part of our readiness to confront challenges. Fear is a stage of preparation alerting us to danger or readying us to perform. Accepting fear's role in your life is a mature and enlightened perspective that can assist in the manifestation and execution of its emotional rival – courage.

> Courage reminds us that even fear has a nemesis.

Courage reminds us that even fear has a nemesis. Courage is the antidote for fear and is probably the most admired and sought-after quality for most people. Many of us view courage as some sort of gladiator quality, confined archetypally to territories of battle or the sporting field. We think someone is courageous when they jump out of a plane, scale a high mountain or perform some other similar feat demanding endurance, risk or fortitude.

While this is fair enough, overly focusing on this 'sexy' form of courage deflects attention from the everyday common opportunities to exercise courage. Ordinary life arouses the need for courage more prolifically than adventure or even combat because of the inescapable realities of life, such as sickness, pain, heartache, regret, struggle, financial concerns, loss, panic and change. Regardless of how much we cling to safety, life serves up endless opportunities to exercise courage.

As downbeat as this sounds, these are all common features of the human condition experienced by millions of people every day. Although these day-to-day examples of courage may appear to be mundane when compared with overt acts of daring, they nonetheless demand all kinds of gallantry and emotional stamina. The often-perpetual nature of these difficult situations can make one-off stunts such as jumping out of planes seem like a more leisurely alternative.

Whereas activities such as base-jumping, extreme surfing or prize-fighting are all self-contained undertakings with a finite timeframe and a probable return to normalcy when finished, facing real-life emotions such as grief or distress can be quite different. The extent of their magnitude and timeframe is unknown, with the only guarantee being that much will need to be endured prior to any respite. To lie in bed with fear at night or awake each morning and sense the return of anguish, grief or sorrow is an experience many of us have suffered. Sometimes, summoning the fortitude to rise anyway and carry on with our day as best as we can is courage in itself.

It is important to distinguish between courage and fearlessness, for without fear there is no need for courage. Courage is essentially the act of faking fearlessness – acting as if there is no fear present. Legendary actor John Wayne once said, "Courage is being scared to death but saddling up anyway." This approach allows us to expand into difficult situations or stand up to intimidating people when we may otherwise be immobilised with worry. Courage, therefore, is not so much a feeling – it is an action or habit.

There have been many attempts to tackle the topic of fear and provide guidance for diminishing its impact on our lives. In my view, there have been no better mentors on this subject than the famous boxing trainer Cus D'Amato. D'Amato became well known in boxing circles in the 1950s and 1960s when he guided Floyd Patterson to become the youngest heavyweight champion in history. Some 20 years or so later, D'Amato became universally known as the man who discovered Mike Tyson, predicting the then 13-year-old Tyson would become the heavyweight champion of the world. Unfortunately, D'Amato would not live to see the outcome of his prediction. In 1986, Mike Tyson broke Floyd Patterson's record by becoming the new youngest ever heavyweight champion at just 20 years of age.

D'Amato was as revered for his philosophical insights as his excellent credentials as a boxing technician. Not surprisingly for a fight trainer, one of his pet topics was the psychology of fear and how to best manage its presence in the emotionally turbulent environment leading up to a fight. There are few – if any – sports where the fear of losing carries so much weight. Boxers can be overwhelmed or beaten up by another man, and it all plays out in the most public of ways. The potential for intense humiliation and extreme embarrassment is high, which only adds to the already considerable concerns of being physically hurt. Irrespective of your view on combat sports, the fear factor in such activities is colossal.

Rather than deny or underplay the fear he knew his boxers experienced, D'Amato instead chose to acknowledge the sense of foreboding fear created. He asserted that being scared in itself was not an emblem of weakness. He rationalised that the difference between a coward and a hero was not that one experienced fear and one didn't. Rather, both the coward and the hero suffered the same fear, but it was what the hero did about it that made him the hero, and what the coward didn't do that made him the coward. In essence, he focused his fighters on affecting the only thing they had any control over (their behaviour), rather than where they had very little dominion (their emotions). Ultimately, he tutored his fighters to use fear as a friend and to embrace its internal alchemic role in the body's combustion engines.

Trying to diminish fear by 'thinking it away' has limited results. Constructing courage in the face of fear involves accepting its presence, rationalising the consequences of action vs non-action, and then taking affirmative steps towards the object or situation. Every step you take towards the fear is likely to incrementally decrease its magnitude. Rarely is the feared object as immense in real life as it is in your imagination.

# It always looks worse from the sidelines

There were many occasions in my early martial arts training where I gained invaluable insights into fear and its counterfeit representations. Sparring or *kumite* is an unchoreographed fighting activity that pits you against another person or persons. While all efforts are made by both parties to fight with a degree of physical and mental control, it is nonetheless the closest thing to having an actual fight without actually fighting. It can be somewhat confronting, particularly when you know that your opponent is highly skilled and/or aggressive. I was not immune to these nerves and often spent entire classes worrying about what might happen if we had to spar before the session ended.

The upside of this anxiety was that it forced me to challenge my internal fears and upgrade the psychological software that had previously specialised in worst-case scenarios. The subsequent wisdom gained from this cognitive transformation is the greatest gift I have received from martial arts.

Here's the best of what I came to realise:

→ Everything looks faster from side on than it does coming at you.

→ Courage is sometimes acting like you're not scared. Act like you're not scared and soon you won't be.

→ During moments of self-doubt, I was more fearful of losing face or credibility than I was of losing to an opponent or getting hurt. However, if I displayed courage by actively facing the fear then my credibility was secure irrespective of the outcome.

→ There was little to no space for fear during the fight – I was too busy focusing on the fight in front of me. Hence, there was only fear in the forecasting, but none in the doing.

→ Even if I didn't do well, the worst I felt afterwards was disappointment and a determination to look for that person again next time around.

→ Disappointment is manageable.

Aside from the everyday fears we can experience such as fear of failure, disapproval or the intimidation asserted onto us by another person, many people harbour deep concerns about their own mortality. While it's true that our pilot light will extinguish one day, there is no need for our minds to overly inhabit that mental space while we are alive.

If we obsess over our inevitable end then all that exists is distress. Being deceased is not something we experience until it happens. Our only encounters with death are when we lose others and face grief. Our own death is not part of our personal experience, and as such we can escape our fear of dying by firstly accepting and then disregarding its inevitability.

In the end, we will either be defined by what we feared or by how we faced it. As the saying goes, "Fortune favours the brave." We must mobilise the fortitude to confront real threats to our wellbeing and cease being terrorised by self-created 'horrorgrams'. Our imagination has the ability to conjure up disastrous fictitious scenarios, but it's clear that fear itself is more to be feared than the majority of actual things we worry about.

# WEAPON #5

# FORTITUDE

FORTITUDE CAN BEST BE described as the 'mind force' that enables a person to confront danger, endure pain or encounter adversity with mettle. This sense of resolve or spirit of tenacity is not something we call upon to steel us through our good times but, rather, we call on it when we are facing resistance, experiencing loss or beset by fears of some description. In the sporting arena, fortitude is described as mental toughness or the 'iron in the mind'.

> Fortitude is described as mental toughness or the 'iron in the mind'.

In boxing, fortitude is the display of character shown by the fighter who remains undiscouraged when the fight is not going his way. Maybe he has taken a few clean shots or been down throughout the fight. Most likely he is tired and hurting, behind on points, but is keeping his hands up, his chin down and continuing to move forward looking for opportunities. He tries through his facial expressions and his overall body language to send a message to his opponent that he is

OK and getting stronger. He wants his opponent to know that he is unperturbed by what has happened, and he is gathering steam to turn the fight. In short, his overall aim is to make his opponent start doubting his own ability and punching power. This is a good example of why fighters insist that winning at the top level is far more about the mental game than the physical one.

Substitute the opponent in the boxing analogy for the multitude of oppositional forces that threaten to knock us down over the course of our lives. Like the fighter who displays resilience and mental toughness in the ring, we must resolve to press on when we are pushing uphill or when the wind is not at our backs. Using boxing parlance again, we must work hard to avoid the 'glass jaw' syndrome, where one solid shot can take us out.

While it may be biologically correct to state that some fighters can take a punch better than others (a naturally thick neck is helpful), the ability to absorb blows with more durability is mostly a product of training and preparation. One need only watch former undisputed world lightweight champion Kostya Tszyu doing headstands for ten-plus minutes at a time, or Mike Tyson arching his back high off the ground as he executed frightening-looking head-roll exercises, to see that these champions fortified every part of their bodies, including their chins and necks.

Metaphorically speaking, it's highly unlikely that one could succeed in any worthwhile pursuit with a glass jaw. Success in any venture comes down to how well we can take a hit and come back. There's also a distinct difference between playing to win and playing not to lose. While the overly cautious or defensive fighter may avoid being hit by refusing to engage his opponent, he will also be unable to win. If he truly seeks victory, then at some point he'll have to step into range and risk being hit. So is the case with our approach to enterprise. Nothing ventured, nothing gained.

It's almost impossible to recognise the virtues of fortitude without acknowledging the backdrop through which it is summonsed. In the same way that the umbrella only becomes useful during rainfall, fortitude's value is maximised during periods of failure or loss. For many people, the natural tendency is to become timid or discouraged after suffering a setback, but fortitude straightens us and urges us to press on, albeit at times under strain. This resilience is easier to preach than it is to practise but, importantly, it is not beyond us. Football player Roger Staubach said, "There are no traffic jams along the extra mile." This reminds us that uncommon rewards and very little competition await those who can persevere in the face of resistance or failure. Fortitude is fortune.

There are many active measures we can take to optimise our staying power in times of trial.

# Discriminate

Author Charlie Tremendous Jones once said, "You will be the same person in five years as you are today, except for the people you meet and the books you read." This means you become like the people you hang around with, and your dominant thinking is determined by what you see or listen to regularly. For this reason, we must be selective about the company we keep and the daily narratives we're exposed to through television, newspapers or social media. Garbage in = garbage out. It is more important now than ever to detect and deflect these negative influences wherever possible whether they present themselves in human form or via some other medium.

It is unwise to conclude that you will remain unaffected by pessimistic or downbeat company, or that being regularly exposed to small-minded or mean-spirited conversation is harmless. Your

> Regular exposure to 'mental candy' will take its toll.

mind is like a bear trap and regular exposure to this 'mental candy' will take its toll despite best intentions and staunch denials. Success in any field demands exceptional drive and a superior mindset, and it's unlikely that these qualities will be given fertile ground to develop in a cynical, parochial or nihilistic environment.

# Attitude adjustment

Failure is nothing more than an outcome where the result failed to match expectations. These expectations are often arbitrary and based on unrealistic ideals or non-empirical data. Exercising resilience in difficult times requires us to reframe our attitudes towards falling short. In a sense, we must aim to become a master of failure because success demands its percentage of setbacks. Acknowledging this helps us to construct a new paradigm that can muster the fortitude to tough it out during an emotional, professional or financial beat down.

Pain, as they say, is a great teacher, but nobody wants to attend its class. Often during a gruelling karate session, we would comment that *pain was just weakness leaving our body,* which was our way of saying *toughen up and keep going.* It was part of our dojo etiquette to conceal physical discomfort wherever possible and to adopt the mentality that we were using our bodies to strengthen our minds. This was a major part of our process for developing mental toughness and a fighting spirit. All of these practices were designed to frame our pain or failures as something to overcome and ultimately be proud of. 'Fail forward' was our mantra, and it amplified the notion that you're not a failure until you quit or start blaming others.

In sport or throughout life in general, there are many types of victories. Defeat, however, always provides an opportunity to learn something and often unveils alternative paths. It takes a mature attitude and good sense to accept that the best lessons are usually the toughest – and defeat regularly qualifies within this category. This urges us to realise that the only true defeat is in letting defeat force us into submission.

The fear of failure is more debilitating in most cases than the tangible fallout from actual failure. Getting knocked down – whether physically or metaphorically – can be everything from discouraging to embarrassing to even humiliating if looked at from the perspective of an unhealthy ego. Winners take pride in the getting-up part, which overrides the embarrassing experience of the going-down part. True failure only occurs when one fails to participate or compete. This is not a naturally occurring mindset or realisation for most people, but one that needs to be cultivated through self-education and personal reflection. Ultimately, if your life is free of failures, you're probably not aiming high enough.

# Defining the win

It's easy to become swept up in the win-at-all-costs attitude when competing. Phrases like 'there's no prize for second' or 'second place is the first loser' or 'nobody remembers who came second' all suggest that winning is the *only* thing that matters. While there's no doubt that winning is more enjoyable – and maybe more profitable – than coming in second, it is inevitable that losses will occur.

Rugby league super-coach Wayne Bennett, in his book *Don't Die with the Music in You*, expressed that there is too much emphasis on winning and losing, even in an intensely competitive sport where the financial stakes are high. He stated that the obsession with winning was, "The most false thing I'm involved with." He explained, "The thing about winning and losing is that you can win and give a mediocre effort, and you can still lose after giving it everything you have. I know which effort I'd be prouder of!"

All forms of competitive activity require us to exercise resilience at some stage. Reframing our view of failure and adjusting our behaviour post-loss are the fundamental elements that endow us with the steel to continue, despite our breakdowns. Renowned American football player and coach Lou Holtz remarked, "You're never as good as everyone tells you when you win, and you're never as bad as they say when you lose."

# A lesson from the Swiss maestro...

In January 2017, tennis legend Roger Federer shocked the sporting world by winning his 18th Grand Slam title at the Australian Open. At 35 years of age, and in his first tournament back after six months away from the game due to injury, Federer defied all the odds to defeat his greatest rival and nemesis Rafael Nadal in the final in five brutal sets. Nadal was widely regarded as the most mentally tough and physically imposing opponent on the tour and, at 1–3 behind in the fifth set, Federer was again staring down the barrel of Nadal's gun forehand and legendary fighting spirit. Federer had been here before, only to be left broken-hearted by Nadal's relentless pressure down the closing straight. In a superhuman feat of skill and courage, Federer unexpectedly reeled off five straight games to take the set and the match in one of the most miraculous victories of his illustrious career.

When asked after the match how he managed to summon the fortitude under such pressure in the final set, Federer revealed a remarkable irony. While he had told himself that his best chance of winning was to 'play free, keep attacking and take it to his opponent', he also acknowledged that his best chance of executing this strategy under pressure was to remind himself that it was OK to lose! In effect, he was playing with the mentality that being too hung up on *not losing* would impede his daring and allow his opponent to dictate terms. In short, Federer stared down defeat and said, "You don't scare me!" This is how elite athletes and other successful entrepreneurs approach their challenges, and it serves as their primary generator of mental and physical toughness.

## Make friends with pessimism

Regardless of our best efforts to evict pessimistic thoughts from our daily life, the reality is that they will be permanent tenants within our head. The good news is that we don't have to wait for our negatively wired minds to be renovated before we can move forward. In some cases, this inherent pessimism can work for us.

Contrary to the popular view, imagining failure can sometimes be a more superior motivator than imagining success. There are times when tracking and checking off little successes along the way has actually led people to do something inconsistent with their greater goal. This can happen because they assume the good feelings they get from acknowledging items on their to-do list will automatically create motivation to do more. But this is

> Imagining failure can be a more superior motivator than imagining success.

not always the case as optimism about the future can sometimes authorise self-indulgence or inactivity *today*.

Perhaps the simple interpretation for this odd psychological phenomenon is that we will do far more to move away from something we don't want than we will to move towards something we do want. While pessimistic thoughts are rarely viewed as inspiring, they can serve a constructive purpose by being an antidote for complacency and by helping us stress test our goals to identify the challenges ahead.

> Be ready to swallow that 'concrete pill' when you need to!

Attempting to banish all negative thinking from your mind is fruitless and unnecessary. Get started now with what you have and be ready to swallow that 'concrete pill' when you need to! For as long as we live, we are never out of choices.

# CREATING TIME

*"Those who make the worst use of their time*
*are the first to complain of its brevity."*

—Jean de la Bruyere

TIME IS A CONTINUUM of 'now' moments that, if well managed, knit together and cumulatively create something special. If not well managed, these moments have no cohesion or greater order, and end up randomly dissipating into unrelated fragments of memory. In most cases, we can make up for ill-conceived comments, health that's been neglected, money lost, trust broken or relationships damaged. Time, however, is unequivocally irreversible and unambiguously finite. Once it's lost, it's gone for good!

The well-worn concept of 'time management' almost passes as an oxymoron, given that there is only so much time and no amount of management can make it more or less than it is. Despite this obvious fact, some people achieve remarkable things in the same time that others fail to make even the slightest impression. The challenge for the inspired and success-driven businessperson, athlete, musician, parent or spouse is how to use the time they have to best effect.

Extracting the maximum value from the time we have is achieved by design and not by default, by choice and not by chance. There is no such thing as being accidentally time efficient.

> There is no such thing as being accidentally time efficient.

As a young man, the concept of maximising my time was a low priority. Like most young people, I found that the inherently finite nature of life failed to create a legitimate urgency with regard to health, savings, behaviour or my general outlook on progress. In too many ways, I was in no hurry! Rather than invest the time I had, I was content to merely spend it. Not unlike money, however, invested time returns a greater value at some point in the future than 'spent' time.

Our attitude towards the value of time is reflected in our choices and our behaviour. I look back at my late teens and early twenties and quietly lament the amount of non-working time I spent watching junk TV and reading vacuous magazines. It's true that we all need to zone out occasionally and pursue our personal interests. Effective time management, however, is about keeping our lightweight activities in their rightful ratio. We can't spend a disproportionate amount of time 'killing time' and expect a stellar outcome. You can't sit down and slide uphill!

Having recently achieved my half-century, I have been invigorated with a renewed sense of determination to prolong my days and squeeze every last drop out of my mortal innings. I have clearly reached a point in my life where there is less time left than has already been, and this has shaken me into the present moment and forced a re-evaluation of my priorities.

Entire books have been written on the subject of time management. The irony of this, of course, is that many people claim they don't have the time – or attention span – to endure an entire book on that single topic. I can sympathise with such a view. Over the years, I have been exposed to many different theories and structures that virtually tried to turn time management into a form of science by breaking it down into small components, micro-steps, priority quadrants and so on. That being said, if I were to approach this topic from a scientific perspective – albeit a simpler one – I would suggest that time management is like a chemical compound that is made up of two key elements: planning and discipline.

While much has already been covered in the area of practising discipline, it is relevant to reacknowledge its importance when it comes to maximising time. The fortune is in the follow-up, and no amount of planning will foster a result without consistent and supportive behaviour. Some would argue that it also takes discipline to put time aside at the start of a project to sit down and create a plan. Needless to say, acting in accordance with your plans – irrespective of whether you feel like it or not – is central to effective time management.

Planning sounds like a simple enough concept, so much so that many people fail to recognise its value and approach the activity too casually as a result. Those who are unable to manage their time well have usually either planned poorly or failed to plan at all. As the saying by Benjamin Franklin goes, "If you fail to plan, then you plan to fail." Many people cite they don't have time to always be planning, planning, planning, because they've no time to lose and must get started straight away. While there are odd times when a goal can be achieved without prior organisation, it is rarely the case.

There are simple guidelines to consider when it comes to effective planning.

# Never start the day until you've finished planning it

Spend the first five to ten per cent of your day establishing priorities and planning your activities. As a very basic example, if you work an eight-hour day, take 20–40 minutes to map out what needs doing, how long each task may take and roughly what order you intend to tackle them. If your major tasks follow more of a weekly or monthly cycle, then adjust your preparation and planning times accordingly.

On a day-to-day basis, by far the best time to plan your day is the night before. This can be done either as the last part of your formal working day, or shortly before bedtime as a constructive way of emptying the to-dos that inevitably build up throughout the evening. Once these tasks are written down, you no longer have to sleep with them.

When prioritising your activities, it is good practice, where possible, to tackle the biggest or most difficult things first. Leaving the challenging tasks until later in the day can often be distracting or even stressful. The metaphorical expression 'Eat that frog' refers to this concept. This suggests that if it is part of your job that day to eat a frog, then it is best to do it first thing in the morning. If it so happens that your job is to eat two frogs, then it's best to eat the biggest one first.

In the absence of any heavy-duty errands, precedence should also be given earlier in the day to any creative work that you may have to complete. Comedian and author John Cleese has conducted many serious lectures over the years where he sighted strong examples of his most creative and problem-solving powers operating at their peak first thing in the morning. By the afternoon, he regularly found that the onset of mild mental fatigue stymied his imaginative capacities, so he planned his creative and procedural tasks accordingly.

# Start the day early

Another approach I recommend every person investigate is something I have read about many times. It was also relayed to me more recently by a very wealthy and successful acquaintance. His theory on effective time management and maximising productivity was to be in bed each night by 8pm and rise each morning at 4.30am. By doing this, he is at his home office desk by 5.30am and has powered through the majority of his intended tasks by the time most people were starting work at 9am. Not only is he able to pursue his daily objectives without interruption during this time, but it also gives him a sense that he has a head start over the rest of the working world.

Those willing to make such time sacrifices will invariably be rewarded. In the past I have always operated at the opposite end of the day and worked in my home office until after midnight watching seminars, studying financial or business-related topics, or training. This was my time to work uninterrupted. However, it naturally lends itself to rising late the next morning. A late rise naturally leads to a late start and it's not especially motivating to be tackling your first diary task at 10am. As the saying goes, "Conquer the morning, win the day!"

Many people are not in a position to choose what time they start their official job, but the above recommendations can still be inserted into a standard working day. At the very least, you can be up early exercising, stretching, swimming, meditating or taking care of personal errands before you need to be at your job. Then, when

> The real cost of your phone or TV is far greater than its purchase price.

you come home at night, you can relax knowing you've already attended to the essential tasks that day.

To earn an above-average income, or just live your best life health-wise, we must be prepared to do more than an average person. This includes converting many of our after-hours entertainment sessions into productive or educational time. It's true that you may miss some mind-numbing videos along the way, but your bank balance and your future self will be forever grateful. After all, the real cost of your phone or TV is far greater than its purchase price.

# Create a physical plan

Irrespective of how organised you feel your thinking is, it is a recipe for stress and poor productivity to keep your key priorities internalised. Even the most methodical minds are a veritable tumble dryer of rogue thoughts, feelings and to-dos. So, don't kid yourself that your brain can miraculously collate priorities into an orderly queue without you writing them down.

Oddly, the proliferation of smart phones and electronic personal organisers has not automatically made us more organised. Technology by itself does not improve discipline, planning or time management. In fact, there is strong reason to believe that our personal devices can actually be an impediment to our productivity if we let the tail wag the dog. Being consistently contactable can be an ongoing distraction and take its toll on clear-thinking and cognitive administration. By using some type of digital organiser, a simple wall planner or a written diary, you will be light years ahead of the piecemeal and scatter-brain patterns typical of the mental-diary guy.

> Technology by itself does not improve discipline, planning or time management.

## Learn how to say no

One of my favourite lines from the *Dirty Harry* movies I was addicted to in my teens was something like, "A man's gotta know his limitations." While the context may have been slightly different, it still reminds us that there are only so many extra things we can effectively take on if we want to perform at a high level. The Russian proverb dictates, "If you chase two rabbits, they will both escape." The key here is to not let your mouth overload your back. Saying no to people's requests can often generate guilty feelings or anxiety, but it can also be liberating.

Some people's main argument for not planning is that other things may come along and upset their plans anyway, so why bother. This is fuzzy thinking and more often a thinly veiled justification for their laziness. It's actually much easier to pivot and alter your plans if you had them well-mapped to begin with. You may even be in a better position to say yes to more things because you'll know exactly when you are available. But irrespective of how solid your planning is, there will still be times when – for the sake of your sanity, health or marriage – you'll need to decline people's requests in order to preserve your priorities and keep *your* main thing *the* main thing.

# Something will master and something will serve

Are you the thermostat or the thermometer? Do you run your dog or does it run you? For those who are self-employed, you either run your business or it runs you. While these distinctions hint that we should be the boss of time, it's unrealistic to expect we can fashion a plan or a timetable that we always hold command over. There will inevitably be unexpected invasions into our schedule that leave us in a state of reaction. The key here is to accept that while there will be temporary forays into chaos from time to time, your plans are your bedrock and will be there to provide the stable structure to revisit once the spot fires have been extinguished.

Many of us are familiar with the saying, "There are those who make things happen, those who watch what happens, and those who wonder what the hell happened!" Planning helps us keep both hands on the wheel, and when we occasionally need to swerve or take an unexpected detour, we still retain control.

# Rest is not a reward

Earlier on in my career, I adopted the mentality that holidays were for wimps, and that weekends and public holidays were for indolent wage-earners who needed a break away from their unhappy working lives. In effect, I had become a success-seeking extremist, jacked up on rah-rah personal development seminars and dismissive of anything that so-called 'average people' did. If I was to have a holiday, then it had to be linked to a specific goal, and failure to

> Effective time management includes effective rest management.

achieve that goal meant no holiday! Even worse, I deemed sleeping eight hours a night to be a symptom of complacency reserved for the lazy and aimless.

Over the years my thinking matured into a more measured view of the above, partly because I started to meet very successful people who holidayed and took recuperative time off regularly. I realised that while there are times to set goals for something or somewhere special, there are also times when you'll need to recharge the batteries irrespective of an outcome. Failure to recognise this inevitably results in burnout, at which point you have ceased to be productive anyway. I came to view rest and relaxation as a weapon that could contribute significantly towards maximising my mental and physical performance. Effective time management includes effective rest management.

# Time is priceless

Days are expensive. When we spend a day, we have one less day to spend. We must treat our days as we would any other invaluable possession. As stated previously, you can always make more money, but you can't make more time. How you spend your time, therefore, is more important than how you spend your money. Most people would be distressed if they lost $1,000 in cash, yet regularly think nothing of wasting an equivalent amount of money in time lost through poor planning or engaging in trivial amusements.

> It's time you made more time for time.

If you're determined to protect a freely available and relatively limitless commodity like money, then it's time you made more time for time.

# 3D COMMUNICATION

MOST MOVIES PRESENT US with the physical experience of two major viewing perspectives: the height and width of the screen. Technically, this is considered a two-dimensional (2D) presentation. The popularity (and extra cost) of viewing the movie on a widescreen indicates there is a greater value when the image is projected onto a larger screen. The assumption is that the more the movie image spreads itself to the extremities of our peripheral vision, the more absorbed we are in the make-believe world we are watching. As an added feature, theatres place extra speakers at the back of the cinema to provide an all-round sound experience. With all this theatre hardware in place and the incredible special effects now present in even your basic films, it is an immersive experience viewing a drama or action movie in a large cinema.

As much as this set-up super-stimulates our senses, it is a whole other level to experience the visceral impact of a three-dimensional (3D) movie. The 3D movie spreads tall and wide within your visual scope *and* comes at you. It can make you feel physically touched when you weren't, make you duck for cover when there was nothing flying towards you, make you feel like your hair blew back from an on-screen explosion and literally give you motion sickness in the middle of the high-speed car chase.

A 3D communicator is someone who has the ability to elicit these same visceral responses in others by expertly conversing with them in a multidimensional way. In essence, they possess a versatile range of communicative tools that allows them to present their point of view in an impactful and captivating manner. The picture they paint is large and in full colour, and their articulated message is loud and clear. The combination of these factors taps directly into their audience's adrenal system. This evokes a strong emotional response and a sense that the message was delivered in 3D vision and surround sound, with the subwoofers turned up to full chest-vibrating strength. Expert communicators cut through the potential bias, egos, preconceived ideas, ignorance, stubbornness, low intelligence or timidity of those around them who they value and hope to influence positively. In doing so, they effectively bypass the comprehension filters that exist across a wide variety of opinions and personalities. They accomplish this by successfully applying the trifecta of effective communication strategies: rapport, state and story.

# Rapport

Rapport is the invisible conduit that allows feelings, thoughts and language to flow back and forth without obstruction between groups or individuals. It represents a sense of harmony or accord that you feel with people inside your social, emotional or professional sphere of influence. I have heard it described as having two guitars sitting side by side, where plucking one string on one guitar automatically causes the identical string on the other to vibrate. This example of harmonic vibration accurately reflects the interaction between two people who are in rapport. It's important to note that both guitars must be in tune for this audible phenomenon to take place. This process of tuning is precisely what rapport is all about.

3D communicators are experts at rapport because they view it as a mandatory preface to all prosperous interactions. As a result, they achieve rapport more deeply and quickly than others, making them masters of the first impression. They understand that perception is everything, and it's not what you say, but what others hear that ultimately makes the difference. Moreover, they know that others are more likely to be positively affected if the message is delivered in their language.

To achieve an elite level of connection with people, our aim must be to study our audience's language patterns and emotional signals. This greatly enhances the speed and depth of the rapport gained. There are a number of models that seek to break this process down. One of the simplest is to view communication and comprehension styles as falling into three broad categories:

- **Visual** comprehension and communication. Broadly speaking, visual people think in terms of pictures. Their ideas, memories and imaginations are represented as mental images.
- **Auditory.** Auditory people think in terms of sounds, voices, words or noises.
- **Feelings or kinaesthesia**. Kinaesthetic people experience thoughts more in terms of feelings and often relate them to physical touch or sensations. This includes the senses of taste and smell.

To gain maximum rapport and influence with people, it is highly advantageous to be mindful of their primary communication mode. Given the other person will not be wearing a lapel badge stating their dominant internal language, it is up to us to dial up our powers of perception and pay attention to the clues they provide. These clues are revealed most noticeably in the language they use to communicate with us.

One of the best examples illustrating how these distinctions present themselves is the home-theatre showroom at your local electronics department store. The *visual* person stands back and takes in the clarity of the picture (these people get sold on 'higher resolution' or 'pixel recovery rates'). The *auditory* person asks for the sound to be turned up and may even close their eyes to better take in the noise (these people get sold on speakers, equalisers and subwoofers).

> Dial up our powers of perception and pay attention to the clues.

The *feelings or kinaesthetic* person takes a seat in the lounge chair provided and imagines how this would feel in their loungeroom (these people often buy the purpose-designed theatre armchairs as well). This is a simplistic portrayal of people's different processing systems, but an effective salesperson will pick up on these cues and focus on what's most important to the customer.

Of course, you personally have your own dominant internal language and the people you find easiest to converse with are likely to be those who naturally have the same patterns. Conversely, it's difficult at times to find a rhythm with people who clearly have a different dominant communicative mode. Auditory people may find visual people a bit over the top, distracting or all 'froth and bubbles'. Visual people may find auditory people to be verbose, boring and not expressive enough. Kinaesthetic people can come across as overly melancholic or internalised for the visual person who likes everything large and out front.

These are generalisations and many people are a combination of different communication modes, but it serves to highlight how two people can fail to be in sync even though they may like each other and genuinely want to converse.

## *Person-to-person communication*

3D communicators are excellent observers and pay close attention to how the other person is expressing themselves. If they use phrases like 'that sounds good', 'I hear what you're saying' or 'a lot of that rings true', then you are conversing with a primarily auditory person. If they use large gestures and exaggerated facial expressions while telling you that 'the future is looking brighter', 'I can see it clearly now' or 'I get the picture' then they will be largely visual people. If, however, they appear more outwardly subdued and choose phrases such as 'it just doesn't feel right', 'that had an impact on me' or 'it all went smoothly', then feelings are the dominant communication and comprehension mode.

# DECODING LANGUAGE

Examples of everyday language clues would be:

**Visual**

We're in the red.

I look forward to seeing that.

He's a colourful character.

The outlook is bleak.

He's looking through rose-coloured glasses.

I take a dim view of that.

She has a bright-looking future.

I was in a dark mood.

Things are looking up.

### Auditory

You'll be happy to hear this.

Can you tell me how it's done?

I can't explain it.

It was music to my ears.

It was a harmonious decision.

Have you listened to what they're saying?

My knees were knocking.

I told myself not to listen to it.

Things clicked into place.

We're in tune with each other.

I was shocked to hear you say that.

### Feelings or kinaesthesia

I can't get a handle on it.

I've been racked with pain.

The whole thing stinks.

It has a touch of class.

You need to get in touch with reality.

We need to taste it first.

I've got a grasp on what you mean.

I sign an email with 'warm regards'.

I was moved by that.

It was a kick in the guts.

Hold on a minute!

It's important to note that you cannot automatically assume you are speaking with an auditory person simply because they told you that something 'sounds good'. However, once you establish the other person's dominant mode, you can subtly tailor your communication to be in rapport with theirs. This is sometimes referred to as 'matching and mirroring'.

Warning: Any attempts to mirror another person's communication patterns need to be very subtle. The last thing you want is for others to feel you are performing a 'technique' on them. Highly skilled communicators make these adjustments on an instinctive level and lock into a rhythm with others effortlessly.

## Catering to a group

It's not that easy trying to determine the dominant language pattern of an audience. In these instances, your best strategy is to utilise phrases that cover a broad range of sight, sounds and feeling themes. In doing so, you take a step closer towards gaining rapport and improving the comprehension of the whole room. Ironically, you are likely to learn more about your audience conversing with them during the coffee breaks than throughout your presentation.

Visual people may comment on how much they enjoyed your keynote presentation. Auditory people may instigate conversation with other delegates first before trying to engage you in discussion. Kinaesthetic people may make an extra effort to shake your hand as well as others in the group. While these are generalisations, they represent the type of cues that the elite communicator aims to detect. In any case, paying attention is the key.

## Using questions to gain rapport

Even the individual with an average level of social skills knows that asking questions gives the person you are speaking to a genuine impression you are interested in their opinion. The sophisticated communicator takes things a step further in a couple of significant yet subtle ways.

> Superficial conversation does not foster rapport.

While the first *gateway* question may start the conversation, the subsequent *expansion* questions establish a genuine rapport. The gateway (primary) question opens the door, and the expansion (secondary) questions are those that prompt people to elaborate on their news or views, which allows you to step into topics at a deeper level. Superficial conversation does not foster rapport.

Good examples of expansion questions could be:

SC (Skilled communicator): "So, what do you do for a living, John?" (Gateway question)

John: "I'm a panel beater."

SC: "Do you work locally?" (Secondary question)

John: "Yeah, the factory's only about five kilometres away in the large industrial estate near the freeway exit."

SC: "OK, I know where you mean. Is it your own business?"

John: "No, but I've been there for over ten years. Maybe one day!"

(Here the SC could use their empathetic skills and ask an even more industry-specific question to completely fortify the rapport.)

SC: "With all the rain lately, you must be getting plenty of work?"

John: "You're not wrong! We've been flat out for the last couple of months, and we're well booked into the New Year."

SC: "Between the weather and all the extra cars on the road these days, it sounds like you'll never be short of work!"

John: "At least until the self-driving cars take over…"

SC: "Yeah, after that, all the accidents will be caused by computer glitches and exploding batteries."

Note: Try to end each 'topic exchange' with either something positive or some form of humour. It doesn't matter if the humour comes from you or your subject as long as there is a shared amusement or positive agreement to cap the topic off. With any of the above expansion questions, for example, John may offer additional related stories that are meaningful to him. As a result, and most likely at an unconscious level, it will register with John that you are easy to talk to and seem in tune with his interests. Furthermore, he appreciates the space you gave him to talk more about himself and what he does.

The socially 'wooden' individual on the other hand has very little capacity to progress any further than primary or gateway questions. In fact, they sometimes float from one gateway question to the next in a vain attempt to keep the conversation alive. These people don't fare well on first dates or job interviews. Instead of Superman, we end up with Superficial Man!

## And… ?

'And' is an often-maligned word. You're not supposed to use it too often and the traditional rules of grammar once forbade you from starting a sentence with it. It can, however, be an effective tool for edifying someone's point of view by building on what they say. Correctly used, the word 'and' communicates that, as a listener, you are *with* the person and they can be at ease. For example, Peter says, "I feel like they accepted me personally as a trusted ally." Peter's colleague then asks, "And do you sense that they fully comprehended your proposals?" This is a much more fluid way to ask the question than to say, "Yes, but do you think they understood what you were talking about?"

The moral of the story is to try and use the word 'and' in place of the word 'but' wherever possible because it implies more rapport and presents as less argumentative. As you've also probably noticed, using the word 'and' can be an effective lead into expansion questions.

## *Pause*

The 3D communicator also understands the value of silence in the rapport-building process. Pausing, or generally allowing space within a verbal exchange, allows the other person time to relax and not rush their next comment. This reduces what can sometimes be a low level of conversational anxiety caused by constantly being cut off or spoken over. By deliberately allowing for pauses, the intelligent communicator also gives the other person the opportunity to fine-tune the information or message they are expressing.

# State

While our astute observations of how a person represents themselves enable us to adapt our communication towards theirs, we should – as a default setting – communicate with as much of our body as possible and as much of our vocabulary as possible. This doesn't mean that we always need to use complicated terminology or bounce unnaturally around the room like we drank too much coffee. What we are aiming for is to generate a peak physical and mental state within ourselves that exerts a similar influence over those around us in much the same way that the two guitars affected each other in the previous example of rapport. This impact can apply in a social, business, selling, leadership or coaching setting.

## INSPIRING THROUGH PHYSIOLOGY – WHAT IS SEEN

If you were asked to act like someone who felt at the peak of their physical powers, what things would you focus on to play that part well? How would you sit, stand, walk, gesture and breathe? How would you use your eyes and whole face? What else would you do?

How much more impact could your message have if it was delivered with such a confident disposition?

## INSPIRING THROUGH LANGUAGE – WHAT IS HEARD

If you were required to write a short story using the most colourful and expressive language within your personal vocabulary, how would this differ from your normal speech?

Aside from your choice of words, if you had to make an audio recording of your writings, what enhancements could you apply to your tonality, volume, enunciation and general cadence that would do justice to the enriched language you authored?

## Simpson vs Spock

One of the easiest models I have used to best explain how to stimulate the attention of others is to imagine that there is a hedonistic child and a pragmatic adult inside every person. For the sake of this exercise, imagine *Bart Simpson* as the serial fun seeker and *Mr Spock* of *Star Trek* fame as the ultimate logician.

*Bart* represents the part of us that closely identifies with new toys, fun, recognition, attention and excitement. He also likes to experience pleasure, feel safe and have routines. *Bart* represents our energy centre and craves stimulation. This part of us lives by the motto, 'If it feels good, do it!'

*Spock*, on the other hand, signifies the logical, rational, more mature (or adult) side whose primary function is conscious learning, discriminating and calculating. *Spock* generally tries to guide the *Bart* within us in a similar way that a parent does to a child. The *Spock* in each of us has the motto of 'Look before you leap', which provides a constant reminder not to test the depth of the water with both feet!

So, what does this have to do with 3D communication? If subdued physiology and only neutral language and tonality are used in conversation, then there is very little appeal to the excitable senses of the other person. In these instances, *Bart* can quickly become bored and leave the conversation. Restrained emotion and anodyne speech are only likely to keep the intellectual, critical, unimaginative side of the brain engaged (the adult) rather than stimulating the imagination and energy centre (the child). Given that *Bart* holds the key to unlocking internal motivation and drives, it is vital to amp up the language, tone and physical delivery of the message if the desired outcome is to generate change or exert influence with others.

By acknowledging that the *Bart* in each of us is both excitable and impressionable when spoken to the right way, we can communicate with others in such a way that appeals to the drives of their inner child, causing a surge of energy within them that elevates their emotional state. At the very least, it makes them feel more empowered and increases the likelihood we will see the best side of them when they are around us. Either way, you are sharpening your communicative tools to become an expert mood-maker and master of persuasion.

# Metaphors, similes and phrases (the story)

*A metaphor* is a figure of speech that makes a direct comparison between two objects or scenarios by using a descriptive word that is not accurate literally to imply a resemblance – for example, *that man is a machine!* A simile performs an identical function but includes the words *like* or *as* – for example, *he's as strong as an ox!* Phrases are common combinations of words used to augment meaning.

These powerful communication tools speak the language of the subconscious and create vivid images beneath the surface layers of the mind through symbols and images. The term 'force field' is a perfect illustration of this.

We are well accustomed to the more common examples:

- A bed of roses.
- Stuck between a rock and a hard place.
- Time is a thief.
- The apple of my eye.
- The light of my life.

Then there are some extended versions:

- She was a couch potato in the gravy boat of life.
- Her purse was a soft-sided rubbish bin.
- He was a stainless steel ruler: tall, straight and always measured in response.
- One day you're the peacock, and the next day you're the feather duster.

Metaphors, similes and phrases present a more colourful, and sometimes partly humorous, impression of a situation by hiding the message in a short story. These stories carry more weight and attract greater attention from the listener than a simple assembly of the facts. We can say more and connect more with these tools than we can ever achieve with a literal description because we are bypassing a listener's conscious resistance and channelling straight to their childlike subconscious (their Bart Simpson). When you are dealing with someone who will not rationally consider your viewpoint, try wrapping your message in a story. Any use of language that encourages a deeper connection or association is more memorable.

> We can say more with these tools than with a literal description.

## MALAPHORS

Like jokes, however, metaphors or similes can fall flat if they're not constructed properly. My wife, bless her heart, often finds herself blending common metaphors, similes and phrases to the detriment of her argument. These constructions are known as 'malaphors'. With her permission (sort of), I have listed some of them here for your enjoyment:

- The place was locked up like Fort Douglas.
- It's a double-headed sword.
- Last night I slept like a Trojan.
- He wouldn't say boo to a mouse.
- He gets under people's goat.
- Don't pin all your high hopes on it.
- He's really gone off the skids.
- I had an email the other day from yours truly!
- It's better than a poke with a stick in the dark.
- I've got her over a loophole.
- She wanted to put things on an even slather.
- It was the white elephant in the room.
- You can't dangle the bone over me any longer.
- I'm boiling under the collar.
- It was like pulling hen's teeth.
- He tried to pull the wool out of my eyes.
- I was flat strap.
- It's time to tighten the belt strings.
- I made sure we had equal Stevens.
- Surprising things come in small packages.
- He was as keen as a cucumber.
- Their arms were all in the air about it.
- He was going full ball.

I solemnly swear that these are all genuine home-grown inventions created in the moment by a flustered mother of three daughters. If someone else has already uttered one of these then it is by pure coincidence. Ironically, the metaphors, similes and phrases they are meant to represent are such a part of our language that you can read all of these and pretty much spot the blend.

We use metaphors, similes and phrases every day in common ways. The superior communicator always searches for a more inventive and imaginative way of using them in different situations to colour their message.

# WEAPON #8

# SOCIAL INTELLIGENCE

THE SOCIALLY INTELLIGENT INDIVIDUAL has the ability to optimise their connection to other people and possesses an acute awareness of the underlying forces that exert influence in social scenarios. Often referred to rather one-dimensionally as 'people skills', social intelligence, at its simplest, is the knack of getting along well with others despite differences in method, opinion or interests.

For reasons which often go unexamined in both personal and professional environments, some people unconsciously exhibit noxious behaviours that inadvertently leave those around them feeling undermined, embarrassed, frustrated, irritated, intimidated or generally flat. Many of these individuals exhibit the people skills of skin lice and literally brighten up the room when they leave!

The socially *un*intelligent often assert that it's either other people or personality clashes that are to blame for the discomfort in many of their social exchanges. Accompanying this (and perhaps causing it) is an inability to ever ask themselves the question "Is it me?" As such, the friction they regularly experience in social settings is no accident. It's like the man who unknowingly had a piece of stinky cheese caught in his moustache and proceeded to complain about the stench in the room everywhere he went.

Aside from these abrasive characters, we also have the 'attention hog'. This person insists on dominating conversations and overestimates other people's interest in their opinions. They may also be overly preoccupied with impressing their audience, with often the opposite response being evoked. These people have the power of speech but have lost the art of conversation.

Then there are those who fall into the 'social desert' category. These 'low temperature' people are the benign lump in the group who create discomfort through either passive non-contribution or via an awkward disconnection with other people's views. As a result, they have the unfortunate tendency to make you feel like you weigh more when you're around them. Unlike the abrasive serial irritant or the attention hog previously mentioned, the social desert can often be an extremely nice and easy-going person and we tend to feel guilty that we can't handle being around them for very long.

It's important to note that the above individuals may still possess high IQs, proving that intellectual capacity is not necessarily correlated with social skills. This should not be news to anyone who sat (or slept) through science classes in high school that were taught by brilliant but boring teachers. Unlike IQ, which is primarily a born attribute, social intelligence can be studied and developed through diligence and astute observation. Social intelligence also requires a certain amount of self-awareness and a conscious recognition of our own perceptions, sensitivities and response habits.

Self-awareness makes us mindful of how we are being seen by others and prompts us to regularly ask ourselves how we can put our best energy into the world. It also forces us to reflect on our own conduct, ensuring we do not engage in behaviour that may undermine our integrity or be destructive to our credibility as a leader or mentor.

This self-imposed behavioural standard is not an exercise reserved solely for organised social interactions. Whether we like it or not, there is no such thing as 'off the record' for anyone who operates in a professional leadership or coaching capacity. Anything that a leader says or does during work hours, at the office Christmas party, the Friday night drinks session or any other impromptu setting where workmates are present will be noted and locked in the memory banks of observers. Of course, nobody's perfect and we all say and do things at times that the best version of ourselves would not be proud of. However, it can take years to build a reputation and minutes to destroy it.

> It can take years to build a reputation and minutes to destroy it.

While reputations can be reconstructed over time in most cases, the self-aware individual invariably manages to curtail the severity of any such falls from grace. They do this by being more attuned to the reaction of others and by monitoring their own performance along the way as if they were one of the observers. These individuals rarely suffer a full-blown reputation meltdown as a result of a social or communicative gaffe.

Ultimately, an individual with sound social intelligence behaves and communicates in a way that makes people feel uplifted, listened to, understood and appreciated. There are some common weapons that socially intelligent individuals possess and use regularly to great effect.

# Humour

*"Some people see the glass half-full. Others see it half-empty. I see a glass that's twice as big as it needs to be."*

—George Carlin

Having a sense of humour is not the same as being funny. The former is essentially the ability to laugh or be amused while the latter is the ability to evoke laughter. Developing a better sense of humour is about opening your mind to the potential for laughter or amusement in even seemingly mundane situations.

Laughter is like magic. It creates a unique explosion of neurochemicals that make everyone in its presence feel good. It is often said that laughter is the best medicine, and in many ways it could be viewed as an integral part of our mind's immune system. Those who aspire to be socially intelligent would do well to study stand-up comedians and pay particular attention to how they construct their stories and deliver their punchlines. It is no accident that they generate laughter, but the uninitiated mistakenly assume that they accomplish this by saying funny things. It's more accurate to say they have found a funny way to say ordinary things. Stand-up comedy is an art form.

There are many communicative benefits to developing humour as a skill – and yes, it is a skill! A tense mood can be lightened, an angry stance can be tempered, and it can be the perfect icebreaker when endeavouring to make a memorable first impression. It can even help you tolerate the sometimes-annoying behaviour of others. For example: "They say light travels faster than sound – that's why some people seem bright until they speak!"

Aside from the obvious psychological benefits, laughter also manifests positive outcomes for our physical health. On a fundamental level, laughter exercises our diaphragm, which allows us to intake a greater volume of oxygenated air and stimulate our lung function. This generates positive vascular health by increasing our heart rate and lowering our blood pressure. It's also an incredibly effective ab workout.

In many ways, our personal *force field* is likened to the body's suspension system, and in this case, the sense of humour represents one of the most crucial springs within that suspension unit that absorbs and redirects the shocks. Individuals without a sense of humour are therefore likely to be jolted harshly by every pebble on the road.

To some extent, humour is like wine – it's not about which form of humour (or which vintage) is best, but more so a case of personal taste. A wine snob can recommend his favourite bottle of shiraz and give you a highly credentialed history of the wine maker, but it's still possible that you'll dislike the taste. In the end, the best wine for you is the one you most like the taste of – and preferably one that doesn't give you a headache the next day!

For someone of my age, there is no greater anthem for promoting humour as a general panacea for the harsh realities of our finite existence than a famous Monty Python song from the movie *Life of Brian*. If we ever needed a soundtrack to accompany the study of how humour could be used to uplift and inspire positive states, then 'Always Look on the Bright Side of Life' would be it. *Life of Brian* is a biblical parody, and this song was performed at the very end by a group of men who had just been hung on crosses and were about to die. I'm unable to reproduce the lyrics here, but I challenge you not to feel a sense of merriment when hearing or singing this number.

One of the oldest phrases to describe something that lacks any jokey quality is to say that it was 'about as funny as a funeral'. This is based on the fact that funerals were notoriously solemn, and it was deemed inappropriate or disrespectful for anything other than sadness to be present.

The more contemporary view of funerals and occasions such as these is to view them as a celebration of life. When this occurs, it often includes tales of the deceased's life that give cause for laughter or at least fond reverie. In fact, the sombre atmosphere of a funeral can often be lightened by a well-placed amusing story about the deceased. This becomes an exercise in remembering the good times and can be a tool for providing temporary emotional relief for the broken-hearted (As a note, 'Always Look on the Bright Side of Life' is among the top ten most popular songs played at funerals).

There is much debate these days about what you should or shouldn't laugh at. When looked at objectively, however, there are very few instances where humour cannot or should not be utilised. The reality is that you have very little control over the things you laugh at. There may be times you find yourself laughing hysterically at something you shouldn't, but by the time you rationalise how unsuitable your laughter was, it has already happened. At the end of the day, it's OK to laugh as long as there is no malice or intent to hurt anybody. It's certainly preferable for our physical and psychological wellbeing to laugh at the so-called wrong thing than to not laugh at all.

> Perhaps, most importantly, we need to learn to laugh at ourselves.

Perhaps, most importantly, we need to learn to laugh at ourselves. Individuals who are self-deprecating generally emanate a charisma and carry an attractiveness that is hard to deny. It's certainly the antithesis of the egomaniac who is almost unanimously disliked. Biology dictates that if we lose one sense, then our other senses are enhanced. That's why some people with no sense of humour often have an increased sense of self-importance.

Broadly speaking, a sense of humour really is the Swiss Army knife of life skills. When effectively employed, it can relieve tension, defuse anger, initiate an instant state change, accelerate rapport, diminish anxiety or depressive feelings, soften heartache and brighten up any meeting or social engagement. It can also reduce your chances of being offended, improve your productivity and provide the perfect 'bubble wrap' for delivering otherwise unwelcome news. It serves as an enduring social lubricant, a built-in coping mechanism and the ultimate performance-enhancing self-help drug.

If asked, most people would say that they had a good sense of humour. The challenge for us all is in possessing enough awareness to realise if this is actually true. In terms of social intelligence, I've never known a person who was funny or who laughed a lot to be unpopular. In fact, the most socially popular people I know have all been funny and/or had a great sense of humour, and I'm talking about a 100 per cent correlation here. While there are some people who aren't funny and don't laugh with people much who have nonetheless still managed to be popular, *all* people with a healthy social sense of humour are popular.

Learning how to laugh regularly with others is the first step. Causing them to laugh is a more difficult but rewarding step. If you make people laugh, then they will feel chemically enhanced when they're around you. Laughing with them is a close second and requires more intention than it does skill.

None of this is meant to imply that serious issues should be laughed off, but more so that we should see laughter as an amazing evolutionary blessing that we can indulge in regularly with no downside to excess. The joke "How do you make God laugh? Tell him your plans!" reminds us that in the grand scheme of things, the negative issues that consume us are relatively insignificant on a cosmic scale. Laughter is a bold and cathartic act and one of our best defences against the outcome that ultimately awaits us all. If there's an opportunity to find cause for a laugh in the midst of something sad, then take it! In a quote often attributed to Francis Bacon, "Imagination was given to man to compensate him for what he is not, and a sense of humour to console him for what he is."

# Empathy

Empathy is the ability to understand and share the feelings of others. The chief tools for achieving this – listening and asking questions – have been previously well-covered, but it would be wrong to view empathy and rapport as one and the same. Beyond the active listening and genuine desire to know more about the other person, empathy involves exercising a form of emotional displacement where, for a time at least, you allow yourself to metaphorically be in the other person's shoes.

This allows us to better understand the motivations behind other people's views that we may otherwise be blind to if only seen through the filters of our own self-centred vision. The practice of 'othermindedness' can allow us to better deal with and tolerate people who don't share the same beliefs as we do. It can also resolve differences and aid in the coaching of people experiencing heartache or difficulty.

Socially intelligent individuals have learned to listen with a respect and naivety that allows them to truly learn about others. They're also prepared to give up the satisfaction of being right. Internally they have the strength, humility and graciousness needed to absorb inconsistencies within themselves and others.

# Comprehension – shut up and listen!

The positive effect that listening has on interpersonal communication is often overshadowed by the more overt act of speaking. Giving someone your complete attention and allowing them time and space to express themselves helps bridge the gap between hearing and listening. This is no small distinction. In many cases, a conversation consists of two people, both of whom are 90 per cent focused on what they each have to say. The pauses between their sentences are often only an effort to appear like they are giving the other a chance to speak. In reality, they are simply waiting for as little time as possible before it may be reasonable for them to start talking again. As the saying goes, "The single biggest problem with communication is the illusion that it has taken place."

It has also been said that the ears are the primary objects of attraction. This is because people in general are starved of the experience of being heard. True listening is different to just hearing another person's voice. It's not dependant on how long you hear them speaking, but more about the level of attention you place on everything they say. It is far more important to be interested than interesting. People care about you less than they care about how much you care about them! When you are fully present, you pay more attention to another's words, their tonality, their volume, eye contact, body movements and level of agitation. In these instances, you truly hear and comprehend *beyond* what is being said.

At times, hyper-alertness may be more attention than a situation calls for, but you will be astonished at how grateful people will be to have received your undivided focus on what they had to say. Contrary to what many people in positions of influence believe, it is the practice of conscious listening that makes them a magnet to others, more so than the sound of their own sage wisdom being imparted. Challenge yourself to pay closer attention next time someone speaks to you. Use this moment as a spiritual exercise of your own and focus on a level above the superficial norm by tuning in to the true essence of the situation.

This skill can greatly enhance one's ability to lead, counsel, parent, sell, coach and manage conflict. It is therefore indispensable for anyone aspiring to a position of leadership or influence.

# Tact and diplomacy

Tact could be best described as a demonstration of concern for others' wishes and feelings and is a critical mechanism for navigating the sometimes fickle landscape of human relationships. Tact is an intelligent virtue that carefully and proportionally exercises discretion, subtlety and sensitivity to a situation. Tact or diplomacy often calls for inaction, which is sometimes a case of thinking twice before saying nothing.

Closely related to tact is the seemingly old-fashioned practice of good manners, which could be described as treating others with consideration. Manners are often dismissed as merely surface niceties or formalities of incidental importance. But manners make up the minor transactions of civilised society and are often only acknowledged in their absence.

> Tact or diplomacy is sometimes a case of thinking twice before saying nothing.

Philosopher Eric Hoffer said, "Rudeness is the weak man's imitation of strength." Those with a low level of social intelligence have little or no ability to discern between frankness (which can be helpful) and rudeness (which is always destructive), hence the aptly named metaphor of 'sledgehammer diplomacy'. Playwright Tennessee Williams once wrote, "All cruel people describe themselves as paragons of frankness." Anyone can be frank, even the thoughtless and unsophisticated, but it can be an expensive outcome if dispensed carelessly.

Another critical feature in relation to diplomacy is to be mindful of an unwritten rule that says we need to give roughly five compliments for every one criticism. I'm sure that married couples can relate to this concept. It would be wrong to surmise that this ratio only applies to those who are overly sensitive. Some people need more than five compliments to feel appreciated and valued enough to absorb just one critical comment, while others require less. In any case, being aware of this relatively common aspect of human nature enables the socially intelligent individual to package their message in such a way as to not leave the other person feeling diminished.

# PART III

## THE

# WARNINGS

### WE HEED

⚠

*"The battlefield is a scene of constant chaos.*
*The winner will be the one who controls that*
*chaos, both his own and the enemies."*

—Napoleon Bonaparte

WHILE IT WOULD BE nice to focus solely on the positives that can propel us towards our desired destination, it would be naïve to disregard the more common objects of destruction that can threaten our momentum and obstruct our overall happiness. It is a fact of life that poor attitudes, negative people or self-defeating behaviours are never far from our immediate experience, which makes identifying their arrival and dismantling their influence an essential part of any success strategy.

The following notes aim to highlight some of the more common enemies of progress. These not only focus on outside forces that can wreak havoc in our personal or professional lives but also include internal affairs, where thought or emotional weaknesses can hinder us just as severely.

# WARNING #1

# DIFFICULT PEOPLE

BEING THE SOCIAL CREATURES that we are, the interactions we experience have an enormous bearing on our happiness quotient. When people say they work for a great company, they're usually referring to the people they work *with* and *for*, rather than making a statement about the value of that company's products or services. If a football player states that he plays for a 'great team', it reflects more on the camaraderie and spirit within the squad than on the sum total of individual talent or their position on the league ladder.

The quality of our interpersonal relationships dictates the degree to which we enjoy our day-to-day lives. The unexpected breakdown of an inanimate object like a car can surely trigger a bad mood, but its emotional impact seldom rivals that of a heated confrontation with another person – even if that person is a stranger.

Difficult people can impose themselves into our lives in many different ways. It could be as a work colleague, boss, employee, friend, teammate, spouse, child, parent, sibling, shop assistant or customer. Unfortunately, we have very little control over the attitude and behaviour of other people. Even our own children, whom we have tried hard to raise in our own likeness, often reveal personality traits or opinions as they get older that we find hard to tolerate.

Nowadays, we are exposed to difficult people in many more ways than we have been used to. Social media, in all its forms, has brought the bigot, racist, serial hater, loudmouth, ignorant, cowardly and the clueless directly into our homes. The ill-mannered and aggressive comments that are frequently spewed out online are often nothing more than a reflection of the perpetrator's low self-esteem, jealousy or blinkered ignorance. Even where they have sound knowledge of an issue, they are still naïve if they think that abandoning the basic human communication protocols in the discussion is going to achieve anything constructive. Many of these people are incapable of portraying strength in person, so they try to portray toughness online where nobody can test them. This is not to say that social media is all bad, but the degree to which the majority of hostile online comments survive unchecked is shocking to me.

> Dealing with difficult people is more about navigation than transformation.

Dealing with difficult people is more about navigation than it is about transformation. You don't need to change them; you just need to get around them! When you focus more on how to circumvent these people rather than trying to fix them, you can move beyond their toxicity and succeed regardless.

There are many categories of difficult people and various strategies for dealing with them.

# Short-tempered

These are the people for whom the phrase 'walking on eggshells' was invented. They unwittingly succeed in keeping everyone around them on tenterhooks and make it difficult to discuss any sort of opposing views. In a sense, it feels as if you have to wrap everything in cottonwool before presenting an opinion so that it doesn't trigger a tantrum. For their part, they usually like to characterise their temper as something they can't help, such as, 'It runs in the family'. These people are impatient, emotionally erratic, intolerant and unapproachable. They make terrible leaders and challenging employees. In general, they probably learned at a young age that if they yelled, stomped their feet and made a big fuss that they would get what they wanted.

*Navigational advice:* Finding the right tone and picking the right time is paramount with these people. Be particularly cognisant of maintaining a relaxed and calming tone yourself, even if they begin to escalate. Also aim to have any contentious conversations in the morning vs the end of the day, and do it face to face wherever possible in order to engage all forms of the communication equation (physiology, voice quality and words chosen).

# Impulsive

Impulsive people tend to cause frustration rather than discomfort. Their serial lack of forethought often sees the faces of those around them being regularly plunged into their own palms. 'Think before you speak' is not a phrase that impulsive people subscribe to, nor do they engage in a 'pros vs cons' exercise very often. Typically, they'll barrel into most tasks in a half-cocked manner and a clean-up team is invariably commissioned afterwards to deal with the wreckage.

Ironically, many impulsive people characterise themselves as 'decision-makers' and dress up their lack of patience as a virtue.

*Navigational advice:* It is sometimes valuable to allow these people to marinate in their mistakes, so they can experience firsthand the negative consequences of their rash decisions or actions. If you care about these people enough, take time wherever possible to link the negative outcomes to the impetuous starting point. Ill-conceived schemes waste money, compromise good health and cost friendships. These types of people place a high value on being decisive. As such, your end goal should be to convey in the clearest terms possible that good decision-makers are not measured by the number of decisions they make or the speed with which they make them, but rather by the outcome each decision yields.

> Ironically, many impulsive people characterise themselves as 'decision-makers'.

# Narcissistic

The narcissist has, in a sense, become the modern-day version of what we used to call 'egotists'. While people often use these terms interchangeably, they are not exactly the same.

The egotist is someone with an inflated sense of self-importance who lacks genuine humility and has a tendency to talk about themselves constantly. They rarely acknowledge their mistakes, don't handle critique well and being the first thing on everyone's mind is their highest priority.

The narcissist is every bit an egotist – but more! Narcissists also have a strong sense of entitlement and a deep need for excessive admiration and attention. They often expect to be acknowledged as superior with or without merit and have a strong tendency to exaggerate their abilities and accomplishments. In addition, they will take advantage of others to achieve what they want, attempt to dominate conversations and often behave in an arrogant and conceited manner. It's certainly not an easy task being around someone who constantly showers themselves with affection and expects everyone around them to follow suit. These types of people are difficult irrespective of where you encounter them.

As it turns out, the majority of people clinically diagnosed as narcissists are men! One doesn't have to look too hard on social media, for instance, to discover that there is a growing community of women who are publicly sharing their tips on how to break up with a narcissist. Aside from this, the workplace or similar type of team environment is where we are most likely to experience ongoing exposure to these types of characters.

If you've ever had to terminate someone like this from their job, then I can pretty accurately forecast their internal response:

- Egotist: If they are kicked off a team or fired – the company will collapse without them it
- Narcissist: If they are kicked off a team or fired – it's because they had outgrown their leaders and the company secretly knew this.

*Navigational advice:* While everybody needs a job, my short advice is to try and detect these traits in others early on, and if you're in any position to remove them from your team then you should. They are not team players, do not take direction well and are very high maintenance. If you're not in control of this person's presence in the group, then play nice but keep your distance. In other words, your outward demeanour should portray neutrality towards them: not unfriendly, but not necessarily a fan. If they don't

> Keep your expectations low and your guard high!

feel a sense of adoration from you then chances are they will gravitate towards others who more outwardly satisfy their craving for attention. Be aware though – if you are too obvious in giving them the cold shoulder, they may begin their own unique brand of politicking, concluding you don't like them and therefore mustn't like anyone else in the team (if you hate them, then you must have something wrong with you).

In any case, keep your expectations low and your guard high!

# Melodramatic

Also known as 'drama queens', these people excel at making mountains out of molehills. Their over-the-top histrionics create hard work for those around them as they blow issues out of proportion by fuelling drama where it's not warranted. The sense of theatre that often accompanies their overblown stories only serves to make problem-solving more difficult, as they do their best to make an otherwise simple issue appear multifaceted or complex.

*Navigational advice:* Stick to the facts – not what the facts 'mean' to someone else. Don't be surprised if melodramatic people shed hints of conspiracy, deception or jealousy in their blow-by-blow accounts of events. Nothing is straightforward to them. We need to ignore the spectacle and become skilled at subtly trimming away the emotional fluff in their stories.

# Negative

These 'glass half-empties' have pessimism as their default setting, habitually rummaging through situations to root out the worst-case scenarios. Fault finding is usually a central theme of their narrative, and they often misrepresent themselves as realists. They'll regularly state that they're just 'telling it like it is' or 'just being honest', which is mostly a vain attempt to make their viewpoint seem more rational or sensible.

Within this group, there are two fairly distinct categories. The aggressive negators (ranters) typically express their negativity through anger and sometimes even rage. These people are externally energised, and their rhetoric is highly critical and often aggressive. The 'gloomy negators' (low-energy people) inadvertently drain the vitality out of others. They are like kryptonite, capable of extracting the most downbeat perspectives and depleting the overall mood of the group. It's not uncommon for these types of people to exhibit more depressive symptoms.

As we all know, things occasionally turn sour in a situation through no fault of anyone, even in the most upbeat environments. Negative people usually see these outcomes as verification of their grim assessments. For the most part, people tend to get what they focus on, attract what they fear and achieve outcomes in accordance with their expectations. This is commonly referred to as a 'self-fulfilling prophecy'.

As the saying goes, "Even a broken clock is right twice a day." Doomsday economists who forecast the coming of the 'next depression' every New Year will probably be right eventually, but to live every year in fear of financial collapse blinds us from genuinely positive opportunities that may materialise along the way.

Within teams or work groups, negative characters can be like a drop of poison in the water supply. In many cases, pessimism is so hardwired into their thought patterns they are unaware of how miserable they sound.

> Negative characters can be like a drop of poison in the water supply.

*Navigational advice:* Don't allow yourself to be dragged into the cynical and distrustful world of the negator. Position yourself as the solution finder in the relationship, and let their fatalistic outlook serve as a helpful reference point from which to always take a contrary view. As is the case in dealing with melodramatic people, pay attention to the facts rather than the pessimist's interpretation of them, and let these simple disciplines create a barrier that shields you from the defeatist's contagion.

# Exploitative

People who are exploitative are so focused on their own interests that they routinely manipulate situations and take advantage of others to fulfil their own aims. It is not uncommon to label this behaviour as being 'Machiavellian' – a personality trait widely acknowledged by psychologists. It is considered to be one-third of the 'dark triad' – the other two being psychopathy and narcissism.

Aside from being very poor team players, their callous disregard for other people's feelings makes them difficult to reason with or coach. While these traits don't necessarily prevent some of them from achieving success in specific fields (politics comes to mind), they are nonetheless a category of difficult people who exploit your weaknesses for their own self-gain and do so with a free conscience.

Because they often possess a strong disposition and aggressively seek superior vantage points over their peers, Machiavellian personalities occupy many management positions throughout the workforce – particularly where their ascension has been driven by success in sales. Unfortunately, it is also very common for top salespeople to fail at management. The empathic shortcomings that help Machiavellians remain sufficiently detached from their prospects during the sales or closing process become a problem when dealing with staff who are expecting their leader to exercise generous helpings of empathy and always act in their best interests.

*Navigational advice:* As a starting point, it would be wise to conceal your vulnerabilities from the exploitative characters in your work or friendship circles. Keep your correspondence on a 'surface' level and maintain an emotional distance. In extreme cases, you may choose to cut them off completely with either no contact or by limiting the amount of information you give them about yourself. At the end of the day, they can't exploit what they don't know about you, so give them nothing personal!

# Two-faced

It's quite likely that people who gossip with you will also gossip about you to others. Not only do two-faced people say one thing to your face and something entirely different behind your back, but in the worst instances they will even bait you into commenting on someone else's business only to then pass on these sentiments to the person in question. Two-faced people tend to be more insecure than they are mean-spirited and aim to gain favour with those around them by purporting a special friendship built on gossip, faux secrets and indiscrete revelations.

⚠

There are a couple of major themes that the two-faced tattler peddles to others that make them difficult to tolerate: personal details you may have trustingly shared with them about you; or things you may have said to them about someone else, presumably as part of a confidential conversation. Of these two scenarios, the latter is potentially more damaging, particularly if it relates to a working environment or a valuable circle of friends.

*Navigational advice*: It takes two people for a two-faced person to thrive. If someone's conversations with you are regularly comprised of details about other people – the content of which either smacks of gossip or inappropriate disclosures – then don't play the game. At the very least, be mindful that your words will definitely travel outside the conversation. As such, don't make any comments about others that you wouldn't be prepared to say to their face, which is not a bad rule to follow irrespective of your immediate company.

The average two-faced individual lacks confidence and is often trying to manipulate their relationships to make others fonder of them. Their thinking here is if they tell you something that would otherwise be confidential, then they're signalling to you that they think the two of you are close, thereby hoping you will requite this in some way.

If this is a work colleague in an ongoing business environment then you've no choice but to call them out, either directly or through your company's protocols. Where no ongoing relationship is mandated, then jettison them from your social interactions wherever possible.

⚠

# Sulkers

Each of us has been witness to sulking in either our family, work or social circles. The moody silence, the pouty face, the single-word answers or the mopey demeanour are all characteristics of the individual who instinctively reacts to not getting their own way by being sullen and grumpy.

We've probably even heard people boasting that they gave someone the silent treatment, and this certainly sounds more mature than admitting they 'cracked the sulks', which is essentially the same reaction.

In many ways, the sulker has a greater intention that goes well beyond the basic act of not talking to someone. Their secret aim is to exact some sort of revenge on the 'target' of the sulk by attempting to make them feel uneasy. Their ulterior motive is to compel the other person to make the first move in repairing the situation, which then allows the sulker to perform their signature move – to initially reject the truce. Then, after what is deemed to be sufficient time with respect to the magnitude of the perceived disagreement, the sulker finally accepts the apology and everything goes back to normal.

> Sulking is an immature psychological game.

Basically, sulking is an immature psychological game that the sulker plays to express their feelings of injustice or to signal a lack of fairness. It serves as a non-confrontational way for the sulker to get what they want without feeling like they are going head-to-head with the other person. At the core of the problem is the sulker's inability to properly express their feelings. They choose withdrawal for their default setting over talking things through.

⚠

*Navigational advice*: The telephone, including texting, is the sulker's best friend, so keep away from using it! In the absence of visual cues, the sulker is more able to leave the person on the other end guessing what all the silence means. Their goal is to make you do all the talking because this gives them a sense of control over the conversation.

If you get caught up in this trap, you will often find yourself subtly adopting the role of the apologist when it may not be warranted. With this in mind, the objective is to find ways of skilfully breaking the silence. For instance:

- "Are you OK to talk to me about this now?"
- "It's unlikely that we can reach a resolution unless we discuss the matter properly."
- "I can't address your concerns unless you can articulate how and why you're feeling this way."
- "It doesn't sound like you're ready to discuss the issue right now, but we need to move on from this as soon as possible. How about we chat again later today once you've had some more time to consider your thoughts?"
- "Perhaps this is something we'd be better off discussing in person. How about we catch up tomorrow for a coffee?"

What you'd really like to say in response to this silence is:

- "I'm afraid my powers of telepathy are a little sluggish today so you're going to need to talk to me."
- "If I wanted to talk to myself, I can do that without you!"
- "Normally when I meditate, I do it alone…"
- "You'll have to cut the petulant teenager routine if you'd like us to achieve a mature outcome…"

Clearly the last few options would be highly inflammatory, but it feels good to think them sometimes.

Wherever possible, deal with the sulker face to face – even if it's via Zoom or similar. This is much more effective than text messaging or phone calls. Given that sulking is a more passive and less demonstrative form of protest, by exercising self-awareness we can also ensure that we are not unknowingly engaging in these behaviours ourselves.

# Bullies

'Sticks and stones may break my bones, but words can never harm me!' This statement really should be true but, unfortunately, it's not that simple. Bullying in all its forms has become a substantial problem in every level of society. Its negative impact in the schoolyard, among peer or sporting groups, within the workplace or indeed online has spawned countless initiatives in both the public and private sectors.

Many books have been written about this one broad topic, and many psychological reviews have highlighted that pervasive conditions like anxiety and depression are often the emotional offspring of chronic bullying. These studies also address the fact that most bullies have themselves been badly bullied or abused.

Cyberbullying is the 21st century incarnation of a much older problem and is understandably where many of today's teenagers, adults and businesses experience this sense of intimidation. Social media platforms have given birth to a galaxy of public abuse that was previously confined to a bully's physical radius. Anonymity gives cowards a rare batch of courage. It provides them with a genuine hiding place where they can conceal their identity and parade their opinions as hard facts. Unencumbered by the burden of proof, these people trample through others' lives armed with a bias, ignorance and sometimes a spitefulness that is virtually invincible.

⚠

While I'm an advocate for freedom of opinion and thought, I don't feel every thought should be expressed verbally, whether it be in person or online. Some thoughts are better kept to yourself. 'If I wanted your opinion, I would've asked for it' is a phrase we are all familiar with, as is, 'If you wouldn't say it to someone's face, then don't say it at all', or the classic, 'If you've got nothing good to say, then don't say anything!'

In the 'olden days', if you didn't like someone then you just didn't socialise with them. If you didn't like the food or the service at a restaurant – while you may tell a couple of friends about your experience – your primary response was not to go there again. If you didn't like something on TV or radio, you just changed the station. The broader online world has provided the so-called scorned with an avenue to exact vengeance on others and things they don't like. This emboldens the bully and provides them with temporary relief from their insecurity.

The belief that social media can be a safe space to express both your opinions and your individuality is a naïve one, because it's likely that anyone who succeeds in creating a popular online profile will be attacked, often (and ironically) by people who are advocates for free speech.

Expressing an opposing view, whether in person or online, is a perfectly acceptable act. It is the malice and aggressive characteristic of the cyber-mob that crosses the line into bullying. It's a weird concept being attacked by a group of strangers who have never met you and who don't have a balanced perspective on who you are beyond the view you're being attacked for.

> Freedom of speech is not a permission slip to be rude.

In essence, freedom of speech is not a permission slip to be rude, nor is it a licence to be a thug! The sociological fallout from this practice

– particularly among teenagers – is truly shocking, with a regular flow of suicides attributed directly to instances of unbearable and inescapable online bullying.

Businesses that promote themselves online are now at the mercy of a starred-review system. This is supposed to be a platform for customers to evaluate their experiences. It seems like a good idea – except there is rarely a platform that reviews the reviewer! The reviewer can leave a scathing account of their experience at a particular business – whether it is valid, genuine, verified or not – and human nature is drawn to that negative review over other positive ones at a ratio of ten to one.

In these instances, the business is forced into damage control which usually includes various forms of grovelling in an effort to dial down the reviewer's anger and persuade them to remove the post. Online bullies often become emboldened by this recognition, as it reinforces that their spiteful and vindictive behaviours can deliver what they really crave: attention and a sense of power! Even worse is that there's nothing stopping individuals who are in competition with that business from posting fake negative reviews or, on the flip side, posting fake positive ones for their own business. These scenarios are not meant to reflect that the customer is always wrong, but more so to highlight the unruly and sometimes disproportional criticism being regularly hurled towards individuals or groups with prominent platforms.

Civilised discourse about contrary views should always be encouraged, but protracted vitriol or deliberate attempts to intimidate others – whether covertly or otherwise – should be called out. While I'd love to devote these pages solely to ideas that would halt the bullying epidemic, the primary intention here is to assume that bullies exist and that the short-term solution is to strengthen our defence against their influence.

⚠️

*Navigational advice:* Many of us are familiar with the old TV and movie tropes where the victim finally stands up to the bully. According to scripts, this typically pressures the bully into backing down and they subsequently learn their lesson, often becoming best friends with the victim thereafter. In the real world, this almost never happens. But it makes us feel better to imagine it.

While a percentage of bullying that takes place within civilised societies is physical, the vast majority is mental and/or emotional. Pain is a more finite and tangible experience than fear, and that's why the argument could be made that being punched or physically pushed around is preferable to being psychologically terrorised over a period of time (although one may accompany the other). Given that non-physical bullying is far more prevalent, there is justification for allocating more attention towards dealing with it.

The irrefutable remedy for all forms of bullying is to strengthen oneself.

The irrefutable remedy for all forms of bullying is to strengthen oneself. 'Standing up to a threat' can represent many different things, not all of which necessarily appear outwardly aggressive or retaliatory. Our end goal is to engage in behaviours and thought practices that stop us from presenting as a 'soft target' to the outside world. Signalling strength to those around you is not about puffing one's chest out or bragging about how tough you are. It is an exercise in developing a thick skin and a perspective that puts other people's threatening behaviour towards you in context. This is an integral part of our force field's composition.

Consider the following:

→ When people verbally attack you, they are technically not 'hurting' you; they are only affecting your ego or sense of self-worth.

→ What other people think of you is none of your business.

→ You give bullies power over you, and you can take it away. Bullies usually confine their attack to those they feel they can dominate. Most bullies are put off if they sense their victim does not fear them. In many cases, it is easier for them to move on to their next target than persevere with someone who is projecting indifference or calm. This is why signalling strength – even subtly – is a useful defence in many cases.

→ Don't make their bullying of you about you! The bully is the one with the problem!

## HOW TO RESPOND TO A BULLY

→ *Be passive*. Ignore the negative attention and see if it will die of starvation. If not, then…

→ *Be passive-aggressive*. Make subtle overtures towards the bully that indicate your wilful resistance to their attention. While this may not present as overtly confrontational, it subtly says to them, 'There's a part of me that's totally prepared to fight but I'm keeping this exchange respectable for now and I suggest you do the same'. Even if your representation is fake (and you wouldn't really want to have it out with them), they don't know that for sure. Bullies generally don't thrive in an environment of uncertainty. If they deduce after a time that their target is not one to back down easily then they will invariably back off – albeit in a way that disguises their concern. If this fails to achieve your desired outcome, then…

→ *Be aggressive*. Aggression does not imply violence or an intention to escalate the issue physically. If the previous two avenues fail to achieve the result, then your weapon of last resort is to bear all and state your position without apology. Metaphorically speaking, this is the 'back off and leave me alone' stage and could be accompanied by suggestions that include professional, legal or lawful recourse. The bully will not always back down at this exact point in the exchange because it will be too obvious that they retreated out of fear. They will, however, be left with a very clear idea of where the line in the sand is, and the residual caution it creates will often initiate a silent and gradual withdrawal.

→ *Take control.* When a bully or toxic person can no longer control you, they may aim instead to control other people's opinions of you. Developing the smarts to detect these tactics will give you the necessary head start to thwart some of these attempts.

→ *Be yourself.* As Dr Seuss said, "Be yourself because the people who mind don't matter, and the people who matter don't mind." If you could reason with an idiot, then there would be no idiots. Also remember in these instances that the word 'awesome' ends with 'me' and the word 'ugly' starts with 'u'!

*Notable Exception:* If the individual attempting to bully you is intoxicated or under the influence of mood altering substances, then either leave the scene as soon as possible or do your best to de-escalate the situation. These people may be incapable of rational discourse so swallow your pride and focus solely on the immediate goal of maintaining your physical safety.

# Adapt and overcome

Each person we interact with brings either a contribution, destruction or a void to the situation. As such, succeeding in any people-oriented enterprise demands we develop strategies to navigate our way around this array of challenging circumstances.

Sometimes, it would be more constructive to define 'difficult' people as simply being 'different' people, thus highlighting that it can be a struggle dealing with others whose views or behaviours are contrary to ours. At the same time, we should be equally mindful that many people may find *us* to be part of *their* 'difficult' group.

Putting this open-mindedness aside, the aforementioned characters will all show up in your life at some stage. There will always be spectators shouting from the sidelines and people who've done largely nothing lecturing you about how to do things. You may one day even be called a 'has been' by someone who 'never was'.

Managing your way through these experiences is a skill that can be acquired and is a much more proactive pursuit than hoping society or legislation will protect you from such trials. Strengthening our own reserves physically and mentally is our only true defence against the politics of competitive human interaction.

# WARNING #2

# SEARCHING FOR HAPPINESS

ON THE SURFACE, HAPPINESS may seem like an odd subject to be appearing in the cautionary category of any book. Many people would claim that happiness is their greatest goal in life, but their failure to tangibly identify what this actually means for them will almost certainly ensure the goal remains elusive. Ironically, the search for happiness, particularly where it relates to the threadbare, modern-day version of material satisfaction and adulation, is likely in itself to be a disheartening pursuit and a probable cause of unhappiness.

It turns out that lasting happiness cannot be directly sourced; it can only be obtained as a consequence of engaging in worthwhile activities that create fulfilment and satisfaction in their doing. Acknowledging this helps us arrive at the practical realisation that for happiness to have longevity, we need to treat it as a verb more than a noun. Happiness is not a thing to look at or to look for – it's an exercise in *doing*. Happiness is achieved as a result of something that you do rather than somewhere you arrive. It is a

⚠

> Happiness is a result of something you do rather than somewhere you arrive.

state to regularly visit rather than a place to permanently reside.

Readily accessible first world pleasures like good food, fine art, music, literature, theatre, endless shopping malls and the finest coffee on every corner, are things that can make us feel great in the moment. Achieving financial success or being awarded a prestigious career appointment can also manufacture happy feelings. The pursuit of happiness for many people is to try and string instances of these temporary pleasure providers as close together as possible in the hope that they create a 'happiness continuum' that fills days and weeks with ceaseless enjoyment. Hmmm… nice if you can get it!

Unfortunately, the quest for unending superficial pleasures can leave us constantly searching for what's next because the feelings generated by these things are invariably short term. This behaviour can resemble that of an addict trapped in a cycle of dependency and a preoccupation with scoring their next fix. This is a common trap that forces us to examine whether or not a deeper form of wellbeing exists that isn't constantly dependent on indulging in good things, visiting exciting places or being in stimulating company.

It doesn't take much effort to feel happy in pleasurable surroundings or at exciting events. The challenge is in being able to experience happiness without the obvious stimulants at hand. Working out what it means to be happy and determining the best way to attain and preserve this desirable state should drive us beyond the acquisition of bling, fame or money. It's OK to pursue and enjoy these objects, but don't expect them to sustain a sense of ongoing fulfilment. A state of happiness inevitably gravitates towards a considered life that values restraint and proportion over excess and indulgence. This is not meant to be a purity test, but more so a simpler alternative for finding happiness than becoming fixated on material surplus.

It's widely accepted in sociological studies that people who are preoccupied with income and/or status are more dissatisfied and more likely to suffer from anxiety, depression and other stress-related ailments than those who pay less importance to these things. This unhealthy outcome is not only due to the temporary characteristic of such material rewards but also because these ambitions are often driven by comparisons to what others have.

The keys to life satisfaction rest on feeling valued for what we do and on having the freedom to choose our direction. This 'freedom to choose', however, is not meant to represent an aspiration for total control, but more so to be content in controlling what we can without engaging in the fantasy that we can control everything.

While these greater perspectives lay a foundation from which to cultivate a more moderated sense of happiness and contentment, there are also choices we can make each day that produce a more immediate sense of joy.

Is it possible, for instance, to *act* happy even when you are not feeling particularly happy? We know the answer to this question is yes since we've all managed to do this for at least some of our working life, or even in social environments where we may be forced to put on a happy face for the sake of exhibiting good manners. This doesn't suggest we should suppress or ignore our true emotions; it encourages us to behave at all times as if we were already happy and wanting to express kindness to others.

The underlying moral is that 'things' only provide a temporary feeling, whereas the sustained practice of worthwhile activities or actions creates a true and long-term sense of happiness. When immersed in a productive activity, it's possible that we may not even realise we are happy at the time since we often fail to appreciate

⚠️

> Happiness is more of a practice than an event.

the true value of the experience until it becomes a memory.

This is precisely why we must realise that happiness is more of a practice than an event. Life is not waiting for us, and happiness should not be habitually postponed or tied to something exciting happening soon. Right here and right now is the place to create happiness and contentment.

# WARNING #3

# CAUSATION BLINDNESS

ON THE SURFACE, THE principle of 'cause and effect' is a relatively straightforward concept. Comedy entertainer Tom Lehrer once remarked, "Life is like a sewer – what you get out of it depends on what you put into it!" This concept is also referred to as 'the law of sowing and reaping'. In its most earthly form, the concept of cause and effect is also the basic representation of karma. When we refer to something as 'karmic', we're usually implying that some form of just and proportional payback has taken place – whether it be painful or pleasurable.

> If you plant sunflower seeds, you don't grow pumpkins.

Buddhists' deepest beliefs about karma extend from one lifetime to the next, but we don't have to subscribe to the idea of reincarnation to embrace our own terrestrial version of karmic fairness. The principle of cause and effect is universal and can apply to things both tangible and relational. If you plant sunflower seeds, you don't grow pumpkins. It's not the sunflower seed's fault that it failed to produce a pumpkin. If you want happiness then

⚠️

engage in positive actions and behaviours towards others. What you wish to receive is the universe's way of telling you what you need to give. Exercising loving kindness towards others is the only guaranteed way to thrive socially and feel love. As the song lyrics by the New Radicals state, "You only get what you give."

Embracing the mechanics of cause and effect in our lives can often be hindered by our own character flaws.

# Failure to take responsibility

If we have manipulated the truth by unduly blaming others for our setbacks, then we are seeking an escape from reality and are destined to repeat past mistakes and relive present struggles. To run from the truth and lie to ourselves in the name of transitory solace is a foolhardy and senseless exercise. If you think your future is more likely to be affected by what other people do for you than it is by what you can do for yourself, then you need to hit the reset button. In instances like this, the most valuable personal growth tool for reclaiming your sense of responsibility is a mirror as it always gives you immediate and direct access to the real boss.

> The blame-game is a lame-game.

Even if you pray to God for things to work out a certain way, it's probably fair to say that the Lord is not going to run, fetch and deliver like your own cosmic butler. The popular quote 'God helps those who help themselves' sums this up well.

The blame-game is a lame-game, whereas taking personal responsibility for your outcomes is one of the highest forms of human maturity. You must never surrender the captaincy role of 'team-you' by appointing someone or something else to be your day-to-day decision-making power of attorney. In accepting this self-leadership role, we come to realise that we can be both the architect and the builder of our causes and thereby exert greater influence on our 'effects'.

# Short-term thinking

The focus of most people's thinking is conspicuously short term. Without a good long-game strategy, we lack the patience necessary to persevere through difficult or repetitive tasks. There's nothing in the cause-and-effect phrase that implies there will be a cause and an *immediate* effect. As hard as we may try sometimes, we cannot bend external conditions to satisfy our need for rapid gratification. Quite often, the 'effects' take some time to emerge so don't sabotage your outcome by expecting results too early.

# Relying on luck

Preparing for good luck is not the same as relying on it! Luck, as they say, is the idol of the idle and has a curious habit of favouring those who don't depend on it. A common superstition is that a rabbit's foot brings good luck, but we should be mindful that it didn't work that well for the rabbit!

While no one could refute the role that chance plays in our lives, it is a gross oversimplification to identify luck as the explanation for most of what happens to us. This is not to imply that good luck or bad luck doesn't exist, or that 'everything happens for a reason' (often it doesn't). Bad things occasionally happen to good people and vice versa. The point is that one should not depend too heavily on good luck when pursuing significant achievements or automatically blame bad luck if things don't transpire as planned.

⚠

> Many people prefer lazy excuses over challenging self-examination.

Unfortunately, however, many people prefer lazy excuses over challenging self-examination. We should also adopt the same mindset when processing other people's success. Rather than instinctively deducing they have been blessed with favourable luck, it should prompt us to examine their 'causes' with a view towards emulating their 'effects'. Ultimately, this can only happen if we recognise *causes* over *kismet*.

# Resting on laurels

Another tendency that often constrains the long-term cause-and-effect cycle is resting on past achievements. If we accept that certain causes and conditions combined to produce our initial desired result, then we must acknowledge that the ongoing success of that project requires either sustaining existing causes or adopting newer, more positive ones. Achieving a fitness target after a period of dedicated action is worth celebrating, but the applause will be short-lived if the causal initiatives fall away. Likewise with business. Many people work hard in the early stages to build a business and establish an initial customer base, but then spend too much time basking in the glory of their creation without enough thought to the natural attrition of customers over time.

This concept is very prevalent within the martial arts industry, gyms and fitness clubs. Through a strong initial focus, the club builds to a healthy number of members, but then sometimes unconsciously alters its processes. This doesn't necessarily mean that the club's team members were no longer busy, it's just that they had unwittingly diluted some of their original causes (actions) which – over time – yielded a proportionally inferior set of effects.

In a sense, they had camped themselves out in the 'effects' world, living off their previous harvest without enough thought or action towards the winter that may lay ahead.

# Hopelessness and low expectations

Cause and effect are not just a result of our physical actions. In many instances, the process of creation begins in the mind and our ultimate outcome is determined by our initial expectations. We are co-creators of our destiny and the subconscious mind is often the point of conception.

The subconscious mind has a childlike innocence and vulnerability. It's also highly impressionable and even gullible, meaning that it accepts anything as truth that its parent-like conscious mind tells it. It has no real sense of contemplation or fairness and is unable to accurately determine what is true or false. Sometimes, our imagination creates a scenario for what 'could' happen that can be more influential to our outcome than the manifestation of our physical actions. This is why we seldom raise to a level beyond our imagined target and why we are sometimes more likely to get what we expect rather than what we deserve. In essence, our expectations are our unconscious rudder. The bad news is that if we fail to define our own goals and expectations then we'll likely just end up becoming part of someone else's.

> Our expectations are our unconscious rudder.

Inexorably aligned with our goals and expectations is something that is often denigrated in personal development literature, and that is 'hope'. "Hope is a beggar," says the cynic, who also says, "Hope is allied to illusion; it is a false dawn that offers lies as truth and

⚠️

traps people in worthless pursuits." Because hope always applies to some point in the future, it is cheaply procured and infinitely renewable. After all, when old hopes die, new ones can be conceived at the speed of thought. Cynics often note the human tendency to entertain unrealistic aspirations and cling in vain to hopes in the face of contrary information.

But the cynic often fails to acknowledge that magnificent outcomes can also sprout from these imaginings. Much of what has moved society forward over the last couple of centuries was born out of hope, and much of what dragged it backwards came from hope being suffocated. For those living in war-ravaged territories, hope is their prized possession and is essential to life. After all, the alternative is to believe that things will only get worse or to expect defeat and anticipate loss.

Hope is the anticipation of better days in good times and a sense of comfort on the bad days. It upholds the idea of reprieve or salvation in the face of adversity. This is why hope has merit all by itself – irrespective of whether or not it is fully realised. It has an inherent worth because it represents a positive attitude that is full of ambitions and possibilities.

> Hope is the lead domino that activates change and alters behaviours.

You can understand more about an individual when you discover their hopes than when you measure their achievements. The undeniable partnership between hope and expectations provides a precursor to most aspirational activities or outcomes. In many ways, hopes are the genesis of the *cause* that creates the *effect*. Hope is the lead domino that activates change and alters behaviours, for better or worse.

# WARNING #4

# LOW SELF-WORTH

YOUR SELF-WORTH REPRESENTS THE overall sense of value, significance and deservedness that you have and show towards yourself. This evaluation has more to do with your perceived worth than it does with your inherent worth. Self-worth, therefore, is not a solid thing. It's an opinion – your opinion!

You can enjoy a healthy self-worth without holding any unique abilities as well as suffering a poor sense of self-worth despite being highly capable. If you fail to appreciate your inherent value or to give yourself credit for your many virtues, then your psychological self-portrait will be decidedly flawed.

Irrespective of how gifted, intelligent or charming a person may be, a low self-worth likely results in the emergence of destructive tendencies that can broadly impair their efforts and damage their close relationships. Learning to appreciate our worth can significantly enhance our emotional and physical environment by altering the actions we take and the choices we make. In the end, we don't get the job or the partner we deserve; we get the job and the partner we *believe* we deserve. We subliminally choose or attract the people and experiences we believe we are worthy of.

> We subconsciously communicate to others how we expect to be treated.

Therefore, as we begin to regard ourselves more highly, other people begin to do the same. In a sense, we subconsciously communicate to others how we expect to be treated through our physiology, tonality and other behaviours, both subtle and overt.

There are many pivotal moments in our lives where our sense of self-worth dictates or affects our decisions. A healthy self-worth may see us take a more righteous path where we work hard, treat others well, choose a devoted and loyal partner and deliberately mix in positive social groups. On the other hand, low self-worth may result in us taking a more errant route, signified by abusing our bodies, sabotaging our professional reputation or accepting a dud partner just because they like us. It's not hard to see how our self-worth motions us to either strive or struggle... to *mess* up or *rise* up.

These choices can impact our educational path, income levels, fitness and wellbeing practices and potentially even our longevity. The self-sabotage spawned from negative self-worth could be represented by substance abuse, spending more money than we earn, overworking to the point of serious fatigue, dropping out of school, tolerating a toxic social circle, working for an oppressive employer or choosing a partner who abuses us physically or verbally. These are general examples that you are likely to have witnessed at some point – hopefully not personally. The people in these situations may consciously still aspire to succeed, but their low self-worth indirectly undermines their desires.

It is indeed ironic that many people who possess the highest standards and principles often have the lowest self-worth because they continually fail to meet their own unattainable benchmarks.

The reality is that we all have missteps throughout our lives, but our worth should not be contingent on us being flawless. Rather than judging our mistakes so critically, we should re-examine them with more self-compassion and learn how to forgive ourselves. We cannot rely on others to provide us with an improved sense of self-worth any more than we can hold them responsible for our self-worth being low. Building or restoring a healthy self-worth is shaped from within and is derived from doing things that are worthwhile.

Of all the factors that impact our sense of self-worth, 'self-talk' is the one we have most command of. If you tell yourself something often enough, your subconscious mind assumes it is true and you will begin experiencing life through the prism of those self-made beliefs. As a result, it is imperative to adopt the practice of substituting derogatory thoughts such as 'nobody's going to find me attractive' with more constructive examples like 'I know there's someone out there for everyone – including me!' Sounds simple for sure, but ingrained impressions can be difficult to budge and sometimes we assume that solutions to big problems must be proportionally grand when this is not always the case.

# The pitfalls of perfectionism

It's not uncommon to hear people refer to themselves as being a 'perfectionist', and we have all met people with perfectionist tendencies. These individuals tend to place extremely high demands on their own performance, as well as those around them. The kindest interpretation of the perfectionist personality is that they set high standards, strive for excellence and are always heavily invested emotionally. In some respects, this can all seem complimentary,

⚠

but deeper inspection reveals that perfectionism can be more of an affliction than a positive attribute.

Most perfectionists can perform tasks to a high level of competency, but these capabilities come with a warning as they are often accompanied by an almost fanatical pursuit of regulation and orderliness that can be intolerable for those within their radius. The greater truth is that fear of failure is the constant lurking behind almost all perfectionism. This fear can easily manifest an unhealthy attachment to winning, a fixation with attracting accolades, a pathological anxiety towards losing or a paralysing obsession with protecting a so-called perfect record.

> Fear of failure is the constant lurking behind almost all perfectionism.

This may be a necessary condition for those aspiring to be the absolute best in their field such as the world's best golfers, tennis players, boxers, sprinters, swimmers or any other sport where fractional imperfections can make the difference between winning and losing.

While an obsession with perfection may drive the world's best athletes to the top of their sport, it rarely serves them as well off the field or after they retire. The rules of sport and the system of ranking that dictates recognition and earning power are very clearly defined: you know when you've won and when you haven't. Adopting a perfectionist mindset is undoubtedly the right tool under these circumstances. Outside this structured environment, however, obsessive or perfectionist tendencies can cause us to magnify our weaknesses, disregard how talented we already are and be a recipe for continual disappointment.

Perfectionists can unfortunately bring a level of intolerance to their own shortcomings that is intensely unhealthy, resulting in negative self-talk, unnecessary anxiety and even procrastination.

In short, perfectionists are very rarely happy or satisfied because perfection in anything is rarely attainable and never sustainable. Author Brené Brown said, "Perfectionism is a twenty-ton shield that we lug around thinking it will protect us, when, in fact, it's the thing that's really preventing us from being seen and taking flight."

There's a fine line between healthy striving and unhealthy obsessing. I used to believe that I could be the best at everything I committed myself to, and that if I poured enough hours into practice I could move from the bottom to the top irrespective of my starting point. This mostly unrealistic mentality was born out of the CANI principle of 'Constant and Never-ending Improvement'. Unfortunately, when mixed with perfectionist tendencies, this invariably produces a feeling of *constant and never-ending inadequacy* and a failure to recognise that being very good at something is a result worth celebrating in its own right.

Chronic preoccupation with peak performance leads to dissatisfaction. We can't be at the top of our game every day; there are always external factors that we are not in control of.

The pursuit of perfection can be so intolerant of failure, it prevents the individual from accepting that mistakes, setbacks and losses are vital prerequisites to improvement. Aside from this obvious shortcoming, perfectionism also fails to accept that some people are just going to be better than you in certain areas.

Perfectionism's relationship to depleted self-worth is irrefutable. It can paralyse us from taking action for fear of not living up to some idealised standard, resulting in us failing to achieve our desired outcome, which in turn re-feeds our already low self-worth. In this scenario, even if you take action, your perfectionist expectations will rarely be satisfied on a consistent basis, leaving your opinions about yourself in a fallen state.

The most constructive opposition to a perfectionist attitude is to simply shoot for good instead. Aiming for perfection often results in a venture never being completed or us never being happy with the outcome. This is why 'the perfect' is the enemy of 'the good'! Focusing on excellence is a far more profitable mindset to adopt if you want to finish the job and turn in work of a high standard.

Perfectionists don't just obsess about their own failings; they also exercise an inflexibility towards the perceived defects of those around them. Finding things to fix in others is their part-time job. If this sounds like you, then take this as advice to resign as general manager of the universe and *let it be!* We must learn to accept that others will have different expectations and rules.

It's not always our job to correct people nor is our happiness contingent upon everyone liking or agreeing with us. Reality can collide with your expectations of others when they are unreasonable, leaving you feeling perpetually unsatisfied or frustrated with your friends or family. None of this is conducive to healthy relationships.

# Surround yourself with supportive influences

It is difficult to maintain a positive sense of self-worth if you regularly associate with overly competitive people who may subtly take pleasure in your struggles. These people invariably get into your head and drag you back into their own insecure worlds. You must be prepared to cut ties with this crowd and spend time with more affirmative and uplifting people instead.

These influences also extend beyond personal interaction. If you spend much of your time reading puerile chat sites, Instagram posts, parochial blogs, gossip columns or mean-spirited forums, then you are unconsciously infecting your mind with toxic thought material. If you wouldn't seek out this sort of conversational compost at a party or in a social setting, then don't seek it out online. Instead, seek out inspiring messages that make you feel good about yourself and more positive about life in general.

# Shut down your internal critic

The destructive personal commentary that can dominate our thoughts and emotions from time to time is most often referred to as 'negative self-talk' or our 'internal critic'. As mentioned earlier, positive self-talk is an indispensable companion for all successful people, none more so than in the field of sports. In the heat of battle when your opponent is doing their level best to take you down, the last thing you need is a second opponent to come along and beat you from the inside out.

If we are to enjoy a healthy self-worth that is not dependent on always achieving exceptional results, our goal must be to come up with a more constructive outlook or perception. Can you still be great even if you fail to win? Consider sporting legends such as Roger Federer, Usain Bolt or Michael Jordan. All of these men have lost at some point, but their internal processing of these losses is one of the main things that sets them apart from the average. Never equate failure with self-worth!

> Never equate failure with self-worth!

It's easy to proclaim these ideals, but we meet resistance when we realise that we cannot really control our thoughts. Where we don't have the option of pausing to meditate on a negative or doubtful thought, one of the best short-term mental strategies we can adopt is to shut down the internal dialogue, much like you would stop another person from unloading their negative views onto you.

⚠

There were countless fights late in Muhammad Ali's career where – by his own admission – he was taken to the brink of physical collapse. His third fight with Joe Frazier – arguably the most brutal and absorbing heavyweight fight in history known as the Thrilla in Manila – was a good example. Ali recalled at the end of the tenth round that he felt the closest thing to death he had ever experienced. Somehow, something willed him on well past what his body thought it was capable of. Deep down, he truly believed that he was the greatest and his colossal mental strength, internal belief and self-worth raised him off his stool, walked him forward with his hands up and drove him to keep throwing punches. Nobody did self-talk like Ali. He really knew how to pump up his own tyres.

> Self-worth is indeed the harvest of discipline.

It's time to talk yourself up! Tell yourself that you're the greatest! Use your self-talk as a performance-enhancing emotional drug and as a reliable driver of your self-worth.

Irrespective of where your sense of self-worth currently resides, it is important to realise that it is not a fixed object. While we cannot wish for better beginnings or a better yesterday, we can start today to create the framework for a better ending. The most effective way to improve our sense of worth is to regularly engage in worthy activities. Self-worth is indeed the harvest of discipline.

# WARNING #5

# HUBRIS

'HUBRIS' IS A TERM that describes an individual or group who suffers from its overconfidence or falls victim to its own foolish pride (or both). Not surprisingly, hubris is often associated with arrogance – whether it be overt or subtle – that ultimately brings about a downfall.

Hubris is an acquired condition triggered by the possession of power or perceived power. This is especially true where power has been kept for an extended time with minimal checks or restraints on the individual. When this happens, the successful person may lose touch with reality by overestimating their own worth, their achievements and their level of proficiency. Most often, this exaggerated pride and inflated self-confidence also manifests as a notable contempt for others.

It is easy to dismiss hubris as an inescapable and unattractive occupational hazard that afflicts powerful leaders or those who seek power in general. After all, a thin skin or absence of basic self-confidence would see the average leader struggle to cope with the inevitable scrutiny that their position attracts. Portraying inspiration, casting a vision, taking risks, putting their reputation on the line, exhibiting boldness and espousing grand expectations are expected components of a successful leader. However, these same positive traits can also present negatively if the leader administers them with a conceited disposition.

> Remaining humble, open and receptive is a natural panacea to the hubris condition.

Taking risks can be interpreted as reckless, exhibiting boldness viewed as impulsivity, portraying inspiration as egoism or taking charge can be portrayed as being drunk with power. Excessive self-admiration and an unwillingness to accept feedback or criticism form a toxic compound that is like a growth hormone for hubris. On the positive side, remaining humble, open and receptive is a natural panacea to the hubris condition.

How, therefore, does one strike the right balance between being strong and being humble – a balance between confidence and hubris? Is there a pattern or early warning sign that signifies the point at which the leader begins to exhibit the vain pomposity that is characteristic of hubris?

Over the years, there have been many cautionary tales about fallen business executives highlighted in management textbooks, and the errors that led them to their failures. With all of this scrutiny, the onset of hubristic behaviour from CEOs or positions of authority should be more easily detected – or so you'd think. Like many things, however, the difference between *proportional* and *excessive* self-confidence often only becomes evident after the fall.

Recognising when the line is about to be crossed from making brave tactical decisions with justifiable conviction to recklessly rolling the dice with unwarranted overconfidence is not as obvious as it sounds.

⚠

There are many different models one could be guided by. The Taoist philosophy of Yin and Yang – although not typically applied in leadership texts – is as good as any. Even a relatively shallow inspection of Taoist principles can illustrate how the dualities of Yin (often represented as the feminine) and Yang (as the masculine) can create a successful harmony within the leaders themselves and throughout the groups they oversee.

Within the basic Taoist framework, it could be said that the person in a position of power can act as a 'warrior' or a 'healer'. They portray their warrior side using force, intervention and by making unilateral decisions – the Yang (masculine) – or, conversely, act as a healer when in a more fluid, open and agreeable state – the Yin (feminine).

# The balancing act

Too much force, assertion or coercive behaviour is often linked to a leader being dismissive of ideas that oppose theirs and will make the group more resistant to follow or to offer suggestions. Leaders whose single gear is to push (too much Yang) presume they are facilitating processes, but they are often blocking them. They view constant interventions as a measure of their importance and a subtle flex of their position. But even if strong intervention yields a successful outcome, there is no immediate cause for celebration. In terms of this group dynamic, there has possibly been an injury.

Leaders who exert influence through inclusion, cooperation, service and encouraging independence (the Yin) will outlast the more short-sighted and bullish approach and will be immune to the onset of unhealthy hubris-based actions. In essence, the Yin *allows* and the Yang *causes*. Neither of these approaches are objectively wrong, but they are incomplete without the other.

⚠

It is the Yin that must ultimately outlast the Yang if hubris is to be kept away. Hubris breeds when egoism and dismissiveness reign and is thwarted where humility and inquisitiveness are practised. The experienced martial artist knows that there is a time to exert force (Yang) and time to yield (Yin), but their ultimate goal is to use the least force necessary to be effective. The leader's touch only needs to be light, and few people realise just how little will do.

## CAUTIONARY MEASURES

- Striving to be a star can make a person ugly and unpopular. Always gauge your audience or immediate team dynamic.
- Style is no substitute for substance.
- Creating an impression is not as important as acting from your central point of integrity.
- The consequences of your behaviours are inescapable.
- Wise leaders keep egocentricity in check and place the wellbeing of the group above their own.
- When leaders become superstars, the teacher can outshine the teaching.
- True leaders don't accept all the credit for what happens and have no need for fame.
- Wise leaders don't rely on applause because they know they'll become dependent on it continuing and anxious when it subsides.
- If you become attached to your reputation, you will lose the freedom and honesty needed for further development and growth.
- Egocentricity injures both the self and the work.
- When a person is humble and calm, complex events become simple.

- Insecure leaders aim to promote themselves. *Impotent leaders* use their position rather than their character to exert influence. It isn't very impressive to be constantly pointing out how impressive you are.
- Being centred means being able to recover your balance – even in the midst of unexpected developments.
- Seek growth over fame and satisfaction over recognition.
- Demonstrating or exhibiting behaviours is more potent than imposing morality through lectures.
- Learn to recognise beginnings.

Preventing the emergence of hubris in an organised setting relies on a culture that keeps confidence in check. Those in leadership roles must not believe they are irreplaceable, nor should they assume they always know better than anyone else. If they are wise, they will always seek feedback from both above and below and won't waste time with articles praising their business acumen or celebrating past achievements. They will make clear to their immediate subordinates that feedback is both welcome and expected and will remain open to voices that challenge their assumptions. They also understand that too much 'thinking uniformity' within a group can inadvertently filter out important data and may cause alternative ideas that could otherwise be worthy of consideration to be overlooked.

Wise leaders also make the formation of a positive team culture a central motivating theme with those they lead, as opposed to being purely fixated on financial gain or a win-at-all-costs competition. Pitting subordinates against each other through internal league tables and contests is also a way of breeding hubris within subgroups of an organisation and can be akin to forming a circular firing squad.

Generally speaking, it's OK to be proud of one's achievements as long as pride does not cause us to look down on others. Inevitably, we all have our turns at failing and, when we do, the suffering it causes humbles us. The good news is that the pain of failure is temporary while the benefit of humility is long lasting.

Humility helps us recognise our mistakes and makes us face up to the consequences of our actions. The phrase 'no regrets' bothers me. As I see it, when people use it, they either have very poor memories or they've made a deal with their conscience that exonerates them from whatever hurts they've caused to others in the past through their own thoughtless actions. So, when you next hear someone asserting that 'they wouldn't change a thing' about their past, you may stop to reflect on how selfish that statement can sound and how much in denial they may be.

# WARNING #6

# BS

*Bullshit: /bʊlʃɪt/ (say 'boolshit) Colloquial (taboo)*
−noun

*1. an account, explanation, creative fantasy, etc., which is fabricated or contrived either to delude oneself or to deceive others.*

*2. nonsense.*

I AM SINCERE IN the view that the inability to detect BS in our media, politics, social platforms or in our daily interactions with others can leave us highly vulnerable. While still technically classed as profanity, the term 'bullshit' (BS) made its way into common lexicon many years ago – nowhere more so than in Australia.

While I can't speak for other countries, Australian culture creates an environment that makes it difficult for BS to survive for too long. As a people, we're pretty good at sniffing it out and bestowing the perpetrator with the quintessentially Aussie title of 'bullshit artist'.

Some could effectively argue that calling BS on something or someone is a subjective exercise. After all, how do we know for sure that we are right and others are the ones talking BS? A term like 'fake news', for instance, is ubiquitous in today's media which makes it more difficult for the average observer to discern truth from opinion. 'Facts matter', they say, but it's also likely that confirmation bias sees two people viewing the same 'facts' and drawing opposing conclusions.

The search for the 'absolute' truth can be frustrating and often brings little reward. Perhaps absolute truth is a bar too high given that it's virtually impossible to know everything about everything. Aside from this, truth can also shift over time with the emergence of new discoveries.

Seeking greater clarity on important issues over the course of your life is a noble pursuit. However, unless it's balanced with a humility that makes room for opposing views then one risks becoming that stubborn blowhard whose boorish sense of certainty undermines their appeal and raises their 'other' IQ – their *ignorance quotient*. The smartest people are those who have embraced mystery, remain open-minded and have developed enough awareness to realise how little they really know for sure.

In the field of politics, for instance, it is a shame when a politician is so quickly branded as flip-flopping if they change their mind on a particular issue. Switching views just to win votes of course is a cheap and nasty ploy, but where a leader is presented with new information that renders their previous ideas obsolete, then they should be applauded more often for exercising an open mind and for adopting a more up-to-date perspective.

The mainstream newsrooms and current affairs programs focus too much on lurid stories designed to make us feel either angry, scared or shocked – or all three. Unfortunately, these emotional states are not known for producing constructive thinking. The angrier or more afraid we are, the more absent our objectivity and the easier it is to manipulate our attention. Much of the time, the 'breaking' news isn't all that breaking. The role of news providers in today's competitive media environment is to make us feel like the breaking news just came out of the oven – and not yet seen or tasted by anyone! It's almost trying to make us feel lucky that we heard it first, like we were in the right place at the right time and, most importantly, tuned into the right news provider! This, despite the fact that their 'exclusive' story is also breaking on every other channel at the same time.

Apart from the obvious baiting strategy that breaking news adopts, it also results in us staying perpetually off balance while we struggle to find context about the topic before the next wave of breaking news arrives. In most cases, we rarely digest the deeper story and simply retain the emotion that the headline created.

Social media is another veritable smorgasbord of BS. Dr Thomas Friedman stated that today's social networks are like open sewers, full of untreated and unfiltered content. He said, "They have diamonds and rubies and gold and gems, and they have toxic waste, rusty cans and broken glass. And if you don't have a population that has the filters to sort out one from the other, you get to where we are today."

Nowadays, ill-informed people can create online media that looks as professional as your nightly network news. Marketing bots can establish a profile based on your social media usage that tracks your interests, and you are then served regular content that fits neatly with your existing views. This information strengthens your existing bias, which in turn causes your critical thinking muscle to atrophy. In essence, it's *your* information, packaged and presented how *you* want it, like only being served your favourite foods every night and day. This constant reinforcement can create the impression that your news source is the only accurate one and generates greater intolerance towards contrary opinions.

Many people now receive all their news from chat rooms, viral emails and social media. If the news agrees with what they already believe, then it must be true, and if it doesn't, then it must be fake! For this reason, the ability to discern fact from opinion has never been more difficult – or more important. This news delivery format threatens to keep us both parochial and insufficiently informed.

BS also broadly includes the array of inane and vacuous online content that people post on their social media pages on the presumption it will be interesting to others. Many of this crowd seem to overestimate how much other people are wondering what they're doing or thinking that day. Or perhaps they're concerned others aren't thinking about them enough, and that this could be rectified by producing an overt display of shameless exhibitionism. Births of new babies or special achievements are wonderful things to share among friends and family on social media, but much of what makes up post content these days is not.

There are many items on the BS menu.

# Fear of missing out (FOMO)

This toxic cocktail of equal parts jealousy, envy and insecurity will lead you around by the nose, constantly looking left and right to ensure that someone isn't having too much fun somewhere else without you. When drawn into this world, you become hostage to other people's aspirations and ignore your own. It is far better to build your own life rather than live vicariously through another's.

At any given time, there's always going to be someone snorkelling at a beautiful reef, climbing a majestic mountain or skiing down a slope in a postcard town – and that's OK. Platforms like Instagram and its army of 'influencers' have been the target of criticism for perpetuating the FOMO affliction and its related insecurities. The argument here is that a false and unattainable lifestyle replete with five-star resorts, high-end bling, luxury brand garments and postcard scenery is being consistently thrust into the minds of young people who have no more than $500 in the bank and a tertiary education debt.

Some may argue that viewing these images will bring forth a wave of ambition in the younger audience, and in a percentage of cases it no doubt would. The downside is in how it hatches the impression that 'everybody else is doing better and enjoying their life more than me'!

As a very young adult, I recall having only a few hundred dollars in the bank and being in no position to travel even interstate within Australia let alone to Ibiza for a rave pool party. Despite this modest position, I was nonetheless happy because I had mates, a girlfriend, a part-time job, a bomby little car and participated in active sports. There was no social media back then to fuel any comparison anxiety by reminding me there were other young men around the world doing better and having more fun in exotic places. I was happy in my bubble and enjoying the life that my semi-adult and still developing brain was experiencing. While the seeds of ambition were being planted in my mind in various subtle ways at the time, they were not being overly fertilised by envy, jealousy or FOMO.

> FOMO is a human problem, not a social media problem.

It's easy to blame social media for driving the FOMO epidemic, but that's like blaming the volume dial on your speakers when you receive a noise complaint from your neighbours. FOMO is a human problem, not a social media problem. It's OK to browse through other people's lives occasionally since they've gone to so much trouble to share it with you. If that post creates positive inspiration then great, but if it makes you hate your life then the only holiday you should take for now is a break from social media.

If you are under the age of 25 and reading this, then I can only encourage you to run your own race and enjoy your own personal bubble for now. You will never be this age again, and the more you immerse yourself in the fake 'happy every day – living the dream' impression created by those who only post their good news, the more you will be living in lack psychologically! The fact that social media platforms have provided opportunities for the itinerant and unemployed to monetise their exhibitionism is not your fault. But believing these glamorous images represent an everlasting existence is akin to thinking professional wrestling is real fighting.

# Political arguments

> Bias is stronger than truth and objectivity in most cases.

Even if you respond to an inflammatory political statement with your most articulate and surgical rebuttal, most people aren't going to budge from their views. As such, only put your time aside for people who will remain sincerely open to your feedback. Even then, be prepared for opposition and keep your expectations low. It's a shame to say it, but bias is stronger than truth and objectivity in most cases. Don't waste your time!

# Conspiracies

These may be fun to entertain but can also lead to excessive cynicism, hostile arguments and an obsessive focus on theories that can never be proven. We'd all like to think that we're nobody's fool, and it's true that men in power have historically engaged in conspiratorial activities to forward their own agendas… but getting too caught up in these stories can be a slippery slope.

No one likes to be told they've got it wrong. As the saying goes, "It's easier to deceive the people than it is to convince them that they've been deceived." Sincerity is not a measure of truth. People who believe crazy things would almost certainly pass a lie detector test because they 100 per cent believe what they're saying. Was there a second shooter? Was it actually all filmed in a studio? Were there explosives already planted in the buildings? Did it come from bats or was it manufactured in a lab? My best advice is to save these debates for the campfire rather than online.

# Internet gurus

While there's obviously an array of genuine and credible experts online, there is also a long list of others whose greatest area of expertise is their digital marketing skills. Many of these people make significant money by running online courses on how to make money online. In fact, it often seems there is more money in the teaching than there is in the method they are teaching! I have been to more than my fair share of these seminars. I've purchased plenty of audio programs and attended the live conventions.

The common schtick of the financial sage is to sell you a product that promises to create life-changing returns. Then when you've purchased what you thought was *the* course and attended what you thought was *the* seminar, it becomes apparent that you have merely entered the ground floor. 'Luckily', you then discover there are many more exciting layers beyond your introductory level, which are certain to eliminate any chance of failing. It's at about this time the coach wheels out a small group of people who have previously joined the 'Elite' program to give firsthand testimonials on why the 'next level' is such a game changer.

It's not uncommon for this 'ultimate experience' to cost five to ten times the price of your original investment. Stock market and Forex Trading products are among the most suspicious here as they attempt to make the world's biggest casino look like a predictable business model – often while stoking the dream that it will replace your job one day. And while this may occasionally happen, it's important to stand back and realise that if the stock market could be consistently traded with such confidence and rewards, then most of these people would remain doing it full-time rather than setting up educational companies.

Are all of these operators questionable? No! But you should do your homework and run them through the BS test before committing to anything. There are people on YouTube right now who are running slick ads portraying themselves as elite Fortune 500 CEOs, who are nothing but paid actors playing a character. It looks so convincing. BS certainly has shape-shifting qualities.

Another type of online marketer is the feel-good guru. They have it even easier when marketing their courses because there is often no quantifiable way to measure the results of their services other than if the individual 'feels great' afterwards. Some of the people who run these mass-coaching events are first-class educators with impeccable credentials. Many others hold a Bachelor of BS, greatly exaggerate their backstory and generate clients by convincing them that their current life is not good enough. According to their underlying marketing narrative, anything short of an amazing life

⚠️

is essentially a life unfulfilled. 'Good' is merely a euphemism for mediocre, average or dull. A good life means you're not trying hard enough and you probably need someone like them to take you from good to great. There's nothing wrong with a good life, so don't let people with a financial ulterior motive convince you that you're not happy as you are.

Many of these online 'life coaches' are also inclined to create tiered courses, with the pinnacle week-long event often held at an exotic holiday destination. It's true that these gourmet buzz-fests can provide a truly unique experience, if only because you've never spent that much money in a week before. Ultimately, however, it's up to our own discipline and follow-through to make sustainable change happen in our lives. That's why it's called 'self-help', because in the end you have to help yourself! Moreover, it's *what you do with what you learned* at the palatial island resort that determines if the substantial investment was well spent.

In my experience, the most valuable coaches are the ones who are there for you along the way. For the same money, you are better off acquiring the services of a switched-on local business, financial or wellbeing consultant and paying them a retainer each week for 12 months to visit and counsel you, track your results and hold you accountable to your goals. This would be a much greater return on your investment because the support and follow-through would be on hand when it really mattered. The benefits of corresponding with this mentor regularly over the year are generally more enduring than the high-octane but short-lived seminar among the pools and palm trees.

⚠

# Dumb rules

'Pseudo' rules are often used to justify poor decisions, validate ignorance or excuse inactivity.

Sometimes you have to call BS on statements or ideas that are as unhelpful as they are common. Well-known expressions or 'pseudo' rules are often used to justify poor decisions, validate ignorance or excuse inactivity. These rules can markedly affect our day-to-day beliefs but are objectively untrue in most cases.

## *Everything happens for a reason*

No, it doesn't! Not unless you believe in the wicked and innately spiteful concept of unending karma! Sometimes bad things happen, and they happen to good people. When bad things happen to bad people, then we say it's karma. But when it happens to good people – then what? By some accounts, approximately nine million children die each year around the world before their fifth birthday, not including an extra three million who are stillborn. This is one of many instances where trite lines like this miss the mark. It's true that some things happen as a consequence, but not always for a reason. This dumb rule is mostly designed to give comfort when something bad has happened – but it rarely does.

## *Ignorance is bliss*

This is rarely the case! What you don't know *can* hurt you. Ignorance is dangerous – emotionally, financially and socially.

## *People have to make their own mistakes*

BS! If kids were smart, they'd listen to advice and learn from other people's mistakes. There's nothing more frustrating than watching your children (or other grown-ups) make mistakes that they don't have to be making. Sometimes, it's like watching a car accident in slow motion; you can literally see what's going to happen before it does and you're powerless to stop it.

Parents and mentors are not always perfect teachers, but teens/ young adults can set themselves back years by being stubborn, ignoring good advice or thinking they have all the answers.

## *You can't just sweep things under the rug*

Yes, you can! And sometimes you should! A wound will not properly heal if you pick at it constantly. There will inevitably be tangles in your life that cannot be unscrambled by thought, excessive meditation or intense discussion. Occasionally, you've just got to let things go and allow time to be your counsellor. The vast recesses of our mind partly exist to store things that we'd rather not look at anymore. Don't resist this tendency – it's not necessary to constantly take inventory of your life's unsettled accounts. Perhaps the rug was invented in part to cover up what lay underneath it?

> It's not necessary to constantly take inventory of your life's unsettled accounts.

Of course, there are always emotional issues that we do benefit from achieving closure on. I'm not suggesting we stockpile mountains of unresolved baggage under the rug. If the pile under the rug becomes too large, we will constantly be tripping over it. At the same time, we shouldn't become too attached to the therapeutic impulse of unwrapping every emotional episode or childhood hang-up, unless we really have to. You won't always know or be able to control why you are the way you are. It's better to just play to your strengths, accept your past shortcomings and fix your gaze firmly forward while taking wisdom from whatever's under the rug.

## *Always follow your gut*

No. Sometimes your gut will deceive you. Assuming your 'gut' refers to your instincts, one may wonder how this could ever lead us down a wrong path. Simply explained, your gut only makes up part of your decision-making machinery. Because it's so tied to your feelings, decisions made only from your gut are heavily influenced by your immediate fears and your overall aversion to discomfort. If a scenario relates to imminent physical danger, then your gut should be given a prominent seat at the table. We often develop uneasy feelings about other people or about our own personal safety in certain environments, and our instincts should not be ignored in these cases.

However, uncomfortable feelings aren't always a signal to delay or retreat. Potentially, there are scores of emotional, professional and financial rewards that can only be accessed by stepping outside of our own personal comfort zone. Sometimes 'something doesn't feel right' simply because we are venturing into unfamiliar territory. Quite often, the thought of taking action makes us feel nervous or apprehensive, but that doesn't mean we shouldn't act. Our gut is hardwired to avoid discomfort, and if we only ever placate the 'nervous Nancy' in our mind, then we may decide that it doesn't feel right to ask that woman or man out, ask for a raise, apply for that job, invest that money and so on. We will, in effect, be frozen by our uneasy gut feeling.

⚠

The intention here is to acknowledge the equal value of our intellect. There are times when our more logical and pragmatic capabilities should be mixed in with our gut reflexes in order to arrive at a well-rounded decision. To some extent, our rational mind serves metaphorically as a well-considered adviser to our comfort-seeking and survival-focused gut.

Our gut and our mind are a team, and the best decisions we make are those where the team work together. It's not advisable to let your heart rule your head and the opposite is no less applicable.

## *It has to be all or nothing*

When a belief system demands that we take only one of these two options, nothing often wins. This is because 'all' is a lot of work. Sometimes, we cannot summon 'all' of our all, and where there is no in-between mode to fall back on, we are therefore left with 'nothing'.

All-or-nothing thinking sounds fully committed and heroic – like giving 110 per cent, whatever that means. But practically speaking, it more often breeds procrastination than anything else. 'If I can't do it five days a week, then I'd rather not do it at all' is a common example of a line proclaimed by the perpetual staller.

Even a small amount of something is preferable to a big bowl of nothing. Starting with minor steps is better than no steps at all. Progress is built incrementally, whether it's related to diet, saving money, exercise, learning an instrument or pursuing a formal education.

## *The grass is always greener on the other side*

No, the grass is greener where you water it! This point requires relatively little explanation. Most of us have come to realise that the 'other side of the fence' is often a mirage. When life gets difficult where we are, it is tempting to wish for a simpler position or to look at how relatively better someone else's life looks. The moral here is to spend more time and energy investing in the enhancement of your job, body, relationship or the professional standing that you have now than to assume things would be better if you just changed jobs, left your spouse, moved to another suburb and so on.

The grass is greener where you water it!

Unless you find yourself in a majorly troublesome environment, then your best move is to plant where you stand. This is where you truly learn how to make lemonade out of lemons. Failure to recognise this could see you carry your problems from one place to the next, falsely believing that a change of scenery is a cure-all for the dissatisfaction that rumbles beneath.

## *Rules based on unexamined traditions*

Just because a belief or particular activity is based on tradition, doesn't mean it is automatically right or good. A traditional view is not necessarily a valuable one. Being old is no guarantee of worth or virtue. 'That's the way it's always been done' is a phrase that indicates a custom, but in many cases, it promotes ritual behaviours that justify the suspension of critical thinking.

G.K. Chesterton once wrote, "Tradition means giving a vote to the most obscure of all classes, our ancestors. It is the democracy of the dead." Blindly following a tradition is like being controlled by a lazy habit that provides comfortable excuses to keep doing things the same way, even if they are irrational.

This is not to say that all timeworn traditions are a waste of time, but more so a call to examine current decisions

> Being old is no guarantee of worth or virtue.

and behaviour in a contemporary context. Otherwise, traditions can be the enemy of progress and of progressive thinking in general. The good old days weren't always good, and some well-guarded and time-honoured customs need to be binned for individuals and societies to move forward.

# WARNING #7

# CONDESCENSION

THERE ARE VERY FEW social experiences more unpleasant than being the subject of someone else's condescending remarks. Displaying an air of superiority or disdain towards others is a highly unattractive trait and one that will almost certainly sever relationships. At the heart of condescension is intolerance for the way that others think or behave, which is to say that condescending remarks are nothing more than the pompous outward expression of an intolerant attitude.

As we grow older, we tend to feel like we are gaining a stronger grasp on how life works and on the way things should be set up. This could include the gradual hardening of your views on politics, economics, the workplace, faith, gender equality, same-sex marriage, abortion, racism, climate change and so on. The more our views become hard-baked, the easier it is to be intolerant of those who do not share the same outlook.

In these cases, those who disagree with your views are failing to see the thing that you've apparently (and masterfully) discovered. Maybe you conclude that they're just not as bright as you or they receive their news from inferior sources. Irrespective of its origin, adopting a patronising or contemptuous manner towards others is the ultimate exposure of intolerance and a sure way to isolate yourself both personally and professionally.

Not saying out loud what you're thinking is one way of tackling the problem, but it's far more effective and long lasting to adopt a more compassionate attitude towards those who don't share your opinions, politics or status. Given that behaviour follows thought, abstaining from condescending expression towards others really starts between the ears.

Developing tolerance and maturity is a noble pursuit for society at large. For instance, we outwardly debate how best to help people who seem unable to support themselves financially or emotionally. In one corner there are those who assert the poor 'did it to themselves'. In the other corner, the crowd is convinced that 'they couldn't help it'. It becomes a debate about self-inflicted vs innocent victim and level playing field vs disadvantaged upbringing. Suffice to say that condescension finds the most fertile soil to grow at the extremities of these arguments where intolerance towards the other side is at its apex.

As mature and balanced people, we have the choice to be humble, and if we don't, we will most likely be humbled. None of us are perfect, and the inevitable likelihood that we will sometimes make poor judgements, commit indiscretions or take wrong turns reminds us to be more tolerant of others' missteps. It is also salient to remember that we live in a world where rewards and retributions are not always allocated by merit. When it comes to personal happiness, the decisions we make as a collective are just as important as those we make as individuals. This is to say that you can only be as happy as the society or community you live in.

The broader truth being highlighted here is that condescension cannot merely be defined as a single patronising comment; rather, it is an attitude of self-appointed superiority over others that compromises immediate relationships and can toxify the mood of wider society.

It is surprisingly common for those with a sanctimonious nature to be completely unaware of how they present. Ironically, these people can also be easy to offend which makes the task of correcting their language and tonality towards others even more difficult. Typically, these people start their defence against any such accusations of rudeness by exclaiming, "All I said was… " They struggle to concede that perception is reality and resist the idea of taking responsibility for someone else feeling demoralised.

Some people are extremely easy to offend, and we shouldn't form the habit of always placing sensitivity ahead of truth when it comes to offering them critique. Some may steadfastly argue that condescension is in the mind of the receiver, and maybe sometimes it is. However, you can be sure that routinely assuming that the receiver is the problem will cost you friends, good employees, professional reputation and, inevitably, money.

> Routinely assuming that the receiver is the problem will cost you.

# WARNING #8

# ENVY

ENVY DESCRIBES THAT FEELING of dissatisfaction or resentful yearning caused by observing someone else's talents, possessions or good fortune. Specifically, it occurs when we lack (or we *feel* we lack) a desirable quality enjoyed by another person. It may even include feeling some pain at the sight of their happiness. Aside from coveting the possessions of others, envy can also leave us disgruntled by the apparent ease with which other people successfully transform their personal, professional or financial lives. Therefore, envy is as much a perspective as it is a result.

Men and women are both guilty of this, although they typically use different units of measurement. When examining the male perspective, men often measure themselves against other men based on the size of their houses, cars, muscles and wallets. None of these are challenges that any man can win regularly, hence they set themselves up for feelings of failure, insecurity and dissatisfaction.

On the surface, envy can seem like the least threatening of the biblical seven deadly sins. It presents as relatively lightweight when compared with the more ominous and in-your-face traits like

⚠

wrath, lust, greed or gluttony. But any face value mildness that envy implies is more than nullified by its insidious nature.

In modern society we have come to believe that nirvana is achieved through the accumulation and ownership of material goods. What we have and how we look mistakenly define our personal identity, and this error is compounded when we begin to measure our wealth against others. While healthy competition can be viewed as a positive driving force for those with an ambitious nature, there is also a fine line between being positively driven and being afflicted with an unhealthy obsession to have more than others. If we overly compare our progress to those around us, our lives can become characterised by greed, discontent and a desire to be someone else.

> If there was no such thing as envy, how much more money could we save?

If there was no such thing as envy, how much more money could we save and have in the bank? How much more time could we have and how much less anxiety? Perhaps the ultimate wealth is in learning to appreciate what we already have. There is a vast difference between genuine poverty and the first world problem known as 'relative' poverty. You don't have to be financially poor to suffer from relative poverty; you just have to think you are poor when compared to those you envy.

Relative poverty is a highly destructive mindset that sets us up for disappointment as it represents a continual competition that we can never win. There are always people who own more or who are better than us at something in the world. This is not a problem! Rather than living in lack, could we instead focus on how well we've done or how far we've come? Trying to keep up with what others have or experience often results in losing touch with what actually matters to us. In the end, we just wind up being led around by the nose, hostage to an infantile comparison trap.

Wanting to emulate or model a successful person with a view to generating your own high achievement is a constructive exercise. Becoming obsessed with what others have and calibrating self-worth based on this negative comparison is a form of social sickness, commonly referred to these days as 'affluenza'.

If you could travel back to the very best societies that existed several hundred years ago, you would discover communities that viewed personal safety, a cosy bed, uncontaminated running water, three meals a day and access to any form of pain relief as absolute luxuries. We've come a long way since those days, but you wouldn't know it sometimes.

While it's easy to belittle envy for all its petty ways, eliminating it from our psyche is easier said than done. Many of us are competitive by nature and probably embarrassed to admit how satisfying it is to be performing better or having more than those around us.

The simple message here is that if you spend too much time looking sideways at what the next person is doing, you run the risk of losing sight of what's important to you. There will always be someone better and always someone worse – so what?! There will be no leaderboard on display at your funeral. When you are confined to your hospital bed during those last few days, it's unlikely that you'll be wanting to look at your investment portfolio account statements or that you'll be quizzing your grieving family about your neighbour's new pergola or his latest car. Envy is ignorance. We all need to be the personal architect of our own destiny and measure our progress in relation to our own potential.

> There will be no leaderboard on display at your funeral.

# WARNING #9

# HEAD WOUNDS

THE LACK OF UNDERSTANDING or clarity around mental illness often makes injuries of the mind difficult to define and even harder to defeat. The debilitating effects of chronic anxiety and depression are well documented and, in the most serious instances, can lead to the contemplation and actuation of suicide. At the very least, they can shrink a life.

Public awareness of mental illness has grown, and you'd be hard-pressed to meet anyone who has not either experienced its effects personally or been witness to them. Thousands of books and a growing – yet still overburdened – mental health system attempt to address these debilitating disorders and their destructive social outgrowth.

What I offer in this section is a combination of foundational perspectives that are communicated by a layperson for the layperson, based on my own personal experiences with family, friends and work colleagues.

The below is intended to be a supportive and practical self-help guide at the very least, or a supplement to whatever additional forms of professional assistance an afflicted individual may be seeking.

⚠

# Stress

Our bodies and our consciousness have evolved over time to experience and manage stress. This is because our early environments in the wild were extremely dangerous. The stress reaction was a necessary adrenal response that kept us alive when our life was under threat – a basic goal being to eat lunch that day rather than being someone else's lunch.

As centuries progressed and evolution continued its forward march, the mechanics of our adrenal system were gradually being refined and polished to suit a more modern and civilised existence. However, despite our adrenal system's maturation, our stress response remained primarily focused on dealing with immediate or short-term threats. While this ability was well-suited to a life where perilous situations were dealt with swiftly – you either escaped or you were eaten – it is less capable of effectively dealing with the long-term ongoing pressures of contemporary life.

Managing stress begins with having a basic understanding of how your nervous system functions. Most people are familiar with the term 'fight or flight', which refers to the mind and body's rumble-or-run response mechanism that is ignited if confronted with palpable danger. This fight-or-flight machinery is a product of the body's sympathetic nervous system. When in this state, the brain automatically alters our body chemistry in order to power up our muscles and fuel our lungs. The body responds to fear by releasing adrenaline and cortisol. This rush of hormones can cause a wide variety of responses, from butterflies in the stomach at one end of the scale to involuntary bowel evacuation at the other (sorry – that's as quaintly as I could put it).

While stress or anxiety can feel uncomfortable, it helps greatly if we can see it as something that is helping us. Stress is the physiological preparation that your body undergoes in moments of distress. You *need* these neurochemicals to be firing at their peak during these times, so embrace the feeling when it arrives; even thank it for showing up when you need it most. View stress as your virtual bodyguard and part of your force field rather than wishing it away when it appears.

The sympathetic nervous system has an opposite – the parasympathetic nervous system – that helps moderate these extreme responses and creates respite during those moments, days or weeks between legitimate crises. The parasympathetic nervous system has been described as 'the fire department of the brain'. It helps the body recover, digest and restore calm. It is the part of our nervous system that helps us regain emotional equilibrium after an episode of acute stress. Effectively, the parasympathetic nervous system pushes the sympathetic nervous system back down when it kicks into gear, and vice versa. It's like a seesaw – when one goes up, the other goes down.

> View stress as your virtual bodyguard and part of your force field.

Problems arise with this system when our minds habitually exaggerate the magnitude of the danger, which results in a disproportionate release of these preparatory hormones. This effectively leaves the sympathetic nervous system turned on as if there were no off switch and causes the individual to feel perpetually anxious. Controlling this on/off switch is more challenging than it sounds, due in no small part to our throwback brain chemistry.

When reflecting on our primitive past, there were two major mistakes that we could make in the wild:

1. We could think there is a predator in the bushes that's going to attack us – but there's nothing actually there.

⚠️

2. We could assume that everything is OK – but there really is a predator in the bushes!

The price you pay for the first mistake is some unnecessary anxiety, but the consequence of the second mistake is a gruesome death.

As a result, Mother Nature has installed an innate warning system that encourages us to make that first mistake a hundred times over to stop us from making that second mistake once. Put even more simply, our minds are very poor at remembering positives and exceptionally good at remembering negatives. This ingrained tendency causes us to overestimate threats and underestimate opportunities.

> Our minds are poor at remembering positives and good at remembering negatives.

A basic starting point for sufferers of chronic stress is to develop a more practical philosophy towards the mechanics of anxiety with a view towards reducing its impact on their day-to-day experiences. While there is no shame in seeking external help from a qualified mental health professional, the greater bulk of an individual's recovery depends on their own internal administration: how they rationalise their thoughts and manage their actions.

How we think about stress dictates how we use it and determines whether or not we receive good or bad feelings from it. It's possible, for instance, that embracing stress might mitigate some of its discomfort. Either way, our goal must be to develop a range of perspectives that can land us on the right side of the anxiety response.

# Perspectives on stress and anxiety

## *Stress is a resistance*

Author Arthur Somers Roche wrote, "Anxiety is a thin stream of fear trickling through the mind. If encouraged, it cuts a channel into which all other thoughts are drained." Stress exists when the mind puts up a resistance to what is actually happening. In other words, the stress is the resistance – not the thing causing the resistance. Stress generally occurs when attention is either dragged into the past to re-examine a negative issue or when it flees into the future to rehearse an imaginary worst-case scenario. It can flow from a state of second-guessing and regret to full-blown catastrophising without stopping in the present for a breath.

## *The nature of the mind*

A Buddhist nun once explained to me that the nature of the mind is clear light and its stains are adventitious. If you're like me, you'll have to look up the meaning of 'adventitious': 'Happening as a result of an external factor or chance rather than by design or inherent nature'. What the nun meant was that the blemishes on a pure mind have been installed by outside events, but they do not become the mind. Too often we view our minds like we observe the ocean where we are too easily preoccupied with waves crashing around the rocks

> The blemishes on a pure mind have been installed by outside events.

and making all the noise (the superficial), rather than the vast body of solid and comparatively calmer water that surrounds it. We are

⚠

not our thoughts, nor should we start a conversation with our negative ones. Again, we must not believe everything we think.

## Something at stake

When stressful feelings arise, accept that there must be something of value to you that is at stake. It's quite likely that any arising stress is your body's way of preparing you to win, defend or survive. Stress doesn't happen to you – it happens inside you. We need to own our stress and embrace the energy of anxiety. In manageable doses, we must view stress as that friend who keeps us on our toes, quickens our mind and sharpens our mental and physical reflexes. Sometimes this means accepting we are wired to be high energy rather than trying to suppress our true nature. Resisting these natural and essentially biological responses is often our biggest problem. Understanding this concept, therefore, is one of the keys to better self-management.

> Stress doesn't happen to you – it happens inside you.

## Anxiety is a bully

Anxiety is a bully and the more you let it shove you around, the pushier it gets. As may be the case when we first encounter a real-life bully, it can be a more comfortable reflex to look away and hope they leave us alone. This may suffice some of the time, but certain people (or thoughts) will continue targeting us. In the end, we need to muster up the courage to confront them. Most bullies are not banking on this.

No doubt, there'll be times when your tough response towards a bully is nothing more than a bluff, but on more occasions than you might imagine, the bluff is enough to keep the bully on the back foot. After all, they're not absolutely certain that you won't follow through. At the same time, you're not 100 per cent sure they won't call your bluff either. Ironically, this often results in a stalemate with neither side outwardly showing fear but both internally feeling too cautious to take the issue any further.

When anxiety bullies us, we cannot cower away – even though we feel like we want to. Step forward, put your shoulders back and confront that thing you fear! In most cases, that thing you fear is not life threatening. Remember, it's more common for us to be frightened than actually hurt, and we can usually handle pain better than we deal with fear.

## Worry

Legitimately painful things can happen to us, so telling ourselves that nothing will go wrong isn't realistic. However, it's quite common that we overestimate the probability of negative things happening when our mind enters a worrisome state. Telling ourselves that things are awful, on the other hand, only dials up the heat of anxiety. Language matters! This is where the acronym FEAR 'Face Everything and Respond' is helpful. You can also replace 'Respond' with 'Recover' or 'Retaliate' – insert the most relevant 'R' for you… as long as it's not 'Run'!

## Attachments

If left unchecked, anxiety can diminish a person's life to almost nothing. The Buddhist philosophy broadly suggests that attachment is the source of all suffering. In their view, if you don't get what you want, you will suffer. Or, if you get what you don't want, then you will also suffer. And lastly, even when you get exactly what you want, you will still suffer because you can't hold on to it forever. This can all sound pretty miserable at first, but the real distinction here is that neither the thing nor the striving itself is the problem. Ultimately, it's the *level of dependency* you have for that thing you are clinging to or don't want. It's the degree of *craving for*, or the *aversion to*, something that creates the neurosis.

## *A peaceful mind*

Ideally, we should aim to be at peace with our minds whether it's filled with positive or negative thoughts in that moment. Either way, it's all just natural mind activity and the most important thing is to avoid mistaking our thoughts for reality. As stated in an earlier chapter, the more we learn to accept that these thoughts sometimes have a mind of their own, then the less we have to worry about changing them. Learning to make the best of our thoughts is a learned skill. In many cases, it is more practical to focus on our behaviour than our thoughts and let the mind 'play' in the background. Positive physical actions and behaviours can serve as a distraction to mind activity and often disrupt any habitual negative patterns present at the time.

What we fear may not happen, and even if it does, we'd most likely find a way to handle it. Unfortunately, anxiety can cause us to overestimate the probability and magnitude of danger and to underestimate our ability to overcome hardship.

⚠️

# HINDRANCES TO INSIGHT
# OR SELF-REFLECTION

Problems cannot be solved at the same level of thinking that created them. Unless we develop greater insight into our own customary thought processes, we will be unable to reflect on the random and uncontrolled views that regularly bubble into our awareness via the subconscious. When addressing this challenge of self-reflection, it is helpful to imagine looking at our own image on the surface of a pond. When the pond is perfectly still and calm, we can see very clearly, and this is obviously our most desirable mental state.

**Desires or cravings** are akin to having dye in the water – the water may be still but it's not pure. This can lead us to see only what we want to see.

**Anger or frustration** makes the water bubble or boil, distorting our reflection.

**Laziness or sloth** is an underlying lack of movement that forms algae on the pond surface, blocking any reflection.

**Restlessness or agitation** creates ripples or waves on the pond surface and warps our self-reflective qualities.

**Doubt** stirs up the mud from the bottom of the pond making the water cloudy. This can manifest procrastination, scepticism or indecision.

⚠️

## *Thinking in degrees*

If we are feeling bad, there's a good chance we are thinking bad. In many cases, thinking errors distort the facts and cause us to make irrational predictions of failure or exaggerate the details of a relatively minor event. An example of this that many parents could relate to would be when you're waiting up for your teenager to come home from a night out. As parents, our minds often wander into the realm of catastrophe, taking a fairly minimal situation and turning it into a horror show. At midnight when they are not yet home, we start to worry and by 1am we are calling all the hospitals. In these instances, we are better served by adopting the thermometer as a model, where we think more in degrees rather than extremes.

> If we are feeling bad, there's a good chance we are thinking bad.

## *Thoughts as theories*

Wherever possible, we should endeavour to treat our negative thoughts as theories to be tested, rather than automatically seeing them as facts. This includes recognising our beliefs and thoughts sit somewhere between the actual event and our emotional response to that event. For example, it's not really your child that made you angry at the supermarket; rather it's your response to their questionable behaviour that caused you to feel embarrassed or annoyed. The meaning we attach to events influences the type of emotions we feel. This is why we need to keep things simple by seeing them for what they are. While we can't be naïve in the face of genuine threats, we should aim to predict positive outcomes and mentally rehearse successful endings (just for a change). Some may view this as wishful thinking, but it minimises the time you spend suffering phantom heartache from imagined outcomes.

## *Let it be*

Barring the death of a loved one or a similarly tragic circumstance, we must otherwise learn to let whatever happens be OK. This requires us to embrace the law of chaos and reorganisation. There are times when resistance is futile as it delays us from addressing the only thing we can affect in that moment – what happens next! As stated in earlier chapters, our internal map of reality is not the actual terrain; it's our impression of the terrain. If what we see is not the same as our mental picture, then our mental picture is wrong. When we learn to let whatever happens be OK, we spend less time lamenting the difference between how we think it should be and how it really is.

## *Feeling concern for others*

Our fear of, or anger towards, another person or group can be greatly diminished by adopting a more compassionate and understanding view of their perspectives. This somewhat undervalued personal quality of feeling concern for others helps to reduce the frustration we can manifest towards them when their opinions don't align with ours. Exercising a sense of loving kindness towards others that bother you rather than exhibiting fear or frustration is indeed a superpower. It's easy to show warm feelings to your loved ones and those who are good to you, whereas the greater test – and in fact the only test of true tolerance and understanding – is to be able to apply it where it would not naturally occur.

⚠

## *Fearing the fear*

There really is such a thing as 'fearing the fear' – it is literally being scared of being scared. If our body knows what it's like to feel the blood boiling and gut-churning grips of anxiety, and it knows who or what the regular triggers are, then we can feel fear at the mere thought of that situation returning. While this can seem like genuine fear at the time, it is akin to the effects of watching a scary movie or being afraid of the dark. Our minds are playing repeats of the scary movie with us in the lead role. In these moments we must recognise that our physical body is not in any danger of being harmed and that the bogey man in this instance is our own imagination.

# Activating the parasympathetic nervous system

Once we embrace the brain's Stone Age bias and natural responses to threats – whether they be real or perceived – the next move is to identify some useful strategies to connect with our parasympathetic nervous system.

Our primary goal is to provide the mind and body with the space to refuel and return to their psychological home base. The best methods for achieving this are a combination of physical practices and philosophical considerations. They start from the premise that the mind is both pliable and in step with the body. Over time, our contemplative exercises allow us to be more aware of the thoughts we dwell on versus those we simply observe and allow to pass by. When anxious feelings begin to dominate, there are a multitude of tools we can utilise.

## Breathing

The most practical and accessible place to start is with our breathing. The parasympathetic nervous system is connected to the act of *exhaling*, while the sympathetic nervous system handles inhaling.

To some extent, this explains why our heartbeat increases when we inhale and slows down when we exhale. Not for the first time in this book, we find ourselves pondering the 'chicken or the egg' scenario. What happens first – do emotions change our breathing or does breathing in certain ways affect our emotions? The answer, of course, is that it can work both ways.

> Our heartbeat increases when we inhale and slows down when we exhale.

If we can learn to mimic the type of breathing we naturally engage in when we are relaxed, then the mind starts to respond in kind by restricting the flow of fight-or-flight hormones and bringing balance back to our nervous system. Exhaling feels more relaxing than breathing in, so we need to place more emphasis on this part of our breath cycle.

As a simple exercise, we can focus on inhaling for a count of three to four, and then double or even triple the count on our exhale. This sounds basic but it is a highly effective strategy and partly explains why it's hard to feel too stressed while you're singing. Conversely, the inability to comfortably blow air out is one of the reasons why asthma is so synonymous with anxious feelings.

## Paper tigers

There are an endless number of triggering external stimuli that can disrupt our brain's peaceful default setting and drive us into a stressful frame of mind. Back in our caveman past, this may have been a charging wildcat, whereas nowadays it is often considerably less threatening like a frown across the dinner table, an aggressive car horn honk, a job interview or an exam.

In the absence of life-threatening worries, our minds often dump an array of petty concerns in this void and inflate them so they take up all the stress 'holding space'. With the value of hindsight and perspective, we often realise that the actual threat level in these instances is very low. We must take root in this enlightened headspace and savour the relative tranquillity it offers. As you practise doing this, you will be priming your memory systems to register these calmer emotions on a more regular basis. This regularity will create new and improved thinking habits which in turn can bring about a change in the brain's wiring.

One of the more stunning discoveries in the field of neuroscience is the brain's ability to create new neural pathways as a result of external events or practices. In these instances, neurons literally begin stitching new patterns of thought together that can upgrade our recurrent thinking patterns. This is akin to replacing a pot-holed and patched-up series of back streets with a brand-new motorway that cuts travel time in half and has a smooth, quiet driving surface. As the brain rewires, it changes its neuro-chemical release habits, thereby helping the mind and body achieve a more relaxed disposition overall.

When reviewing this cycle, we come to understand how conscious actions can restore calm to the mind, which, when practised regularly can reprogram the brain's internal processor... which, subsequently reroutes positive chemicals back into the nervous system... and so the positive cycle continues.

## Be like a zebra

In his book *Why Zebras Don't Get Ulcers*, author Robert Sapolsky highlights how prey animals like zebras experience stress that is mostly 'episodic' rather than 'chronic'. For the zebra, the primary response to danger is flight and it relies on a surge of adrenaline to outrun the stalking predator. The lesson for humans, in observing the zebra, is the zebra's ability to literally shake off their peaking anxiety once they've escaped the chase. The zebra physically shakes the tension out of its body, much like a dog who has just run out of the surf.

While humans are a different species, there is enough of a similarity in the make-up of their nervous systems to draw some useful parallels. We too can experience degrees of relief from stressful situations by moving our bodies and shaking the tension loose that commonly builds in our arms and chest. Walking, running, dancing or jumping can help to disperse the emotional congestion. It also encourages our respiratory system to activate naturally as when we are highly stressed, we tend to breathe in deeply and breathe out incompletely.

## Distractions are gold

Actively diverting attention away from our anxiety triggers can give us periodic respite from the debilitating ruminations associated with acute stress. This can seem like an avoidance behaviour to the purist, however, while it doesn't pretend to tackle the root causes of our anxiety, it does take us on a brief emotional holiday from the intense discomfort. Each time we shift our attention away from the problem, it tends to reset our stress at an incrementally lower level than it was before.

⚠

We cannot remove a negative feeling unless we replace it with something (or someone) else. We cannot just 'think' negative thoughts away. We need to let the body help the mind by walking us out of the stressful environment to see and hear other things – even if only for short bursts. This includes staying actively distracted or busy. As the biblical saying goes, "Idle hands are the devil's workshop!"

When we suffer from anxiety or depression, we may also feel like withdrawing socially, but this is usually our problem-solving mind preferring that we stay alone to think more about the issue. It's as if the mind wants to keep re-examining every facet of the situation to be perfectly prepared for any threats or to keep testing our body's response to the trigger. In a way, it's like a cold sore that we keep agitating to see if it is any better than it was five minutes ago when we last checked.

> We shouldn't wish too hard for the day that all problems will cease.

In short, our mind struggles to accept that sometimes there is no imminent answer or solution to a problem – mainly because it craves control, demands conclusions and has a major aversion to limbo states. At times like these, it is useful to remind ourselves that someday when we are in the ground, we will have absolutely no problems. In fact, we will have nothing of anything. We must accept the highs and lows of life and shouldn't wish too hard for the day that all problems will cease.

The good news is that our primitive brain has developed its social functions over time and relies on the concepts of cooperation, teamwork, community and bonding to feel fulfilled. Exile or solitude mostly work in opposition to recovery from mental illness, just as they are a death sentence for species of prey animals like zebras.

Mixing with other people to talk about things unrelated to your personal issues is an invaluable practice. Don't wait to feel better before being around others – put yourself around others so that you can start to feel better!

# Self-management instructions

Aside from giving attention to these broad philosophical viewpoints, it is also useful during bouts of high anxiety to ramp up our positive self-talk. There is no shortage of self-talk already in play during periods of peak stress, but rarely is it positive or healing. To the best of our ability, we need to take control of that internal conversation by crafting an opposing narrative: one that can deliver a counterpunch to the negative chatter that dominates our mind when suffering from chronic worry.

Once we dissect the reasons for our suffering and author our own personal declaration, it is imperative to recite these directives many times a day. Simply stated, we must hold onto the belief that if negative self-talk can make us feel miserable, then positive self-talk can make us feel good.

Below is a group of simple affirmations I have used during stressful periods in either my professional or personal life. The affirmations provide examples of mature and rational thoughts that serve as self-defence techniques for the mind.

→ Assume the physiology of a confident and strong person. Stand up as tall as you can and put your shoulders back and chest out. Use your body to transform your mood.

→ Don't sit around waiting for more bad news or for the problem to escalate. Assume there's nothing more coming. If you've done all you can for now, look away. If something negative comes back, deal with it then.

→ Worrisome thoughts will try to interrupt your happy pattern from time to time. Your mind will prompt you not to forget about the problem you were recently dwelling on – it doesn't want you to get over it and will keep testing you to see if you still care. Use your positive actions and regular disciplines to interrupt this worry reflex.

→ It's in the nature of things to experience problems from time to time. If you are not in any physical danger, then relax!

→ Even as you edge negative issues out of your mind, there are times when they seem to come back even stronger. It's quite natural for this to happen. Notice the arrival of these thoughts and resume what you were doing. It will be temporary, and you can deal with it. It may be hard to bear, but not unbearable.

→ You don't need to have all the answers to every possible scenario. You are not perfect and that's no problem. In fact, it's a relief.

→ You can't be a leader in a people-oriented business and not have to deal with difficult situations from time to time. Accept that it comes with the territory and separate yourself from the issue. It's not always about you!

→ Your greater goals must be bigger than your challenges. What you want to achieve must maintain priority over any difficulties ahead of you on the path.

→ Your problems are not global emergencies that require hours and hours of constant thought to analyse and unscramble. Sometimes the best thing to do while you're waiting for an outcome to transpire is something else!

→ While anger is not a positive emotion to carry around permanently, it is often superior to feeling fear and can be used in a constructive way to help you face intimidating tasks. Don't suppress the anger when it emerges from a previously fearful place. Let your anger stand over the fear and use this strength to motivate, mobilise and move on.

# Anger

While anger often precipitates a more empowering response to a situation than fear, it is still a mostly destructive energy. One of the major roadblocks to reducing anger is that it gives us a temporary surge of strength and even feels good sometimes – it's certainly preferable to being scared.

While we can be triggered into anger by external events or other people, we can also be guilty of generating anger where it needn't have existed. Even more common is the tendency to exaggerate the magnitude of a situation to justify an inflated response. Perhaps the most accurate label to give this behaviour is 'ranting'. It's hard to deny the short-term buzz that a good old-fashioned tirade can provide, although it's rarely a pleasant experience for those around us.

The real truth is if we compiled a list of all the things that made us angry over the past six months, chances are that 90 per cent or more of them would have a first and last name. Dismantling the things that initiate our angry thoughts is less about correcting other people's behaviour and more about adjusting our own expectations of others.

While conventional wisdom claims that 'it's better out than in', there is a more positive and enduring path that lies beyond the mere act of venting. There is a Buddhist phrase by Lama Zopa Rinpoche that states "No anger inside means no enemy outside." This quote reminds us that anger is an 'inside job' and throws light onto how reactionary we can be towards externalities that we don't agree with.

⚠

The mature philosophical response to this is to acknowledge that the person who is causing you discomfort or harm is probably not in control, and that *they* may be suffering or afflicted in some way. Even if people are throwing anger directly at you, it doesn't mean you have to catch or accept it. You can be a target of bullying, but you don't have to be a victim.

A normal human response to negative triggers is to feel some degree of irritation. This trigger may initially generate a 4/10 feeling (with 10 representing insane rage). At this point, we could characterise such a scenario as a mere 'gas leak', with the most serious consequence being a bad smell. The last thing you would do in the event of a gas leak however is light a flame, which in this case would be represented by the rant. The rant is literally the cheerleader that transforms moderate annoyance (the 4/10) into a full-blown explosion (the 9.9!).

___

Anger is an 'inside job'.

___

Getting to 4 out of 10 in the first place may not always be avoidable but ramping the 4 up to a 9 usually is. Our goal is to short-circuit the ingrained reflex that's responsible for manufacturing the bonus anger by resisting the urge to purge. Chronic anger is destructive; it raises our blood pressure, makes us more irrational and measurably less attractive. Comedian Groucho Marx said, "Speak when you are angry, and you'll make the best speech you'll ever regret." The heightened stress levels that accompany anger also weaken our immune system.

The most sophisticated assessment of anger is that expressing it vigorously is the only option for those who have never learned to decouple their thoughts from their actions. There is a difference between a negative thought and the outward expression of that thought. Not everything we're thinking needs to come out of our mouth.

A negative thought or view coming into our consciousness is akin to new life. If we give it oxygen, then it will grow and begin to drive otherwise positive thoughts to the side. We must therefore aim to catch these thoughts on their way out of our mouths so as not to nourish the anger and negativity.

> Not everything we're thinking needs to come out of our mouth.

Mark Twain said it best: "Anger is an acid that can do more harm to the vessel in which it is stored than to anything on which it is poured."

# PART IV

## —— THE ——
# WAYS
## WE PRACTISE

道

# 道

## 道

*Do*

*– the way, or to embody*

'*DO*' IN JAPANESE TRANSLATES similarly to the English definition of the word 'do', although its scope is broader. 'Do' commonly appears within the name of well-known Japanese martial arts such as judo, aikido or kendo and is meant to represent 'the way' or, more specifically, 'the way of'. When used as a suffix to the word karate as in 'karate-do', it literally means 'way of the empty hand' ('*kara*' is 'empty' and '*te*' is 'hand'). However, when 'do' is used in this context, it implies the art of karate should be viewed as a total way of life that extends well beyond its self-defence applications. Its deeper meaning, therefore, is to symbolise an active pathway where one embodies a set of holistic practices in an authentic and consistent manner.

WAY #1

# THE ART OF PRACTICE (JUST 'DO' IT)

FINDING FULFILMENT IN LIFE is not about finding the way *to* anywhere, but more about observing and practising the *way of*. Even the two most cherished and sought-after emotional states – love and happiness – can be regarded more as practices than feelings. That is if you want them to last!

Guitarist John Mayer wrote a song called 'Love is a Verb', and it's in this vein we should be assessing all of life's most coveted sensations. At school we were taught that a verb is a 'doing word'. In acknowledging the value of 'the way' (do) concept, we should no longer view things like love, happiness, health, confidence or friendship as they'd technically be categorised, which is as nouns (naming words). Instead, the way being proposed here urges us to treat them all as doing words because they demand regular action to maintain their existence and potency.

道

# Where the rubber hits the road!

People are always talking about what they want and what they intend. However, we are not what we think, what we say, how we feel or what others think about us – we are what we do.

When assessing the value of those around us, we must pay less attention to what they promise and focus more on how they behave. When all is said and done, more is said *than* done. It's easier to talk than act, and in the moment, talking can sound just as courageous. But the reality of daily life sorts out the talkers from the doers. An often-quoted axiom from the world of boxing says, "If you cheat on your roadwork in the dark of the morning, you'll get found out under the bright lights."

The disconnection between what people say and what they do should not shock us. They regularly confuse thoughts and intentions for actual change and attach undue significance to promises. According to the Irish proverb, "You will never plough a field if you only turn it over in your mind." Even an old children's song reminded us, "It's not the whistle that pulls the train." In other words, an ounce of practise is worth more than a ton of preaching.

> It's not the whistle that pulls the train.

It is said that knowledge is power, but it is more accurate to believe that knowledge is potential power. From a basic scientific view, 'potential' energy is 'stored' energy. This draws parallels with how we manage the accumulation of knowledge and information: if it is not acted upon then it is simply stored, and like anything that's been stored away, it has limited value in that state. Our goal is to convert our potential energy into kinetic energy – to gain and build more energy through activity or movement.

This concept plays out in all facets of our lives. One of the more fascinating examples of how only a modest value is allocated to knowledge is illustrated in the pricing of many coaching books. Despite the considerable wealth of information that many of them provide, they only sell for around 40 dollars. This scenario also applies to many forms of learning, including our own health. We all understand the advantages of a balanced diet, regular exercise and sufficient rest. The key information pertaining to wellbeing and longevity is not locked away in secret chambers or scribed in code.

Whether we are learning about money, diet, fitness or any other significant condition, the real value remains hidden (or stored) until we start walking the path and engaging in 'the way'. To quote author Jim Rohn, "New life only comes from labour."

If we intend to move up in the world then we need to fully appreciate the difference between 'education' and 'training'. To accentuate the incontrovertible difference between these two, how would you react to the following?

- Your 16-year-old daughter comes home from school and reports that they had a sex *education* class.
- Your 16-year-old daughter comes home from school and reports that they had a sex *training* class.

As a typical father, I'd be terrified by the practical inferences of a 'training class' whereas the 'education class' sounds like nothing more than the sharing and storage of knowledge.

# Practice becomes the goal

Within the martial arts, achieving your black belt is a major accomplishment. The mental and physical challenges a student faces within the dojo over many years to achieve this belt is a character-strengthening exercise. It takes something out of the ordinary to reach this initial summit, but what lies beyond is in many ways more important.

One of the things that characterises the road towards black belt is an intense and ongoing scrutiny of technique: the length of your stance, the shape of your foot when kicking, the straightness of your wrist, the defensive position of your hands or just generally how to maximise the power output of your body. These are all examples of micro-feedback that students have to process and correct if they are to shape up for their *Shodan* (the first black belt rank). With the focus on getting all the little things right and an expectation of continual growth, it's easy to develop the slightly obsessive attitude of constant and never-ending improvement (CANI).

We all know people who have become CANI zealots, and it's likely that many martial arts students and athletes inadvertently develop obsessive tendencies throughout their formative years. No doubt this intense self-focus is more than partly responsible for them being able to mould their bodies around the strenuous techniques demanded of them in their sport. While striving and obsessing about endless improvement can be of value in the initial growth phase of a new discipline, it is likely that the exponential growth in ability that characterises early training flattens out at some point. Perceptible improvement is harder to detect as one progresses beyond the intermediate stage.

Therefore, once the initial goal of black belt has been reached, it is necessary for us to reframe our ideas of progress from that point on. The scale of this adjustment seems to be more relevant for those who start a new discipline later in life. These are the students who have begun to feel the physical effects of age-onset conditions that impede their ability to *constantly improve*.

Quite often when you speak with active sportspeople over the age of 40 and ask how they're going, they mistakenly think you asked them how their injuries are going! This often features personal stories that include phrases like 'bone on bone', 'frozen', 'locked', 'fused' and 'prolapsed', not to mention a whole lot of other words that end in 'osis'! As author Gordon S. Livingston MD said, "The problems of the elderly are frequently serious, but seldom interesting!"

Irrespective of whether you experience an injury, an unwanted break from training or something resulting from the natural process of ageing, there is still an opportunity for you to steer your focus towards the only thing that really matters – training! The practice of training – which formerly may have been viewed as merely a means to an end – must now actually become both the means *and* the end!

The higher you venture into the senior karate grades (or any advanced stage of a sport or activity), the more you need to recalibrate your unit of measurement for progress. Superficially speaking, technical improvements are not as distinct – and progress will be reflected and measured in the smaller refinements that quite often only the experienced practitioner is qualified enough to detect. This lack of conspicuous physical improvement often causes discouragement among the higher grades as they ponder whether or not they have reached their peak and have now begun the inevitable decline that seems synonymous with having another birthday.

While there is nothing wrong with pushing yourself physically to improve beyond a certain level of any activity, it is important to shift thinking from being progress-based to being practice-based. In essence, practice

> Making practice the goal creates an indestructible mindset.

becomes the goal and while you are practising, you are achieving your goal. Growth or improvement is a secondary target that presents visible evidence from time to time, but which we shouldn't overly rely on for our enjoyment of training.

道

Making practice the goal creates an indestructible mindset that is unable to be deterred by the various plateaus and troughs that may otherwise slow us down along the way. This message is really nothing more than observing the deeper meaning of the phrase 'do', as in karate-do! When we learn that 'do' means the 'way of' we realise that in the long run, the spirit of the martial art is in the training and not dependant on always experiencing CANI.

One of the other related discouragements for longstanding black belts (or sportspeople) is the possible loss of reputation. As martial art senior grades, we build up a presence in the dojo and perhaps more widely throughout our club. When we cannot perform at our physical best for whatever reason, it is easy to use this as an excuse not to perform at all. After all, we wouldn't want to look bad and diminish what other people think of us. It is vital here to remember that character is more important than reputation. Character is who you really are, but reputation is merely who other people think you are. It's training and practice that builds character, and in the end it's character that earns more respect over the long term.

> When it comes to energy, it is better to be spent than saved!

As we get older, we should be thankful that we still have energy, flexibility, speed and stamina, no matter what the quantity. Eventually, it will all be taken from us anyway so we need to stop complaining about not being able to do what we once could and start enjoying what we still can do. Don't store your best away because it's not as good as last year's best. When it comes to energy, it is better to be spent than saved!

## The Budo spirit

Adopting the warrior spirit towards your training is far more important than yardsticks and certificates. Having a warrior spirit means doing whatever you can whenever you can with all that you physically have available to use. Many martial artists glamorise the idea of the warrior. Much focus is placed on a warrior's incredible skill, composure and fighting spirit. 'Budo' is ubiquitous within the martial arts and roughly translates as 'the martial way' or 'the way of a warrior'. This is all well and good, but the undeniable reality is that most of us are not currently living in a highly feudal society.

While there is always a risk for anyone in developed countries to experience physical danger inflicted by others, the much higher likelihood is that our spirit and courage will be tested in non-physical and personal ways.

The 'do' in 'budo' is the same as the 'do' in karate-do, judo, kendo and so on. Budo reflects the way of the warrior, the practices, the habits and the decision to place the act of training at the highest priority. The modern warrior accepts that lessons are repeated until they learn them and if we don't learn the simple lessons, then they become gradually harder. This is likely to be a 'two steps forward and one step back' scenario, and this too is part of the way. In fact, it is the regular practice of Budo precepts that makes the warrior, more so than any fleeting symbols of recognition (like belts) bestowed along the journey.

Many people, however, are fearful of being stretched and tested, and gravitate towards a more undemanding life. These individuals may quietly desire growth in their lives but essentially do the same things today that they did the day before without changing. They literally need to find their 'way'!

We can't always control the outcome, but we can always control our activity and the amount of effort we are willing to give. Tennis

道

player Arthur Ashe said, "Success is a journey, not a destination." This is just another way of saying, 'The way is the means and the end – and each measurable end is also part of the way!' Long-lasting fulfilment exists along the path – not at the end of it.

Don't be put off by where you are now if things aren't going well. Do your best to develop a different outlook towards your goals. Happiness comes from engaging in activities that are in themselves worthwhile and which are not necessarily dependent on the achievement of a specific end goal. Sprout where you are planted – and begin now!

# WAY #2

# CODES OF PRACTICE

IN MANY TRADITIONS, BESTOWING faith in specific tenets or codes provides a catalyst for maintaining priorities. The idea of organising one's essential values via a basic doctrine – whether formal or informal – is obviously not a new one. Probably the most well-known of such lists is the Ten Commandments, which were supposedly written with the finger of God on tablets of stone. Whether you believe in the origin of these commandments or not, their enduring veneration only emphasises how valuable a behavioural code can be to people who are seeking an enlightened path and practice throughout their lives.

If you were commissioned with the task of creating a basic set of rules that could be taught to young people as they began their transition into the contemporary adult world, what directives would you include and what would you leave out? Stepping outside the realm of youth, mature and reflective individuals of any age could – and probably should – devote time to organise their own guidelines for optimal living. This idea lies in opposition to a purely spontaneous and potentially less reliable existence, where a lack of preconceived personal objectives could see one's life buffeted about without the solid guidance of a moral or ethical rudder.

At various difficult times throughout my life, I have felt driven to lay down a set of principles that I could rely on to navigate my way out of a cycle of negative thinking that was burdening me. During these times, I identified my greatest weakness was a major loss of perspective – I was making the big things small and the small things big! The key to regaining a more composed view of my circumstances was to create an accessible checklist that organised my thinking and guided my attention back to a better emotional and behavioural balance point. My personalised formula – my 'ten tenets' – acts as a daily meditative baseline theme, the practice of which greatly enhances my positivity, energy levels and interactions with others.

## The Ten Tenets

Remain Calm

Stay Present

Pay Attention

Be Patient

Exercise Boldness

Practise Brevity

Listen More, Speak Less

Be Aware of Posture

Make Sleep a Priority

Rise Above Minor Issues

## 1. Remain Calm

This is a simple request to myself that I adopt an even temperament towards potentially negative situations.

Practising and exhibiting a sense of calm is particularly important when diplomacy is called for to facilitate the resolution of a conflict or disagreement. I've seen many people in management work very hard to improve their communication skills yet fail to remain calm when faced with even the slightest pressure or opposition. In most cases, people cannot access their newly acquired communication tools if their defensive, impatient, intolerant or anxiety-ridden temperament intervenes when they are under duress.

It's easy to be calm when everything's going well, and I'd be the first to encourage a departure from calm if it is a shift towards the high excitement end of the spectrum. The ultimate goal is to be an all-weather player, and the challenge is to stay connected to this state of calm even when your immediate environment becomes strained. If you can maintain this mental stillness under pressure, then you will always retain access to your best thinking and training.

## 2. Stay Present

This is a self-instruction to improve my attention span and concentrate more on what's in front of me. Being able to slow down the mind's perpetual bounce from past to future is a true superpower.

Living in the now is an epic weapon that generates a laser-like focus capable of enhancing almost every part of our lives. When we are in the present moment, we are not thinking about our environment – we are experiencing it. Being fully attentive to the experience of this moment decreases our inner turbulence and prevents us from pointlessly wrestling with circumstances that are beyond our control.

When we allow ourselves to be drawn away from the present moment, we are exercising our memory and imagination. While there's nothing fundamentally destructive about these two functions, repetitive indulgence in either will see our mental focus dominated by the rehashing of past events or the anxious anticipation of future dilemmas – many of which will not occur. The horrors of chronic anxiety and depression are caused by living anywhere but the present. The more we can make each day a series of 'nows', the sooner we can feel truly alive and attentive to everything around us.

In the martial arts, this practice of one-pointed attention is addressed through the concept of Zen. Whether we perform *kata* (meaning 'form', which refers to a pattern of martial arts moves performed alone) or are fighting, we experience a profound respite from the noisy mind. Thoughts do not stop arising during these moments, but we no longer acknowledge them. Their power to distract our attention or deplete our resolve is greatly diminished.

To enhance the frequency and depth of our mindful states, we need to use our bodies to feel the raw uncontaminated reality of the many moments in daily life. By learning to be deeply aware of our physical senses, we can greatly increase the clarity of our mental and emotional experiences. As psychiatrist Fritz Perls said, "Lose your mind and come to your senses."

The past no longer exists and the future has not arrived. The only moment we can tangibly experience – the present moment – is the one we most often seem to avoid. From a spiritual perspective, all moments should be treated as special – at the very least because they are finite but also because they contain the opportunity for powerful insight, heightened instincts and sublime peace.

In observing this tenet, I constantly remind myself to adopt realistic expectations. I have come to accept that my mind will be constantly dragged away from the present moment, and this has helped curtail any frustration or negative judgement I may make about myself on days where – for whatever reason – I feel unalterably scattered.

## 3. Pay Attention

Remaining calm and staying present are important precursors to *paying attention*. This is because developing the skill to live more of your day in the present can profoundly transform both your memory and level of concentration. When you truly experience the totality of the moment via your full range of senses, you will be astounded at the new landscape. There is never 'nothing going on' even in what seems like the most mundane moments.

Unfortunately, what we tend to experience instead is a mind that resembles a TV running all day. This TV alternates from the forefront to the background of our attention, frequently changes channels, and increases and decreases in volume. Occasionally, we are drawn away from the internal TV and give attention to what's taking place in the *actual* world around us. More often than not, however, we are unwittingly dragged back into our fake internal TV world without fully realising we've returned.

If ever I have been driving along a highway so lost in thought that I miss my turnoff or can't remember anything about the last 15 minutes, then I know I have fully experienced the thought salad of random and unfocused attention. The 'pay attention' tenet is therefore a reminder that I have the power to direct and maintain my focus on a fixed point, thereby disrupting the internal background stories and incessant mental chatter that is constantly on hand to prompt distraction.

A great example of this ability to pay close attention to our environment is the experienced tracker. When walking through the bush or a forest, the bushman will notice specific plants, wildlife, foliage, footprints and habitat, and hear sounds that the average person is effectively blind and deaf to. The same scenario applies to an expert chef who can taste each individual ingredient in their dish (or be able to detect if something is missing). Paying attention is a reminder to be mindful in everything we do, at least as much as we possibly can. Like many things, our ability to pay attention is something that can be developed through practice and can, in turn, also generate a greater sense of calm. Consciously developing the depth and length of our attention span will likely result in us becoming a better spouse, parent, coach, communicator and leader.

## 4. Be Patient

One would think that the benefit of exercising patience is pretty self-evident, but it is as much a rarity as it is a virtue. As is the case with many of life's higher values, patience is much easier to talk about than to truly practise. Perhaps the biggest misconception that naturally driven individuals suffer from with this topic is that they equate patience with passivity. However, being patient is sometimes the most positive action to take and is more likely to equip us with the long-haul stamina to make an enduring project succeed.

When studying geometry at school, we are taught that the shortest distance between two points is a straight line. Unfortunately, life has a way of unravelling this theory as it frequently creates detours and road closures that force us to back up and reroute. Each time our progress is stymied, our patience is challenged and our determination to continue towards the target is tested.

The process of *construction* has always been slower and more complicated than that of *destruction*. If we believe in that sudden transformation, the big score or the overnight success, then we are less likely to pursue the harder and less immediately satisfying work of gradually becoming better at something, including becoming better people.

In modern society, most individuals' focus is disappointingly fleeting, with the greatest threat to their sense of achievement being the need for rapid gratification. The short attention span that dominates popular culture rallies against the notion of patience and subsequently takes most people away from its time-tested value.

While it is clearly unnecessary to purposefully wait longer than needed, there are both obvious and significant long-term flaws in an attitude that demands instant fulfilment with little or no tolerance for delays. In contrast to standard mathematical theory, the new cautionary paradigm for contemporary society should be that the longest distance between two points is a shortcut! With very few exceptions, we should also concede that only negative things happen quickly.

The general deterioration of people's patience is visible everywhere. This includes aggression on the roads between drivers, irritated behaviour while waiting in queues, the relatively instant frustration at being put on hold, our intolerance for anything less than turbo-charged internet speeds, and people expecting their texts or calls to be instantly replied to.

The increasing inability of many people to save money throughout their lives is also a product of impatience in most cases. The contemporary mantra among many in the community is 'I want it now!' Why save? Why wait until you've earned it when you can just own it now and pay later? This back-to-front rationale has enabled a generation of instant gratification seekers to rack up an unhealthy level of debt on items that are not prone to capital growth.

Images of quick success and instant wealth are also pervasive on multiple online platforms, with YouTubers and associate marketing spruikers flashing their new Ferrari as evidence of expedient and easily found abundance for seemingly little effort (the crypto world comes to mind).

道

> Skill without patience is like talent without discipline.

While I would be the first to assert that sustainable financial success is achievable for most people in developed economies, any financial coaching strategy which fails to prioritise the concept of patience would be unreliable. Skill without patience is like talent without discipline. Even for those who appear to have achieved an impressive financial position in a short time, it is likely that persistence played a major role in developing the venture to that point. Persistence is the positive outgrowth of patience!

Aside from these financially driven motives, we come to understand that patience is also the ultimate antidote for anger. Many Eastern cultures believe that anger is the most negative and socially destructive emotion because, at its heart, it is usually intended to land on others. As a general rule, we tend to tolerate other people best when we learn how to tolerate ourselves. If you're rarely satisfied with your own results, then you are also likely to be regularly displeased with the efforts of others. Acknowledging this tendency helps us to develop greater compassion and patience towards ourselves and will spawn a more charitable attitude towards those around us.

Patience also reminds us that there is no great advantage to hurrying through life. After all, it will end soon enough and when it's over, it's over! Even if there is an afterlife or such a thing as reincarnation, you can't come back as *you*; be with the people you love *now*; or resume the career you are currently engaged in. Ultimately, the 24 hours that make up the earlier days in our youth are quantifiably identical in duration to the 24 hours we will quietly cherish and beg to slow down later in our lives.

When someone asked me recently what my New Year's resolution was, my answer was "to make this coming year seem longer than the last". Life is short and time is relentless, so every chance I have to consciously slow things down, I take it. Do I still get impatient? Absolutely! But success and happiness are long-game strategies and demand that patience is an invaluable part of my wellbeing practice.

> There is no great advantage to hurrying through life.

## 5. Exercise Boldness

This instruction acts as a counterbalance to my inherent sense of caution. In pure Australian terms, this tenet screams at me to 'have a go': to be game and disregard petty concerns and self-conscious hesitation. Timidity – the opposite number to boldness – is a known deterrent to growth and often leaves us lumbered with disappointment about the things we wish we'd done.

Moreover, this tenet acknowledges that many of life's most memorable experiences float just outside our comfort zone. Boldness is a quality that goads us into the undiscovered space and reminds us in many ways that it's better to regret something we did than something we didn't do! Step into the light – don't back away into the relative safety of the shadows. Try new things, risk failing and enjoy the fact that you aren't afraid of the outcome. It's a liberating feeling.

## 6. Practise Brevity

Comedian George Burns said, "The secret to a good sermon is to have a good beginning and a good ending; and to have the two as close together as possible." I included this instruction on brevity to overcome a biological verbosity that seems to run in my family. As a coach and instructor to others, I discovered the hard way that what I had to say wouldn't be very helpful if it took me too long to say it. People's favourite voice is invariably their own and even your closest friends and family are turning the hourglass upside down when you begin talking. Don't be fooled either by those who do a great job of concealing their boredom with your waffle. Just assume that you have a time limit on their attention and always aim to package your message in the most concise and punchy way possible.

The comprehension and effectiveness of most messages is directly linked to length. Ironically, authoring a short speech on a rich topic can sometimes be more difficult and take longer than writing a longer speech on the same subject. Trimming the fat and getting to the point more efficiently takes preparation and practice, but the time dedicated to developing this skill will be worth it. Practise the 'less is more' strategy and you will see the difference. Wherever possible, we should follow the advice of Franklin D. Roosevelt who encouraged others to "Be sincere, be brief and be seated!"

## 7. Listen More, Speak Less

As a natural flow-on from the previous tenet, this message reminds me not to hog conversations, and that people will be much more inclined to hear what I have to say if I allow them the space to express themselves equally. At the end of the day, people would much rather be listened to than spoken to and keeping an informal track of your personal talk time in conversations will ensure others 'feel the space'.

> People would much rather be listened to than spoken to.

## 8. Be Aware of Posture

Posture is much more than just sitting up straight as it reflects our physical relationship to gravity in both stillness and movement. Posture also affects digestion, breathing and energy levels. While it may not present on the surface as a personality or communicative object of self-improvement, I became aware of just how closely linked my moods and emotions were to my physical posture. On the one obvious hand, I noticed how my body alignment was compromised whenever I was under stress and how it was more upright and symmetrical when I was feeling confident. The greater discovery for me was that this correlation could also work in reverse. Hence, if I deliberately chose to adopt the posture that represented self-confidence, then my nervous system seemed to conjure up the matching emotion. In other words, our bodies associate certain postures with certain emotions. If we uphold a posture of strength and certainty, then we can create an internal change that exudes zest and vitality.

Pretend, for instance, that you are attending a drama school and the teacher asks you to adopt the body language and posture of an extremely confident and energetic character. The resulting mental and emotional change it generates will easily outperform our caffeine intake and should remind us to again be in awe of our nervous system's magic chemical dispensary. Try it the next time you feel lethargic, have an attack of the 'yawns' or even in the early onset of a headache.

## 9. Make Sleep a Priority

I'm aware that this tenet will already be well-tended to for many readers. For way too many years, however, I have treated sleep as nothing more than an annoying necessity. The more work or activities that I could squeeze into the day the better. As a result,

道

I have spent many years battling to stay awake during the day, particularly in the afternoons when Red Bull unfortunately became my life support (I don't enjoy coffee sadly). There are obviously some people who can perpetually survive on very little sleep, but for most of us, sleep is an essential element in the trinity of good health, along with diet and exercise.

The half-groggy feeling that often accompanies insufficient sleep in many ways mirrors the symptoms of being intoxicated – a state not known for its sound judgement. This woozy condition results in an inability to recruit the sections of the brain that would normally be concerned with long-term goals.

As stated in an earlier chapter, this scenario can have significant bearing on even simple daily decisions such as healthy vs unhealthy food choices or sensible vs reckless spending. If we lack vitality, then we are going to find it very difficult to summon either our 'will' power or 'won't' power. Conditions such as stress, cravings and temptations will be emboldened by the inadequately rested brain as it de-couples us from our core values. In this state, the disciplined decision-making mechanisms will be un-plugged from our brain's optimum functionality and will be more inclined to choose the chocolate over the apple, procrastinate or waste time. The simple message here is that you can't do the heavy lifting when you are under-fuelled! If you're not planning for adequate sleep, then you have no intention of performing at your best, either physically or mentally.

My conscious decision at the late age of 46 to start making sleep a priority was born out of the realisation that I was struggling physically and mentally to sustain a high output in my work and training. This more than nullified whatever advantage in yield I thought I was gaining by spending less time in bed.

In any case, I finally succumbed to the idea that a solid and regenerative sleep unlocked all of my talents, quickened my mind, increased my physical vitality and sharpened my reflexes. Lack of sleep literally was my kryptonite!

I also discovered that there were a number of other unexpected positive side effects attached to gaining more sleep. Good sleepers for instance are statistically more likely to eat fewer calories and also have healthier immune systems. They are also less likely to suffer from conditions such as inflammation, depression, weight gain, diabetes and a host of other ailments.

More hours of sleep and doing what I can to make those hours better quality sleep is now part of my plan for increased concentration and productivity. It also facilitates a more effective execution of other tenets on this list such as being more patient, present and attentive.

## 10. Rise Above Minor Issues

This instruction serves as a reminder not to make mountains out of molehills or be drawn into other people's melodramas. It's about distinguishing between imaginary threats and legitimate ones: to metaphorically discern between the *thought* of a tiger attacking me versus *actually* being

> We spend much of our lives in an ongoing threat assessment.

attacked by a tiger. Without realising it, we spend much of our lives, both professional and personal, in an ongoing threat assessment. While we're not faced with mortal danger on a daily basis, we are nonetheless exposed to the machinations of other people's issues and their intersection with our lives. This is where the anxiety can lurk.

This tenet prompts me to regularly ask myself a few important questions:

➢ Am I in any physical danger right now?
➢ Is anyone I care about in any physical danger?
➢ Will this issue still matter in a month's time?

In a sense, this tenet helps me keep a lid on my natural negativity bias by categorising issues into their rightful level of severity. This could be likened to the way in which meteorologists categorise cyclones by virtue of their destructive potential. In any case, it's likely that life will give you your fair share of real problems over time without you exaggerating the less significant ones.

Social media now provides a multiplying effect for this problem as we become more exposed to other people's agitations. The tendency for many to share their open wounds online can draw us in like a tractor beam and before we know it, we are experiencing second-hand anxiety. It is frighteningly easy to be drawn into the scheming and politicking of interpersonal conflicts and this is why we must do whatever's possible to float above them.

In exercising this last tenet, we will find it easier to remain calm, stay present and be patient. It's also worth noting that anxiety is highly contagious and learning how to insulate ourselves from these emotions, while still being helpful to those who are suffering, will undoubtedly increase our value among family, friends and work colleagues.

# WAY #3

# SELF-DEFENCE PRACTICES

AT THE RISK OF sounding like a tagline on a martial arts brochure, I truly believe that everyone should engage in some form of self-defence training if they wish to fortify their own personal force field. This recommendation includes young children to the middle-aged and beyond, both male and female.

There is much contention online over which is the ultimate form of self-defence training. The martial arts and competition fighting industries tend to generate excessive amounts of strutting and posturing about who the head rooster is. This can make it difficult for the average person to decide which form of self-defence to practise.

Despite my obvious bias towards karate, almost all martial arts styles are effective in improving your ability to protect yourself in the event of a physical attack. There are a variety of styles: stand and strike, grapple and choke, some almost exclusively kick, others use an open hand while others use closed fists. If you go back in time far enough, you will see that many of these unarmed combat styles originated from only a few places and were developed in climates of lawlessness. It was not uncommon in the past for top practitioners to travel around to other combat schools to challenge the rival instructor. These were often life-or-death confrontations that took place in times and countries where the culture revered a noble death, and where male pride would prefer dying than surviving a loss.

Thankfully, our current Western way of life has moved on from this feudal mentality and the majority of confrontational activity we experience is confined to sporting contests. While many martial arts purists deride the existence of sports karate, judo, jiu jitsu and some others, they should be thankful that this outlet exists since it provides a more manageable and civilised environment for testing our skills.

Sports and competition aside, the infinitely more important reason every person should learn some form of self-defence is to enhance their ability to deal with confrontations, both physical and emotional. In short, it can give people more practical tools for dealing with fear, whether these be real or imagined experiences.

All of us are born with a need for safety and security. The highly renowned psychologist Abraham Maslow is best known for creating Maslow's Hierarchy of Needs – a theory for identifying and ranking the most important factors contributing to the psychological health of an individual. His model proposes that we cannot be driven or motivated by some of the higher-level desires such as self-esteem, love or self-actualisation until the more fundamental needs have been met. Feeling safe and secure appear at the most basic level within Maslow's model, and few could argue with this viewpoint.

I am of the view that self-esteem begins with self-defence. When someone learns how to protect themselves physically, it creates a positive flow-on effect that strengthens many other non-physical components of their lives. Commonly, the practitioner's bolstered self-confidence sees them walk, talk and generally carry themselves differently, making them less of a target for negative attention. Given what we now know about the psychology of bullying, it also makes them less likely to be the perpetrator of threatening behaviour.

There are countless positive initiatives being implemented in many countries throughout schools and workplaces to curtail all forms of psychological and physical bullying. National and global foundations designed to shed light on domestic violence are also more prevalent now than ever, as are task forces focused on eradicating cyberbullying. While I support any program that draws attention to these social problems, I'm also realistic as to how much impact they can exert by themselves.

At some point, we have to concede that there will still be a tendency for individuals to foster dominance hierarchies within groups or workplaces. Some will instinctively target the timid or threaten and commit acts of physical violence against those who are weaker. It seems there will always be gutless and insecure men who intimidate women, and manipulative and sociopathic women who psychologically torment men. There will be those in positions of authority who become drunk with power and exert it inappropriately towards subordinates. These undesirable human traits are alive and kicking in our genetic make-up. Endeavouring to change such primal and deep-seated negative social behaviours is a worthy pursuit, but it's not a problem that can be fully eradicated by legislation alone.

For this reason and many others, I feel very strongly about each individual taking personal responsibility for their own physical and mental wellbeing by *putting in the time to build their peace of mind.* Don't wait for the world to change and become more civilised

> Don't wait for the world to change and become more civilised.

around you. Don't expect governments to regulate your safety or act as your de facto bodyguard.

In saying this, for most people, being physically attacked by another person is statistically unlikely. Even if you find yourself being targeted by an aggressive person, you still maintain the power to walk away. Regular martial arts training in groups also reminds us that nothing is certain in a fight. An attacker may also be a trained fighter, high on drugs or a complete psychopath. In order to think clearly and retreat from antagonism, it is necessary for our ego to step aside. This may not generate good feelings in the short term, but it is preferable to the outcomes that can result from voluntarily accepting a physical challenge: either the aggressor beats you up or – even worse – you experience the short-term rush of victory before being charged with assault or murder and being separated from your family as you move to a 'new address'.

# Internal strength

Aside from physical threats, what is way more likely to stoke anxiety and challenge our sense of security are the everyday trials that take us well out of our comfort zone, such as a job interview, audition, court appearance, altercation with a crazy neighbour, overbearing boss, aggressive and volatile employee or school bully, or a verbal encounter with a road-rage moron. While there may be an absence of actual physical danger in some of them, our sense of inner security can nonetheless be threatened.

Training in a martial art or some form of self-defence is a vital life skill that's more like learning to swim than just participating in another sport. We learn to swim so that we feel more safe and secure in the water, and we engage in self-defence training so we can feel more safe and secure out of the water. Martial arts training is a highly effective way to enhance coordination, concentration, flexibility, self-control, discipline, courtesy, respect, tolerance and humility. It's also an excellent form of stress relief and is highly regarded by potential employers as a representation of a strong character.

While continual abuse or other forms of psychological intimidation can cause emotional harm, fear of physical danger is mostly our greatest personal anxiety. Effective self-defence training gives us a series of constructive alternatives to freezing with fear. This can help people of all ages transform their day-to-day fears into assertive fighting energy and temporarily suppress feelings of inferiority and weakness. The flow-on effect in their daily lives is invaluable as it frees them from the manacles of shyness, self-doubt and dependence upon others.

To young children who lack confidence, the schoolyard can feel like the jungle, with predators potentially lurking behind every tree. When children feel unequipped to protect or stand up for themselves, the resulting sense of helplessness makes feeling comfortable and learning at school very difficult. Self-defence training forces a practitioner to face hypothetical threat scenarios, essentially helping them to rehearse their responses over and over. While there's nothing quite like the real thing, acting out imaginary attacks builds confidence to respond more capably if or when the time comes. This is why the military engages in so many drills, sometimes using live ammunition, to simulate the real dangers within an operation.

The disciplined and safe training environment of a good martial arts school allows its students to build their coordination slowly and provide a 'failure-friendly' code within the dojo. The self-discipline instilled into the student combined with the practical self-defence drills is what breeds self-confidence.

More than ever, people are spending small fortunes on themselves and their children in a quest to build healthy self-esteem. I can assert from experience that engaging in any effective form of physical self-protection or self-defence training should be central to any personal empowerment strategy. Its greatest value is in its practicality and in how it can positively reprogram an otherwise compromised mind–body relationship.

An ideal accompaniment to learning a form of self-defence is undertaking weight training. Putting in the gym work to build stronger muscles is another way of letting the body strengthen the mind. It is helpful to adopt the mindset that each repetition you do with that dumbbell, on that bench or with that squat is placing another brick into your wall of self-confidence in your force field. For men, the connection between muscle growth and personal safety is an easy one to make. Simply put, if you look bigger and more muscled, then you are statistically less likely to be prey for a predator seeking weak victims. Even without self-defence training, physical strength alone still holds currency in combat. No doubt, a similar scenario would apply for women. Strength, agility, fitness and strong legs give any male attacker a hard time.

Irrespective of the specific art or physical strength-building activity, the real magic is in the practice.

# WAY #4

# SPIRITUAL PRACTICE

BROADLY SPEAKING, SPIRITUALITY REPRESENTS the way in which we seek meaning or purpose within our lives as we pursue a greater connectedness with something bigger than ourselves. For some, this includes a desire to feel a more profound bond with Mother Nature. For others, it is to seek a divine relationship with a deity. Irrespective of the specific pathway chosen, the quest for contentment, inner peace and a deeper sense of harmony with the things and people around us is the common denominator.

> View spirituality as an activity or practice – not as a state of mind.

I have previously been guilty of viewing spirituality as a 'flowery, head in the clouds' type of concept, but I came to realise through practice that it was a profoundly grounding exercise. Perhaps the most important and relevant distinction to make on this topic is to view spirituality as an activity or practice – not as a state of mind.

There's no question that spiritual study can take one into deep waters with a seemingly bottomless well of experiential stages, belief systems and dogmas. Adopting many of the principles I have learned through reading, attending retreats and participating in regular spiritual workshops has provided me with a new solidity and served as an ideal counterweight to an otherwise churning mind that constantly seeks to overperform. Spiritual practices also frequently provide remedy for some of my more destructive personal traits such as being impatient, ultra-competitive, perfection-seeking, overly sensitive and stubborn. While taking time to reflect inwardly can leave us very much alone with our thoughts, it forces us to confront both the workings and weaknesses of our own mind.

From its most practical perspective, spirituality should therefore symbolise the pursuit of peace and purpose that allows us to connect better with others, maintain a more calm and thoughtful approach towards problem-solving, move more into alignment with the natural world and optimise our day-to-day experience.

At the very heart of all spiritual practice is the pursuit of balance.

## Balance

Ancient Greek philosopher Aristotle proposed the theory of the Golden Mean which represented the most desirable middle ground between the extremities of extravagance and frugality, excess and deficiency.

Taking a centrist position these days is too often framed as flaky or limp. For example, it is common for many of life's more dominant issues to be conceptually framed with a polarity that encourages us to position ourselves on one of two distinct sides. Even where a genuine consensus is attempting to be struck on a prominent balance-based issue such as gender equality in the workforce, we are still faced with the debate between equality of outcome vs equality of opportunity.

Balance implies that we position our outlook on life's most pertinent matters well away from the extremities at either end of the judgement scale. It suggests that the most enduringly fulfilling lane is the one that travels towards the middle where the best from both sides is within reach, and where we form opinions about important matters without being influenced by the team, party or individual who proposed them.

One of the most paranoid and indeed short-term concerns about adopting a more balanced outlook is that some people feel it may be too conservative and prevent them from reaching their full potential (maybe they'll never find out what 110 per cent means?). On the contrary, aspiring to achieve outstanding long-term results can exist in harmony with an adherence to a balanced way.

I appreciate this approach may be too measured for the mavericks and freewheelers of the world, and that's OK. Every now and then, one of these single-minded individuals takes off and achieves incredible success in a relatively short time. I have much respect for the courage of those people, and I admire their willingness to lay it all on the line. We must remember, however, that history is written by the victors, and for every one of these success stories there is a large percentage of human wrecks that lost it all along the way. Since failures don't usually publicise their losses, you won't hear much about these cases.

The central theme of balance is to build and sustain a more even-handed foundation around striving, and to exercise a degree of patience that allows the process to bloom over time. Maintaining an acquaintance with spiritual practices while pursuing your career or financial aspirations ensures that your truly important values are also given the attention they need along the way. As such, there's a high likelihood that you'll reach the progressive signposts of success without leaving a trail of personal destruction.

We must all accept that our actions have consequences either instantly or sometime further into the future. Preserving a sense of connection with nature, things and with the people around you provides the balance needed to handle the pressure of making big decisions, taking risks, working long hours and dealing with setbacks.

# Meditation – the indispensable practice

Irrespective of how heartfelt or genuine our intentions are to pursue a more spiritual baseline each day, there needs to be an accompanying structure that supports these ideals. This practice must ignite collaboration within our subconscious mind to allow for spiritual perspectives to become both recurring and instinctive.

The practice of meditation can facilitate many positives and is regarded as an essential custom among highly respected performers in the fields of commerce, entertainment, sports and politics. Unfortunately, it also appears to be greatly misunderstood, which leads many people to deduce that they either don't need it or, more commonly, can't do it. Without pun intended, meditation is indeed a deep subject, but it is not necessary to delve heavily into its ancient origins for it to be of practical use in our fast-paced secular culture.

It is often the rigours of a busy and stressful life that first draws people towards meditation. Sometimes viewed as being like a glorified executive stress ball, the layperson's initial intention in seeking out meditation is to find some way of quietening or slowing down their mind. The only problem is that it often doesn't work.

In fact, many people's initial foray into the practice will invariably result in the mind appearing to get busier.

## *Meditation 101*

There are various ways to meditate and many different traditions that one could follow. My experience has been primarily connected with the Mahayana tradition of Tibetan Buddhism. This is not to imply that one method or tradition is superior to others, but rather to recognise the origin of much of the source material herein.

Believing that virtually all human problems in the world originate from untamed minds, the Buddhist tradition broadly advocates meditation for the purpose of gaining further insight into your mind's habituated trains of thought – particularly where they produce negative emotional outcomes. For Buddhists, relaxation is a by-product of meditation and not the chief purpose. However, this does not stop us from gaining a greater sense of calm by engaging in the practice, particularly in the early stages of our meditative development.

> Meditation is more about tuning in than tuning out.

Meditation starts with paying attention and, as such, is more about tuning in than tuning out. When you give full attention to anything (or to nothing) it becomes a spiritual exercise. The overall practice consists of two simultaneous processes: insight – the recognition and discernment of arising thoughts; and surrender – the letting go of any attachments to these arising thoughts (as opposed to clinging or becoming affixed to them).

It is also important to determine the motivation behind your meditation. Generally speaking, one can either be seeking a greater sense of relaxation, the reduction of stress or they may wish to contemplate an issue or challenge with a quieter and more stilled mind.

## SIMPLE MEDITATION FOUNDATIONS

- Sit in a balanced, stable and comfortable posture with your spine straight and your shoulders relaxed. This can be done sitting cross-legged, on your knees or in a chair. It is also possible to meditate lying down although this can more easily lead to falling asleep.
- Your hands may be clasped gently together in your lap or placed either palms up or palms down on the knees.
- Keep your eyes closed, unless you find fixing your gaze on something visually calming to be more comfortable.
- Place your tongue on the roof of your mouth and keep your lips together. Breathe in and out through your nose.
- To better draw attention to a singular focal point at the start, begin the meditation with three to five deep, long breaths. After that, resume normal breathing.
- Choose a specific object of attention to focus on within yourself. It may be on your breath, a mantra (something you quietly repeat throughout the practice), a visual image (whether it is actual or imagined), internal or external sounds, or body sensations (itching, tingling, heat, pain etc.) As a general rule, it is best to focus on only one of these areas each sitting rather than multiple ones.
- At more advanced levels, attention can move away from your physical senses and be placed on your thoughts: the arrival of the arising thought, the nature of the thought and even the departure of the thought. Beyond this 'observation' level, attention may otherwise be deliberately directed towards a

    specific topic or issue of importance where you are seeking clarity.

- Irrespective of which physical or thought-based area of focus is given attention to, your breathing can always be used as a 'home base': a fixed point to come back to if attention wanders from your primary point of focus.
- You may initially find following a guided meditation soundtrack is the most productive way of beginning your meditation practice. After a while, however, you are likely to favour the silence of sitting without an external narrative as it allows you to more attentively notice your own thoughts and insights as they arise.
- There is no 'ideal' duration. Some say it is for as long as you are interested in sitting, while others suggest defining a particular length of time and using a stopwatch or alarm. The general consensus is to work up towards the 20-minute mark and to sit at least once per day. I stress the words 'work up to' because endeavouring to start your meditation duration at 20 minutes can invariably lead to frustration – and for some, sleep!

I started my formal practice by attending meditation classes once or twice a week for a period of three years. Each class was one hour long and involved a combination of theory and practical with short meditations. For the first six months, I'm pretty sure I fell asleep at the four-to-five-minute mark of every single meditation. Growing ever frustrated by this, I asked one of the monks for some sage advice on why this was happening. As I prepared myself for a dose of philosophical mastery, the monk summoned all of his insight and wisdom and said to me, "You must be very tired!"

Aside from my inherent drowsiness, I discovered that meditating effectively for 20 minutes is something I could gradually condition myself to in much the same way as being able to swim continually for 20 minutes. Start with five minutes, then work your way up. In the end, you will discover that the duration of each sitting is not as important as the regularity. A little bit of something on a regular basis is better than a lot of something practised sporadically. While 'an apple a day keeps the doctor away' may be true, it's not the same as eating no apples from Monday to Saturday and then attempting to gorge seven apples on a Sunday.

## Key meditation insights

### The witness

As we sit with the spine straight and the body relaxed, we notice our natural cycle of breath. As thoughts, emotions and body sensations arise, we assume the role of the witness – a non-judgemental and detached awareness that transcends the normal inner commentary, observing all, allowing it to be as is and clinging to nothing. There need not be anything to fix, as taking time out to observe your passing thoughts is its own reward.

### Placement vs analytical meditation

In many spiritual traditions, there are two primary types of meditation. Placement meditation focuses on bringing your attention to a specific point such as those listed earlier (breathing, sounds, body sensations and thoughts). Its chief purpose is to create what is sometimes referred to as a sense of 'calm abiding', which is generally meant to represent a stable and clear state of mind. The patient and methodical separation from constant mental chatter helps over time to manifest a greater sense of space and quiet in one's daily mind activity. Attaining a quietened sense of stability through placement meditation is a necessary forerunner to effective analytical meditation.

Analytical meditation focuses on a specific theme or topic. It follows the view that all psychological afflictions are born out of confusion, ignorance or attachment. Analytical meditation is training the mind to exercise greater reasoning and logic towards the development of daily thought patterns, reactions and the ability to problem-solve. We can select a topic such as compassion, gratitude, patience or wisdom or, alternatively, the topic could encompass a more specific issue or set of principles. Ultimately, wisdom is the antidote for ignorance, and meditation provides the foundation of stability to foster an enlightened outlook on all things.

Like any physical exercise or discipline, meditation can be a means to an end and an *end* in itself. It therefore should be seen less as a path towards enlightenment and more as the practice of enlightenment.

## Common obstacles

### 'I can't think of... nothing'

This statement reflects a major misunderstanding about meditation's basic premise and is the most commonly used reasoning for not starting or sticking with the practice. Despite our best intentions and our adherence to the ideal meditation methods and techniques, thoughts will continue to arise. Some days they will be busier than others depending on our external circumstances, and we may struggle to concentrate on one area for more than a few seconds at a time. If your mind is relatively 'normal', it relentlessly creates stories that tempt you away from any single point of attention.

One of the most important instructions I received regarding this was not to 'touch the story'. In other words, let it float by like you just walked past a television playing a movie. You don't have to stop walking and become attached to the story or the dialogue of the actors. You can – if you choose – just notice it and move on.

## Impatience

Arising mental distractions are not an obstruction to the practice of meditation – they are a part of the practice. Training your mind to be still is like training a puppy. It takes patience and a recognition of the puppy's natural tendencies to persevere with its restless behaviour.

> Training your mind to be still is like training a puppy.

Do not allow your pursuit of calm and peace to be challenged by your thought machine. Your busy mind is doing what it's been designed to do – imagine, remember and solve problems. Keep bringing the wandering mind back – and do so with patience, compassion and perhaps even a sense of humour. It's not necessary to control your thoughts – nor should they control you.

## Attachment

Meditation allows you to notice the difference between who you really are and who the stories that play out in your mind say you are. The point of the practice is not to try and erase these stories, but to be at peace with them and accept their lack of substance. Thought distractions are part of the meditative process and it's a small victory each time you notice that you've been distracted. In other words, the successful observation of the distraction is progress and an achievement in itself. Most of the time we become part of the story we have created in our minds without realising we have been unknowingly recruited into it.

## Striving

For the sake of maintaining a meditative practice long term, it is important to develop patience and kindness towards yourself during the times your focus drifts away from your breath or your desired focal point. For many men learning meditation, their natural ambition and driven nature serve them well in the early stages but after a while this intense striving becomes more of an impediment. Being OK with whatever shows up rather than having to solve the problem or be constantly improving is the key. We can try to perfect our technique up to a certain point, but after a while it becomes more about *putting practice over progress* than anything else.

Wisdom is developed on a foundation of strong concentration. The still and calm mind creates the necessary space for a deeper sense of contemplation. True wisdom is ultimately reflected in one's decisions and behaviours. Therefore, our more settled mind needs to serve us in the normal course of our daily lives, and not just when we are sitting under a waterfall. It's all very well to meditate like a Buddhist monk or pray like a saint, but what purpose has it ultimately served if we cannot access this inner inspiration while we are in life's difficult situations or extend it towards other people who rely on our good nature?

# WAY #5

# LEADERSHIP
# PRACTICES

*Leadership*
/ ˈlidəʃɪp/ *(say* ˈleeduhship)
−noun

*1. the position, function or guidance of a leader.*
*2. ability to lead.*

WHILE SOME MAY VIEW leadership as being solely related to a formally recognised coaching role or professional position, it includes all forms of constructive influence. Over the last 30 years, I've had to learn the best ways of helping other people navigate the minefield of challenges and setbacks that lay along the path of any worthwhile goal. From a corporate perspective, this included coaching and mentoring others on how to recruit new staff, generate new business, manage teams, maximise profitability, deal with decline, encounter competition and how to be self-driven. As is the case with most sports coaching positions, my role as a karate instructor was about helping students develop the physical and mental skills that equipped them to overcome adversity and remain resolute in the face of negative encounters.

This all sounds very detailed and comprehensive when you itemise the full scope of a professional coaching role, but it's been nothing compared to the leadership demands of raising three daughters. Success in almost any valuable pursuit requires the exertion of a positive or inspiring influence over those around you, whether it's your staff, players, students or children.

Leading others starts with leading ourselves. Having your own house in order is an essential prerequisite to being an effective leader. What you know about your specific coaching field will enhance outcomes to a certain extent, but the degree of followship you enjoy from those under your influence depends on your credibility. Credibility is described as the 'quality or power of being trusted, being convincing and being believed in', and is much easier kept than recovered. Its strength is reliant on a healthy aggregate of the following attributes.

# Integrity

Nothing is as corrosive to a person's credibility as a double standard and there are few human attributes that arouse more contempt than hypocrisy. Speaking and doing must be the same action if we hope to be respected in any leadership capacity. This requires us to adopt unswerving behaviours and values whether we are in the immediate presence of our cohort or not.

In this day and age of social media combined with the proliferation of phone video cameras, we should adopt the view that there is potentially very little in our lives that is truly off the record. If we expect to maintain our integrity as a person worth following, we must then endeavour to live our lives such that we wouldn't be afraid to sell our pet parrot to the town gossip! How you behave in your personal life will most likely have ramifications in your professional life and vice versa. The online scammer cannot be exonerated from participating in deceit and corruption by sending his mother flowers every week.

> Nothing is as corrosive to a person's credibility as a double standard.

It is the same as with parenthood. Children have never been very good at listening to what their parents say, but they never fail to imitate them. Therefore, example is not the main thing in influencing others – it's the only thing. Parents who smoke or drink excessively will always struggle to lecture their children on the dangers of nicotine or alcohol. This is not a judgement on smoking or drinking, but an uncomfortable observation that we are being followed even when we don't realise it.

Ideally, the goal of an honourable leader should be to create an environment where standards are high and fear is low. This culture can be moulded by the way the leader behaves around and communicates with others. Unfortunately, the inverse is also true. Dishonesty or arrogance displayed by a leader will have a cascading effect that can toxify even the most inherently optimistic workplaces. Commitment to honesty, respect for others above and below, and a sense of duty to act in a professional manner is what separates the ethical leader from those who just happen to occupy leadership roles.

道

# Humility

Humility is an easy trait to overlook when discussing leadership because it seems on the surface to act in opposition to some of the more widely accepted expectations of strong leaders such as confidence, strength, decisiveness and an overall healthy ego. But humility does not need to be associated with low self-regard. The humble person can still possess a healthy appreciation for their own strengths and values, provided they also maintain a proper perspective towards their weaknesses. They don't have to advertise their flaws, but more so acknowledge them internally whenever their reflex to judge others emerges.

Some who find themselves in leadership positions seem to forget where they came from and fail to acknowledge the role that both good fortune and other people have had in their rise to their influential position. These folks are hard to love. Australian culture is very good at spotting this delusional arrogance, and the tall poppy syndrome has been a natural creation of a society that frowns upon people with a 'big head'.

But, moreover, the focus of humble individuals is regularly oriented towards others, and they have the propensity to put themselves second when appropriate. They won't view themselves as 'above' others, even when they occupy a position of leadership.

The ability to be confident in one's own skills, yet reflective and accepting of one's own shortcomings, is a balance that prevents the credible leader from being offended by criticism or hiding from uncomfortable questions. None of us enjoy criticism, but the humble leader accepts they can still be wrong even when they are certain they're right. Listening to others who disagree with or criticise us is essential to dismantling the allure of certainty. Leaders who never think (or admit) they are wrong, or who never let people question their decisions or viewpoints, are a danger to organisations and the people around them.

If you try to dam a river unnaturally, then it will burst its banks somewhere else. Whether in a corporate environment, a team or within a family, if we fail as leaders to provide adequate ventilation for ideas and concerns, then they distil into smaller components and spread laterally or downwards.

My mother always reminded me that if you make it too hard for people to tell the truth, then they will lie. This is almost certainly why children habitually lie to their parents. In these cases, they are doing more wrong things than their parents would be willing to accept – and they know it. Teenage daughters hiding their new boyfriend from their dad would be a good example here.

This plays very much into the difference between authority and leadership. With authority, people will do what you say simply because you're in charge, but they will rarely follow your vision or do anything over and above what you have asked. Right or wrong, teenagers don't much like to hear the words 'because I'm your father', and if the only way your child has complied with your wishes is due solely to your position, then they will be more likely to lie and scheme behind your back in future scenarios. Leadership, on the other hand, fosters a desire to follow that is motivated by respect and a sense of feeling valued by the leader. People follow because they want to, not because they have to.

Parents are always shocked when they discover their child has been routinely lying to them (if they ever find out), but the roots of this deception are often caused by the parent routinely portraying an outward objection to objections! If the innocent but contrary views of your teenage child, your staff or your players are viewed with a habitual resistance, then they will soon label you as unapproachable and begin to air their frustrations elsewhere, or just do something you don't like without telling you.

It's a wise practice to never speak to other adults in a way that implies they are inferior to you. This simple rule lies at the heart of humble expression and will draw more respect from those in subordinate roles.

# Charisma

Personal charisma is a composite of sophisticated emotional and social qualities that allows individuals to influence others at a deep psychological level. Charisma is the ability to draw people towards you.

> Charismatic leaders are dealers in hope.

Charismatic leaders are dealers in hope and tend to express their feelings in a very spontaneous and genuine way. This allows them to positively affect the emotions and moods of others. They are also excellent in reading these moods which helps them to form a greater emotional connection with the people in their care.

Truly charismatic individuals also have the ability to control and regulate their emotional displays. They don't often fly off the handle so those around them will feel more comfortable and be less likely to exhibit any ill-tempered behaviour themselves. Furthermore, charismatic leaders are excellent emotional actors, who can turn on the charm when called for.

There is also high charismatic value in being an excellent conversationist. Knowing how to talk a little bit about a lot is an undervalued quality. It can help the people you speak to feel comfortable very quickly. An invaluable feature of this quality is tact, which is the charismatic leader's inbuilt sensitivity radar.

Anytime a leader is called upon to discuss delicate information, or even to discuss relatively benign information with sensitive people, there will be a need to exercise this subtlety. If, for instance, someone under your guidance is in a dour or sulky mood, you could say, "What's wrong with you?" or, put another way, "Is everything OK?" You could also say, "You've been grumpy-looking around the office lately. What's the matter?" or "You don't seem like your normal self of late. Can I ask if it's work-related?" These examples ask the same thing in different ways. One of each pair draws the subject open and there'll be appreciation for the leader's caring, while the other is likely to evoke a defensive response and heighten irritation. In fact, if you're in a leadership position and you routinely enquire about concerns in an insensitive manner, then chances are that you are part of the original problem.

It's a much easier task to make others feel comfortable in a relationship when there is no need to ask for more effort, commitment, staying power, better results and so on. Whenever we feel the discomfort of having to deliver critical feedback or ask for results or behaviour to improve, it is important to remind ourselves that leadership is not a popularity contest.

> Leadership is not a popularity contest.

Charismatic leaders must accept their responsibility to be truthful and to act in the best interests of their subordinates wherever possible. The charismatic leader finds an easier passage through these somewhat difficult conversations via their skilful and disarming delivery and the enhanced rapport they share with those they lead.

# 道

# Connectivity

Many leadership roles involve the bringing together of groups with the intention of creating a collective force that is greater than the sum of the individuals in it. Teamwork has become a highly clichéd term in management and coaching culture, but this should not detract from its fundamental value. The bonds that fasten a team together rarely evolve naturally; they are planted, watered and fed by an effective leader. Positive team spirit is developed more as a result of good practices than from just repeatedly proclaiming that 'we all need to work together'.

> The bonds that fasten a team together rarely evolve naturally.

One of the more banal phrases thrown around in management coaching circles is: "There is no 'I' in team." Maybe not, but there are two in 'team spirit', two in the word 'motivation', three in the word 'responsibility', one in the word 'commit' and a big one in the middle of the word 'win'! The 'no I in team' phrase attempts to highlight that the individual's needs should never be elevated over those of the collective, but it deeply disregards the average person's need to be noticed, feel significant and receive recognition. The uncomfortable truth is that it's very unlikely for an individual to place the priorities of others ahead of their own. We all see the world from the inside out to some extent, and people rarely vote against their own financial or emotional self-interest. Failure to acknowledge this within a group rarely yields maximum output.

In many cases, therefore, the acronym of TEAM, which stands for 'Together Everyone Achieves More' could be more accurately expressed as 'Today Everyone Appreciate Me!' This egocentric model implies that the average individual's desire to contribute to the greater group and its shared objectives is dependent on what's personally in it for them. This isn't to say that there are no truly selfless people out there, but the effective leader always operates under the assumption that each individual team member needs to feel personally valued, significant and recognised. Even the most altruistic team member enjoys personal feedback which means there is no downside in making this your default leadership setting.

The positive irony in this methodology is that if each individual has been primed with an important task and is being held to account for their achievement, then the inevitable success of the whole team will naturally create the sense of 'team spirit' that was being sought in the first place.

Perhaps a more productive approach to adopt when attempting to obtain optimum yield from a group is to never deny a person their personal ambitions, but try instead to align their goals with the team's objective. In other words, find a way to insert each individual's aspirations and desire for personal recognition into the greater organisational cause.

In the same way that individual performance can be enhanced by embodying a personal code of practice, team bonds can also be strengthened by the presence of common protocols. These group rules create a sense of motivation and pride among the team driving it forward beyond its aggregate capabilities. While some of these rules can come precariously close to being hackneyed expressions, they nonetheless fuse the players together by activating the dual elements of responsibility and accountability. This urges each player to carry their own weight for the good of the collective while still providing individual praise for outstanding contribution.

The following page outlines the team success code we have always adopted within our karate organisation:

道

## TEAM SUCCESS CODE

1. Professionalism is our brand.
2. We take full responsibility for our current position and our future direction. If the buck doesn't stop with us, then the buck doesn't stay with us.
3. We will apply a 'do whatever it takes' work ethic and adopt the MASH principle – Make Awesome Stuff Happen.
4. We will display the same level of professional courtesy and respect towards our workplace team members as we would show towards another student in the dojo. Our martial arts ethos will provide a valuable overlay onto our professional team environment.
5. We will value each team member's contribution and be generous with recognition where warranted. The firefighter holding the ladder is just as important as the firefighter holding the hose.
6. We will turn 'mindset' into 'skillset' by being action-takers.
7. We will demand a high level of self-discipline from ourselves and remember that the pain of discipline is nothing compared to the pain of regret.
8. We will lead by example – not by position or proclamation.
9. We will remain teachable at all times, both inside and outside the dojo. In doing so, we acknowledge that our professional success will only grow to our level of personal development.
10. We will use our detractors as fuel and remember that the opinion of the majority is not the measure of what is right.

A team code is only a team code if everyone follows it. It requires all of us to construct and preserve the agreed tenets, and there needs to be a sense of solidarity among the senior members of the group to ensure that a positive and encouraging environment is upheld. The code is everybody's responsibility.

In addition to fashioning a collective attitude protocol within our working environment, we also implemented a short list of ethical behaviours for our students and instructors known as a *Dojo Kun* (training hall rules). Every new member received this document, and it was later printed onto the back of membership cards and on the walls of our full-time centres to keep it front and centre in our minds. It even succeeded in improving the behaviour of some parents which was an unintended benefit.

義

Pursue the
highest
standards
of personal
character

修

Cultivate
a spirit
of effort
and
perseverance

礼

Exercise
courtesy
and respect
towards
others

制

Refrain
from
reckless or
violent
behaviour

誠

Be honest
and
sincere in
everything
you do

These five tenets create the appropriate mental framework within which to teach people physical techniques that could cause harm to others if used irresponsibly. They also ensure the dojo is a comfortable learning environment for all. Alongside the dojo environment are the greater expectations that students carry these attitudes into their daily school, work, social and family lives.

You don't need to be a martial artist to adopt these principles. In fact, they should resonate strongly in all homes, school environments and workplaces.

## Selectivity

Cultivating a positive team environment is made easier by firstly selecting suitable people. Searching for the right person is much easier than trying to convert the wrong person. To quote a memorable scene from the film *Chariots of Fire*, "You can't put in what God left out!" In other words, you can only light a fire in someone if there is at least a pilot light there to begin with.

This, of course, can only apply where you are able to have some say in the selection of the people you lead. Even where you don't have complete control, there will be some who stand out as being more trustworthy, sensible, positive or capable than the rest. The best leaders are able to identify these individuals and subtly form closer bonds with them as a means to establishing a more effective influence over the whole team.

One of the easiest ways of identifying the key people is to ascertain what their place in the group means to them. If they are indifferent about their job, the outcomes of the committee or the performance of the team, it is difficult to exert any significant influence over them. If they have no inherent concern about not having that position, then their level of buy-in to the overall goals of the group will always be on the flaccid side. Ideally, we should never allow someone to be our priority while we are just their current option!

We will rarely be able to affect each of our subordinates equally. Some of them will be influenced more by what their peers are doing than what their leader is preaching. In their eyes: "Of course the boss can do it – they're the manager!" In these instances, the lower performing members of the group or team will only start to lift their game *after* seeing someone on their level begin to excel. This is not something that the leader should resist, but rather accept it as a standard phenomenon within groups and set about selecting the best potential within the group to cultivate, fertilise and maximise. As the old saying goes, "The rising tide lifts all ships."

Where a leader has dominion over the choice of personnel they lead, then finding and selecting the right people is paramount. Competence and diligence are not necessarily aligned with intelligence. Aside from highly technical or strategic positions, most employers will opt for a reliable, teachable and professional individual over someone with a high IQ. This should be comforting to any employees reading this since competence and diligence are within their control, unlike intelligence which is essentially innate.

# The practice of good relationships

Even if we have meticulously followed the necessary steps to select the best available employees, team members, spouse or friends (and especially if we haven't), the ongoing success and longevity of this productive alliance becomes more about management than anything else. The peak state that accompanies the beginning of any positive arrangement will diminish and it will be left to the habitual behaviours of each party towards one another to keep the environment productive over time. The incredible expansion of the human resources field over the past 30 years or so highlights the importance that corporations of all sizes are placing on selecting the best people and maintaining a cohesive team environment for their employees.

One of the main reasons why many smaller businesses fail within the first few years of operation is that the otherwise technically proficient employer – whether the business is trade- or technology-based – was unable to navigate the task of hiring and retaining good staff. Many business owners are unprepared for the personnel challenges that accompany even a small workforce, and often conclude after a time that life would be easier if they went back to either being an employee or a sole trader.

> Relational leaders pay attention to little things that others think are unimportant.

This is why a more relational leader can thrive where others stumble. Relational leaders pay attention to little things that others think are unimportant. A great example is the emphasis they place on something as fundamental as good manners – a concept which appears to be in global decline. Prioritising good manners within leadership communication acknowledges that the method of delivery is as important as the subject being delivered. Good manners are also knowing when to mind your own business and accepting that other people are allowed to have different views.

Large workplaces, teams and friendship circles are mere microcosms of the wider community of which they are a part. Our goal, as effective leaders, is to promote mutual tolerance and respect among a group by first demonstrating it ourselves. Ralph Waldo Emerson once said, "We must be as courteous to a man as we are to a picture, which we are willing to give the advantage of a good light." At the heart of this sentence lay the ideals of tolerance, patience, diplomacy and compromise.

Sometimes it's important to prove you are right and sometimes it isn't. Acknowledging the importance of compromise in relationships forces us to ask ourselves if we would rather be right or happy, given these two things may not always be attainable together. The old proverb "Better to lose the saddle than the horse" reminds us to be long-game thinkers when it comes to dealing with conflict and maintaining a solid working or personal relationship with others. Keeping all parties emotionally engaged and valued is key. If you fail to recognise their efforts or respect their views, then they will surely begin to disconnect. This puts the leader in a compromised position, given that all relationships are under the control of the person who cares the least.

# WAY #6

# TARGET PRACTICE

*"A good archer is known not by his arrows but by his aim."*

—Thomas Fuller

AS DISCUSSED IN AN earlier chapter, establishing a clear motive at the start of any project is paramount to its ultimate achievement as it defines the direction and lays out a broad trajectory. The ability to visualise outcomes well beyond our current experiences requires a healthy imagination and a recognition that we are not limited to our existing level of knowledge or resources. Ultimately, however, while it's motive that conceives the target, it's the execution of an accompanying plan that gives birth to the desired outcome.

Top performers in life decide what they want to achieve, and then figure out how they are going to achieve it. This includes who they need to work with, what they need to learn and how they're going to measure it.

The greatest benefit of having a specific and empowering target is its ability to recruit our emotions. Without emotional engagement, an individual may not persevere through repetitive tasks or engage in activities that hold no special appeal. In essence, many of life's regular activities could seem mundane when we only focus on the actual task itself. We all understand this conceptually, but appreciating the concept is not enough. Unless it is practised it is pointless.

Visualising an exciting future can spawn an everyday optimism which makes each working day, step or activity seem part of something greater that we value emotionally – as opposed to believing we only work to pay the bills. Without a future target in mind, it's too easy to get stuck in head-down, bum-up mode and fail to experience any emotional reward or recruit any emotional fuel from the duty at hand.

These days, everybody likes to talk about their 'journey', and the quote "Success is a journey, not a destination" is sometimes brandished to excuse the absence of a solid target. But within each journey, there is still an inherent call for meaning and for small wins that signify progress. These targets help us arrive at a point where, as philosopher Horace Kallen puts it, *"The going is the goal."* In the end, it is the subconscious mind that generates the drive towards a target and it is our responsibility to make sure it is aiming straight.

However, the existence of an inspiring goal by itself does not separate the achievers from the non-achievers. Once the target has been set and an emotional attachment connected to its successful outcome, we must then go to work on our methods.

It is broadly accepted that there are three basic components to setting a solid and meaningful target:

1. The end result (outcome).
2. The behaviours or activities required to move towards the end result (process).
3. The performance criteria (benchmarks).

While appearing distinct from each other, these components are connected and lack effectiveness without synergy.

# The target

It may seem counterintuitive to start at the end, but this is the place to begin and build backwards from there. An end goal needs to be easily identifiable, unambiguous and set without too much preoccupation about how it will be achieved. It's important to note that setting the end target is only one part of the equation as goals are always at risk of being affected along the way by outside factors such as competition, health setbacks or unexpected financial challenges. Because of this, final outcomes are the part of the process we have the least control over, which demands we have a superior level of patience and flexibility in our quest to achieve them.

# Required action

The activities required to achieve our targets become a series of process goals or mini targets. As a bigger goal is broken down into its components, we set smaller goals that keep us focused on one key thing at a time. The sum total of achieving these smaller progressive tasks is the key to the ultimate success of your greater project.

An excellent example of this was expressed in an interview several years ago by an Olympic swimmer. He was asked if breaking the world record was foremost on his mind when he stood up on the blocks just before the starting gun. He explained that not only was this *not* his main thought at that particular moment, but it was not anywhere in his mind at the time. He revealed that all he thought about when he was on the blocks was executing a technically sound dive. After that, he was focused on settling into a good rhythm and following his race plan.

In essence, he was saying that he trusts in his preparation and the technique-based processes he and his coach planned to employ throughout the race because he knows this will maximise his chances of winning and breaking a record. Adopting this approach is no less important for the average person trying to achieve even the most basic of outcomes. Author James Clear describes in his bestselling book *Atomic Habits*, "You do not rise to the level of your goals. You fall to the level of your systems." This observation acknowledges that the vast majority of reasons why we achieve goals are practical ones.

> The vast majority of reasons why we achieve goals are practical ones.

## Progress targets

Progress or performance targets are benchmarks or predetermined standards we intend to achieve along the way towards our final outcome goal. To use the example of the Olympic swimmer again – an 800m race that involves 16 laps of the pool will see the swimmer and their coach break the race into 16 individual split times.

Both the swimmer and coach will have established what sort of split times are necessary to win the race or break an existing record. These progress times provide valuable feedback to the swimmer during their training, and signal whether or not the current methods, strategies and techniques are positioning them in alignment with the desired outcome.

# HOW TO MASTER TARGET PRACTICE

Irrespective of whether we are focusing on progress targets, process requirements or the end result, it's helpful to consider the MASTER strategy.

The goal must be:

**M**easurable
**A**chievable
**S**pecific
**T**imelined
**E**xciting
**R**enewable

As I write this chapter, it is 29 December. In three days there will be literally millions of people worldwide who assert to themselves and others something like, "This year I'm going to lose weight and get fit!" This statement of intent is a nice start, but by itself lacks the ingredients needed to change the outcome in any meaningful or permanent way. If we applied the MASTER principles towards this intention, however, then it could read something like this:

- The Outcome Goal – between 6 January and 5 July, I will lose 15kg by dropping from 90kg to 75kg (goal is measurable, specific and timelined).
- The Process Goals – from 6 January onwards:
  - attend three gym classes per week (Monday, Wednesday, Saturday)
  - drink at least 1.5 litres of water each day
  - walk in the morning for 30 minutes on non-gym days
  - only have alcohol one day per week

- create a diet plan here (one you can stick with is the best one)
  - go to bed at 9.30pm (to avoid late-night hunger)
  - in other words, *get specific!*

- The Performance Goal – this can be measured in different ways:
  - 26-week plan
  - start weight: 90kg. End goal: 75kg (achievable when broken down into segments)

- Performance Breakdown:
  - lose 3kg in the first two weeks, then lose 2kg every four-week block for 24 weeks thereafter (six blocks in total)
  - 3kg + (6 x 2kg) = 15kg less by 5 July
  - reset goal at each signpost point if progress targets fall behind (renewable)

- Reward:
  - A two-week holiday in Bali at a five-star resort (exciting)

Note: This example is for illustration purposes only, but its structure can be replicated with equal effect towards a weight-gain program, a skin-care regime, breaking a long-term bad habit, learning a musical instrument and so on.

# Mechanics over magic

The absence of one or more of the components making up the MASTER list can render us inert when it comes to developing the necessary forward drive towards a target. Even something as simple as writing down your goals is a step out of the comfort zone for many people. Seeing things in your mind's eye rarely puts the wheels in motion as well as seeing it for real on paper or a screen. It is commonly held that if putting pen to paper is too much trouble for you, then achieving the corresponding end goal is well out of reach.

There have been attempts over the years to portray the creation of goal folders or colourful vision boards as some sort of 'magical gateway' towards achieving ambitions. Theories espousing the intervention of metaphysics into the goal-setting process aim to convince us that a mystical power may combine with our thought vibrations to miraculously produce the desired outcome. While I'd like to think that the universe is on my side and will chip in occasionally to help little old me achieve my career, income, wealth, health or relationship goals, it is nonetheless incumbent on me to pull my weight and follow the practical steps that have been laid out to achieve my goal.

If you have a strong desire to one day buy your dream house, then there's nothing innately wrong with mapping out your desired inclusions or even displaying bright and colourful images of this idyllic residence on a prominent wall in your house or office. Marching to the beat of a distant drum is a powerful lure and can help conjure up the adrenaline to push on when the chips are down.

However, once this stirring image has been formed, emotionalised and internalised, then our focus must switch towards executing the habits and behaviours required to move us towards the target. Essentially, we cease fixating on the outcome and give our full attention to following the process we have set, periodically measuring our progress.

In the same way that the swimmer was primarily focused on his dive and technique, we must also focus on the activities, techniques and habits that propel us towards our desired end result. This highlights the difference between plans and goals.

If there does happen to be some other esoteric form of magnetism dragging us towards our targets, then I choose to assume that – at best – it will meet me at the halfway line. In other words, when I run towards it, it will run towards me. If I sit still, it will mimic my lack of movement. I believe this to be the closest thing to divine intervention there is when it comes to the achievement of any major life goal.

# Fear – an uncomfortable ally

While fear is often attributed to many of life's underachievements, it can also be manipulated in certain situations to contribute positively towards achieving a goal. This involves using both our rational mind and our imagination to invent a plausible sense of loss or pain in the event that our goal is not achieved. 'How will you feel when you achieve your goal?' is an obvious question used to stoke emotions and create excitement around the project. However, 'What will be the cost of *not* achieving this goal?' is more than an equal proposition. We will mostly do more to avoid pain and anguish than we will to attract pleasure or victory. In most cases, we hate to lose more than we love to win.

> In most cases, we hate to lose more than we love to win.

Rather than trying to reverse this biological leaning, we could use it for what it is and keep the negative consequences of not achieving the goal in the picture. For many boxers, their dominant dream in the lead-up to their next fight is that they lose or get knocked out. It's often the fear of losing that drives them to train like demons while they are away from the spotlight, more so than the thrill of pending victory. There is an obvious parallel here for us irrespective of the goals we set.

## Review and renew

Adopting a resilient mindset towards the pursuit of any significant goal will equip you with the most constructive attitude towards setbacks. It's highly likely that outside elements (or internal weaknesses) will occasionally knock you off course or cause you to stray from your plans. For many people, these cracks in their plans soon turn into irreversible structural damage, and they are too quick to tap out of their assignment.

In most cases, the timeline can be reset and the target can remain intact. Stick to the game plan is the message here, and only adjust the process goals if there is clear evidence that the plan is not working.

Whenever we find motivation towards a goal waning, it should be viewed as a subtle siren urging us to revisit both the excitement of achieving the goal and the revulsion felt if not met.

## Celebrate your wins

In the same way that we create incentives (bribes) for our children to steer them towards good decisions, such as 'If you eat your vegetables, you can have ice-cream', we should endeavour to design proportional rewards for ourselves as recognition of a goal's achievement. This doesn't just apply to the end result goal, but also to providing positive reinforcement to the progress goals as an acknowledgement of our adherence to the required tasks.

To again use the weight-loss example, a small reward could be introduced on a regular basis for successfully sticking to the

> You don't have to win every minute of the game to be victorious.

game plan: 'If I successfully follow the desired behaviours for two weeks then I will book myself in for a massage or go see a movie', or something similar. In other words, don't make earning a reward solely contingent on the achievement of the final outcome. To optimise the chances of accomplishing major goals, high achievers construct an environment that mimics a game or a competition. This not only cultivates at least some sense of fun into the exercise, but it also provides a subtle reminder that you don't have to win every minute of the game to be victorious at the end.

## Make friends with the process

Assuming the goal has been sensibly set, then failure to achieve that goal is rarely the fault of the goal. In many cases, those who achieve and those who don't achieve both desire the same outcome. Desire is not their point of difference. This realisation draws attention to the fact that the magic is in the work – how seriously and consistently we implement the necessary activities is what incrementally builds our anticipated outcome.

Giving our full attention to the development of good habits – as opposed to just ruminating on the end result – is likely to hard-wire us for future success. We form our habits, and then our habits form us.

# The verb

There's a good reason why the topic of goal achievement appears in this section of the book. While defining motive as a 'weapon' in our arsenal and acknowledging that embracing the goal-setting concept reflects a greater wisdom, actually achieving goals is all about practising good habits and constructive behaviours. Target practice is indeed a practice, and it's in the doing of these worthwhile and relevant activities that manifests the sense of fulfilment we seek. When we pay more attention to the practice, we become less dependent on the end result for our contentment.

'When I achieve my goal, I'll be happy' is not a sustainable position to take because it resists experiencing any joy or encouragement until the very end – assuming that the end works out exactly as planned. However, when you focus on the continuing practice and develop an affection for the process, then you'll be able to experience happiness along the way.

> *"Though no one can go back and make a brand-new start, anyone can start from now and make a brand-new ending."*
>
> —Carl Bard

# WAY #7

# CLOSING PRACTICES

WITHIN THE PROFESSION OF selling, the term 'closing' refers to the final part of the process where the salesperson aims to draw their presentation or proposition to a conclusion, with a view to evoking action from the customer. Ultimately, it's about arriving at a decision one way or another. Old-school sales training (pre-digital marketing era) enforced the notion that any decision was better than indecision. In other words, even 'no' was better than 'I don't know'.

On the surface, this may seem like flawed thinking. After all, isn't it better to leave the prospect still considering your offer than to have reached a definite decision not to proceed? Not necessarily, as it turns out. The reason for this is that giving people the opportunity to think about it almost always statistically results in the prospect not proceeding anyway. The theory here is that the prospect's desire or motivation to make a decision to buy, join or start is never going to be greater than it is while the sales consultant is there in front of them. In most cases, the urge is likely to diminish exponentially by the day, or even by the hour, after the salesperson's pitch.

With this in mind, the salesperson's primary objective is to prompt action at the end of their presentation while they are there with the prospect. Many customers are ready to buy at this point but instinctively baulk due to one or more of the following reasons:

- the reflexive need to 'think' more about the decision
- fear of making a decision – specifically of making the wrong decision
- fear of change
- lack of trust in their own ability to follow through and use the product or service.

Anyone who has worked in a person-to-person selling environment will tell you that there's a vast difference between somebody interested in buying, someone intending to buy and someone who actually buys something. All the signing of forms, making of promises or positive posturing from the prospect can give the novice salesperson a false sense of security that a decision has been made. In the final analysis, however, no real decision is made until there's a significant and tangible commitment. In the case of business transactions, this commitment equates to money being put down – the payment made. Even those who have never ventured into the field of sales know the difference between intention and execution.

One of the most common training tips put forward by many of the best sales trainers is: 'At the end of every presentation, a sale is always made'. Either the salesperson 'sells' the product or service to the prospect, or the prospect 'sells' the salesperson (and themselves) on why they can't buy or make a decision

If the salesperson genuinely feels that the prospect wants the product or service and would benefit from it, then they will do their best to help them 'off the fence'. 'Closing' is the mechanism used by the salesperson to combat indecision or irrational procrastination from the prospect, and it's something you do *for* people – not *to* them. Procrastination is a silent killer, that could be best described as the thing you do just before you're about to do nothing!

> Procrastination is the thing you do just before you're about to do nothing!

This section is not specifically about the selling profession, however. The greater aim is to explore the dynamics that exist between the salesperson and prospect and draw parallels between this and the duelling voices inside our own minds. Whenever we contemplate the start of something new, there is usually a motivating voice triggering the emotion and driving the change – our internal salesperson. Often, there is also a judicious and partly opposing voice attempting to exercise caution – the inner customer or prospect.

While there is always a good argument for considering important decisions, many people use this rationale as an alibi for not making any new decisions at all. The term 'analysis paralysis' accurately describes the overthinking that prompts an all-too-familiar stall reflex for many people. As such, we need to become 'closers' with ourselves. We should learn to strike when our own iron is hot and recognise that starting and not finishing is better than not starting at all. Doing something is better than thinking about doing something. The greater wisdom that comes from this approach is that the more decisions we make and the more we initiate immediate action, the better we become at making decisions overall.

We should also acknowledge that we are very capable of talking ourselves in and out of any new initiative. This includes sometimes being unable to choose between two good options for fear of not picking the best one.

道

Closers are always prompting something to happen. They don't just seek to provoke thought and are not overly burdened by the fear of making the wrong decision. In many contexts, they'll view 'staying the same' as a bad outcome and will appreciate that developing starting power is a pretext to staying power.

We don't have to be strong to get started – but we do have to start to become stronger! When you come up with a good idea, start it! When you're contemplating the best eating plan to live by, start one of them asap and test it empirically rather than being bogged down with forecasted outcomes. To echo the title of a Richard Branson book, we need to become better at saying, "Screw it, let's do it!"

*Moral:*
*Close → Start → Measure → Continue or Change → Repeat!*

# LET'S GET IT ON!

THE TERM 'LET'S GET IT ON' has a number of different meanings. Its significance as a phrase for me came from veteran championship boxing referee Mills Lane. Lane refereed some of the biggest championship fights in history and was renowned for being a no-nonsense third man in the ring. Apart from his experience as a referee, he also became known for his pre-fight speech when giving both boxers their final instructions in the ring: "Let's make it a tough clean fight… Protect yourself at all times… Any question from the champion? Any questions from the challenger? Let's get it on!"

Essentially, 'let's get it on' is about standing up to life's challenges; it's about adopting a 'bring it' mentality to life and most of all about taking action. It's about staring down those things and people who endeavour to hold you back. It signals that you're going to run at that thing you desire – and attack those things that want to stop you. It implies a willingness to mix it up with life's fears and expand into those moments that test your courage. It's about always showing your obstacles that your feet are planted, your hands are ready to throw and that you'll be a handful for whoever or whatever stands in your way. You will advance on your enemies – both real and imaginary. In doing so, you will take away the time, space and oxygen they need to bully you. 'Get out of the way or get hurt' becomes your mantra! In boxing parlance, 'You're going to fight like a Mexican'!

I concede that this may sound somewhat aggressive, but sometimes you can't think your way through to the other side of a problem – you have to be prepared to kick the door down. Paradoxically, I acknowledge that our overarching goal in life and the primary message of this book is to achieve a balance between inner peace and outer force. This reminds us that thoughtful acceptance, patience and non-resistance is sometimes the most effective strategy, while at other times it is the deliberate show of mental or physical strength that beats a path forward. This is the essence and fundamental composition of the personal force field.

> The primary message is to achieve a balance between inner peace and outer force.

Most importantly, adopting a let's get it on attitude creates a siren call to get moving and constantly pushes against the gravitational grift of procrastination.

From this day forward, adopt the mindset of a dynamic force of nature whose eyes are cast towards their gifts and powers rather than on their burdens and flaws!

Get it on!

# ACKNOWLEDGEMENTS

IF WE ARE SINCERE in our intention to adopt a student's mentality towards our life experiences, then everyone we meet and every scenario we are thrust into, whether good or bad, can be instructive and represent a potential teaching moment. It's a shame that the negative interactions carry more weight in terms of our desire for self-reflection, but perhaps that's the silver lining which lies at the heart of the phrase, 'It's an ill-wind that blows no good'.

This book represents an amalgamation of my most valuable encounters with customers, students, employees, peers, leaders and teachers. It also draws insight from outstanding authors, athletes and sportspeople who have broadened my philosophical outlook and challenged me to venture outside the herd and think independently.

I will be forever grateful to my wife, Sonya, for her patience and understanding as she listened intently to the long-winded version of many a chapter's first draft, prior to its inevitable brevity exam. Additionally, the glacial speed at which the book progressed, combined with its evening and weekend writing schedule required sacrifices to our family and social life that she was always willing to make.

Alex Fullerton and the team from Author Support Services – Joanna Yardley, Louise Zedda-Sampson, Sylvie Blair and Natasha Higgins – were also an invaluable part of this project. Their encouragement and guidance throughout the final stages of its production kept the light on at the end of the tunnel and carried me over the finish line. Many thanks as well to the very talented Francis Fenlon for his patience and design of the cover art.

Finally, to all those who guided, tested, trusted, acknowledged and supported me – as well as those who ignored me, bothered me, intimidated me or fought me – many thanks for your contribution to these notes!

# ABOUT THE AUTHOR

GAVIN SAMIN IS THE Vice President, COO and Assistant Chief Instructor of Go-Kan-Ryu Karate, an international martial arts organisation with over 35,000 students and 2000 instructors worldwide.

Aside from teaching and training in karate for over three decades, Gavin's extensive experience as a high-performance business coach, leadership mentor, communications specialist, strategic planner, keynote speaker and change architect has made him a highly valued leader and sensei.

*Force Field* is Gavin's debut book.

For more information about *Force Field*, visit:
www.forcefieldbook.com

www.ingramcontent.com/pod-product-compliance
Lightning Source LLC
Chambersburg PA
CBHW052108030426
42335CB00025B/2884